To

Stuart

[signature]

Best Wishes

[signature]

18.3.2016

Principality of Sealand

Holding The Fort
By
Michael of Sealand

Published in 2015 by the Principality of Sealand

www.sealandgov.org

ISBN 978-0-9933200-0-2

This book is dedicated to friends and family who have given support through thick and thin over the years. Apologies to those who have taken part in the Sealand adventure that I have failed to mention. It has been a long journey and I have written this with surprisingly little help from the faded memories of others.

My greatest thanks to my sons Liam and James who's many hours of editing my scribbling has made this book possible.

Absent friends: Captain John Crewdson, Barry Harcus and my best pal 'Willy' Gordon Wilkinson

And last but not least my dad 'Prince Roy of Sealand', Roy to his friends.

I have been asked many times if the stories contained in this book are completely true; my time with Sealand has been a rollercoaster, I have no need to embellish or add to the story.

Contents

Prologue

The pilot pushes the stick forward and the little 'Alouette' helicopter hurtles out of the dawn-lit sky towards the raging North Sea, it's tiny airframe buffeted by the strengthening gale. I look over his shoulder my heart pumping out of my chest. From where I'm sitting in the back, directly behind him, I can see the dark shape of our target, growing larger and larger by the second. We are screaming in at a 120 mph and the deafening roar of jet turbines and the clattering of whirring rotor blades produce a cacophony of noise and vibration that hammers my senses. Levelling off, the pilot tips the machine nose down for maximum speed and we are racing towards our final objective little more than a metre above the foaming wave crests.

Fumbling in the wind filled aircraft, I snap open my safety harness, reach under my camouflage jacket and feel the reassuringly heavy weight of a sawn-off shotgun, hung around my neck on a parachute cord lanyard. It's 'grapeshot' loaded, with the breech slightly cracked open to prevent accidental discharge.

Taking a deep breath, I carefully grab the coil of rope from my lap with my left hand while taking care not to tangle the coils. I climb out of the doorless aircraft onto a small step just below the cockpit. I am concentrating one hundred percent on what I am doing. There is a blur of rough sea below my feet, but I see nothing beyond my hands and my feet.

I have to get this right; there will be no second chance. I know one small mistake and I am dead. The pulse in my head is pounding.

Hanging on to the seat frame on which I had been sitting moments before. Stretching my leg down as far as it would reach my toes just make contact with the aluminium landing skid below me. Lowering myself further and putting my full weight on the skid my foot slips sideways on the rounded metal, nearly sending me hurtling into the raging sea. Grabbing the airframe to steady myself I readjust my footing against a cross member on the downward tilted skid.

From nowhere this urgent voice in my head says, *"What the fuck are you doing here Bates?"*
"Are you really going to do this?"

At that moment I remember why I'm here. I remember the dangerous and violent people I am about to get to grips with, and how they had cheated, hurt and humiliated my family and me.
Fury engulfed me, the red mist descended; there will be no turning back.
Head down, no hesitation, do or die, get on with it Bates.
Time of thought process? Probably five seconds!

The Old Man

Why on earth would a man want to create his own country? A tiny Principality in the North Sea? A 20th century enigma? Or just an act of pure eccentricity?

There can't be that many families that have been talked about by world leaders in government institutions around the world, debated in the UK houses of parliament, been the subject of secret meetings with the Prime Minister of the United Kingdom and his Ministers' lawyers and the subject of countless documents marked top secret and confidential.

My father was one of six children, two boys and four girls, of which he was the only survivor. The others all died of various ailments. There was cot death, one got sunstroke and one was even dropped by the nanny. I wonder what her references looked like when she went for her next job. To say he was lucky is an understatement.
His earliest memory was of waking up with the family doctor prodding and examining him, before turning to his weeping mother and pronouncing that he suspected a twisted bowel, and didn't expect him to last the night. I have heard him say the war was a walk in the park compared to his childhood. But then again, he also said the worst part of his war was being shaved by an Italian barber who had eaten too much garlic! My old man bless him, was a master of understatement.

His parents were constantly fighting and as a child he would push himself between them, on one occasion being hurled into the open coal fire unnoticed by them as they battled away. His refuge was under the grand piano that his mother used to play to entertain her friends, where they would struggle to reach him when trying to give him a clump. There was no radio or televisions in those days and people would entertain their friends and family playing the piano or singing. There was also a huge interest in the afterlife and trying to contact lost relatives, probably a result of the horrendous losses of family and friends to the madness of the First World War. Dad said his parents were very much into such things and would have regular séances at their house, inviting a multitude of like-minded friends to take part. They would all sit around a table holding hands asking *"is there anybody there?"* and *"can they send us a sign?"* He tried to help out as much as possible by giving the table a nudge or kicking one of the table legs to please them.

My father, a handsome, tall, athletic man with jet-black hair had always been one to look for a challenge. As a very young man he made his own way down to the Spanish civil war in search of adventure. Sitting outside a café on Barcelona's 'Las Ramblas,' a machine gun opened up. Everyone else dived for cover while my old man foolishly stayed in his chair thinking himself indestructible as an Englishman abroad. Weeks later he was deported to Gibraltar and then sent home to the UK, still defiant and harbouring a growing appetite for adventure. I guess in Sealand he found the ultimate challenge; taking to task the British government, which had hundreds of years experience in politically and physically suppressing insurrection with military might and gunboat diplomacy. Maintaining and successfully running the biggest empire the world has ever known.

Whilst serving an apprenticeship in London's Smithfield meat market he was once locked in one of the huge fridges for several hours when he was asked by his employers to break a strike. The unions were all-powerful in the markets and did not take kindly to people interfering with their business. He recalled seeing a crowd of men standing in a circle one day. When the crowd broke up and dispersed there was a body on the floor. A man had been kicked to death for some misdemeanour. Life was cheap in those days.

Prior to the outbreak of the Second World War my father was in the employ of Lord Vesty being trained to go to Argentina, where much of the worlds beef came from, to run cattle ranches.

When the war came along he couldn't wait to volunteer for the infantry. His war took him to the vast swathes of Africa, Syria, Iraq, Italy and more countries besides. Wounded several times he was proud to serve king and country.

He said when they were in the desert the army would send them warm clothes and when they fought in the freezing Italian mountains they were issued shorts.

His service found him fighting in Italy alongside the Ghurkhas at one of the most famous battles of the Second World War: 'Monte Casino', a hellish hard fought siege against Germanys crack troops.
Other times he would be sent to attack small Beau Geste style dessert forts in the Middle East rushing across the sand clutching scaling ladders they had made themselves with whatever materials they could find to hand, charging up them like medieval knights assaulting a fortress under siege.

"See these wrinkles around my eyes," he would say with an exaggerated flourish of his hand as he raised it to shade his eyes from the sun, *"I got them staring into the distance defending the four corners of the British Empire."*

One of my favourite stories of his was as a young subaltern in Syria with a dozen or so men; some native cavalry, commanded by a French officer, confronted him.
He got his men to 'dig in' under the relentless heat of the midday sun. The men swore and cursed him, as soldiers had their officers since time immemorial. Sweating as they burrowed away into the hard ground with their trenching tools and placed his two 'Bren' guns at either end of the trench. These were backed up by the other infantrymen's standard issue slow rate of fire bolt-action .303 calibre Lee-Enfield rifles.
The French officer gave the command and the cavalry charged across the plain towards them.

As they came closer and closer, at a great rate of knots and a thundering of hooves, my father clambered out of the trench and held his hands up for them to stop, pointing to the 'Bren' guns on either side, silently imploring them to stop. The charging mass feinted, turned and galloped back to their original position without a shot fired.

Then through the dust filled air churned up by the charging mass of horses and men, he saw the fat French officer riding up and down the ranks of horsemen, slapping their backs with the flat side of his sabre to drive them on for another go.

Once again they thundered across the plain intent on impaling my old man and his comrades on their wicked lances. Once more he climbed from the trench and pointed to the 'Bren' guns, with the probably misplaced confidence of a young Englishman in a foreign land.

Yet again they feinted and retired. This time they kept going and left the field of combat, a broken and disillusioned troop.

I was astounded when he told me this story as a young man. *"Why did you not just stay in the comparative safety of the trench and mow them down? Surely you felt threatened by all the tons of horse flesh and steel charging at you with deadly intent? Why did you put yourself at risk? Why did you do it?"*

His understated answer was more British than British.

"I thought I had the situation in hand. More importantly, I didn't want to kill the horses!" he exclaimed lost deep in memory of that long ago day.

It must have been one of the last cavalry charges of the Second World War and there will be a few good men alive today that can be thankful we come from a nation of animal lovers.

He served as an officer in the Eighth India division and somewhere along the line even became blood brothers with a Ghurkha.

He ended the War a Major in the infantry and probably would have gone further if it wasn't for the fact he kicked his colonel up the backside while being rebuked for doing something *'his way'*.

He was in the Royal Fusiliers City of London regiment, whose regimental headquarters bizarrely enough are the Tower of London.

As a boy sniping came into the conversation. *"Messy business!"* announced the old man. *"Don't ever get involved with it in your life. Not a good thing to do."* He said with an air of certainty in his voice. Some years later while sharing a beer with him the same conversation came up. *"Did a bit of that"* said the old man off handily.
"Did a bit of that?" I responded shocked. *"You told me you wouldn't get involved in such a messy business."*
"No" he said sarcastically *"I told you it was a messy, business and you shouldn't get involved with it."*
I can imagine he would have been put forward for such a thing, as he was a crack shot. As a boy I remember him reading in a book about someone managing to hit an old fashioned six pence at twenty yards. He couldn't wait to try this out in my grandfather's back garden with a .22 bolt-action rifle he was licensed to own. I proudly kept the bent and buckled coin for years.

It would be fair to say that my father enjoyed the war. He even admitted it sometimes. It was to him just a huge adventure. It did however take a great toll on his health. My mother asked me to copy a letter from the Veterans agency. It makes for interesting reading. It explains that war veterans are to be given priority treatment by the National Health Service. It then goes on to itemise his injuries during the war:
Malaria
Gunshot wounds to the face (multiple)
Gunshot wounds to the limbs (multiple)
Bilateral sensory neural hearing loss
Sand fly fever

Frostbite to feet
Desert sores of hands
Bilateral Dupuytren's contracture

They fail to mention the snakebite he received in Iraq while sitting on a rock lobbing stones at a couple of snakes. He later realised they happened to be in the process of mating, and didn't appreciate coitus interruptus induced by the old man's bored stone throwing. Naturally he carved a great chunk out of his leg with a razor blade, to try and remove the poison and drank a bottle of whisky. All the things we are now told you shouldn't do under such circumstances. I remember seeing the livid scar on his thigh the size of a fifty pence coin. His excuse for always keeping a bottle of whisky in the house was *"You never quite know when you might get bitten by a snake!"*

After the war my father met my mother, a stunning beauty, at the famous Southend Kursaal. He was with his friend Jimmy 'the frogman' Simpson who he elbowed out of the way to get the first dance. He was totally smitten, and proposed within a few days, even though he was at the time engaged to my mother's friend. They married at Caxton Hall Registry Office in London soon after. They were devoted to each other from then on.

I think his war experiences must have left my father with, shall we say, somewhat of a short fuse. He did tell me he came out of it with a very aggressive survivalist attitude, and didn't tone down for several years. Some years ago I was introduced to a man called Jimmy Dickenson, who had risen through the ranks to become the assistant chief constable of Essex. As a young constable in the 1950s, he was called to break up a fight on Southend beach. He told me that when he and his colleague got to the scene there was my father in dinner jacket and bow tie, standing on the beach squaring up to three similarly attired gentlemen. He dispatched them one at a time, one after the other with the panache and style of a professional pugilist. *"It was like a prize fight"* said the ex policeman. *"We couldn't break it up as it was such a spectacle."*

Having said that, he was the kindest and softest father one could have, with a great sense of duty and care, and always wanted the best for us. All be it the best as he perceived it.

I suppose when you read on its ironic the challenges he gave me as a youth, yet didn't allow my sister or me a bicycle when we were younger, because he considered the roads too dangerous. Even though my maternal Grandfather had always had one for going to the pub on. However now I think about it, he was found on more than one occasion, laying in ditches with the bike; the victim of over indulgence or a jealous husband driving him off the road.

As kids we would have to borrow our friends' bicycles and pedal them on roads and pavements where we thought he wouldn't be. Needless to say this culminated in disaster when riding along a road near to home one day, enjoying an illicit biking moment on my pal's bike, I heard a vehicle come up at speed behind me. I pedalled furiously to get away from it, but it was still there close behind me. The sound of the revving engine made my blood run cold. I realised then that my father had been right all along, and that the roads really were too dangerous for bikes.

I stood up on the pedals and gave it all I had, when all of a sudden I clipped the curb I was trying so hard to get so close to, and flew over the handlebars into the road with a painful crunching of bones and scraping of skin. 'This is it' I thought, 'I am dead'. The car behind me couldn't possibly stop in time and was surely going to run me over. Dad was right all the time. There was a deafening screech of rubber as the vehicle swerved to a halt, and all went quiet. You could have heard a pin drop. Then like the sound of the falling guillotine to its victim, I heard the all too familiar scrape of a sliding van door opening. I didn't have to look around.

I had heard that noise so many times before in the past, in fact I think my dad must have had three of those bloody vans in a row!

He plucked me bruised and shaken of the road, and made me push the bike back to my mate's house. All the time following behind in the van, smug in the knowledge that he had been right all along.

My paternal Grandfather Harry was much the same. Exactly six foot tall (so he told me) with a fine muscular physique, and bald in the middle of his head. He had been a 2nd Lieutenant in the Royal Horse Artillery during the First World War and had been presented with the military cross or 'MC' by King George V at Buckingham palace for an act of bravery during an artillery duel in France. The citation announced in the London Gazette dated 11 January 1919 reads:

"2nd Lieutenant Harry Michael Bates Royal Field Artillery:

For conspicuous gallantry and devotion to duty;

When his battery was responding to an S.O.S. call, his section suffered heavy casualties from shellfire. He kept both his guns firing, and eventually, with the help of a gunner, he fought one gun after the rest of the detachment had become casualties. The man with him was severely wounded, and the gun put out of action, so he reported for duty at the next section, after dressing the man's wounds under heavy artillery fire.

This was his first action and he came out of it with flying colours."

- Stirring stuff to read about your Grandfather nearly a hundred years later!

Harry had been on a troop ship crossing the English Channel to France when it was torpedoed by a German U-Boat. He found himself in the water and was kicked in the head by a drowning horse. I can only imagine that his uncanny knack for surviving sticky situations once again prevailed.

After he came back fro the war, Harry suffered long-term breathing problems having been the victim of German mustard gas attacks while he was in the trenches.

He was also known to have funny turns; he would wake in the middle of the night, run into the bathroom turning on the taps and shouting; *"Fire number one gun! Fire number two gun!"*. My father later realised that he must have been suffering from shell-shock; a condition not recognised or treated in those days.

He was no doubt a little *'potty'* and would sponsor aspiring young boxers whose talents caught his eye. He would bring them back to the house, give them my father's bedroom and put them into training. There were rumours of women in London and a double life. He definitely had a taste for the high life, and had aspirations of being on the stage. As a boy I saw him fooling around at Westcliff railway station and I can assure you it wasn't Michael Jackson that invented the 'Moon walk', the old chap was doing it years before and had some very nifty dance moves!

When the train arrived in London, he flung the heavy door open too soon and it swung back, squashing his thumb flat with a solid and sickening thump of heavy metal door against the solid frame of the carriage, he hardly batted an eyelid. It made me break out in a sweat just looking at it, all flat and bleeding and turning the colours of the rainbow.

He was as mad as a very sophisticated, well dressed March Hare. He would fight any man at the drop of a hat, getting my father into endless trouble. He was anti-Semitic, anti-Black, and anti anything else that took his fancy at the time, and was not backward in saying so.

He was as fit as a fiddle until the day he died of a massive heart attack and collapsed at home aged 79. Only the week before, he had thumped his upstairs neighbour for beating his wife. The fellow must have been half his age and was certainly considerably bigger than him.

My father being on Sealand when he died, it was down to me in my late teens, to go round and sort him out. My father asked me to dress him in his best dinner jacket for the occasion. (My old man doesn't just like a challenge; he enjoyed handing a few out as well!) I went around to his house with Joe, an old man in his seventies, who did a little work for us now and again. Joe, not very happy with the situation, grabbed his feet and I lifted his top half under his arms. We carried him carefully from the lounge into the bedroom, laid him out, then grabbed an arm each and sat the old chap up to, try and undress him to fulfil my father's wishes. Suddenly, he let out a tremendous belch that I should think could have been heard at the end of the road. Joe immediately turned ashen coloured, his eyes popped out on stalks, his jaw dropped and before I could say anything he had disappeared out of the door with the speed of a startled gazelle and legged it off down the road, not to be seen again for several days.

Strangely, when my parents married, they found that both their fathers had been in the 'Royal Horse Artillery' and both stationed for a time at Shoebury barracks in Essex. They had both fought at the battle of the Somme. My mother's father was the regimental sergeant major. But the weirdest thing is they both had the same toe blown off the same foot by shrapnel while fighting in the trenches. Exactly the same injury, the second toe in on the left foot. Bizarre!

So I suppose these tales give some insight to the man who at times has been accused of being unpatriotic because of Sealand. Nothing could be further from the truth if he had been young and fit enough my father would have done it all again to defend Queen and country. That's not to say he wasn't somewhat disappointed the direction that his motherland had taken as I am sure many are. That is what we have to accept in a democracy, but as the French philosopher Voltaire said

"I do not agree with what you have to say, but I'll defend to the death your right to say it."

The Early Days: Pirate Radio

The four 4500-ton Navy forts were originally built at Gravesend in Kent on government instruction, at a cost in today's values of some £6 million each, after it was decided that too much damage was being inflicted on convoys arriving in the Thames and waiting to discharge at London docks, or forming in the Estuary to carry goods elsewhere in war torn Europe.

The Thames in those days was the gateway to London and the rest of the United Kingdom. It was imperative that the waterways were kept open so that ships could anchor safely before discharging their precious loads of food and other goods in London docks. The docks were vast and covered miles of the London riverbank with huge basins lined with vast cranes for unloading them, a prime target for the German bombers who simply followed the river to their target. Hitler had given orders to the Luftwaffe to close the river to shipping, to starve out London and bomb it flat to break the will of the British people by doing so.

Army forts were built in the upper reaches of the river, but the Navy were the service charged with the defence of the outer reaches of the Thames and North Sea.

The Naval forts, built in an arc across the outer reaches of the Thames from Harwich to Margate, were linked by a telephone cable that came ashore at Felixstowe and were thus able to communicate information of enemy ships or planes spotted, with each other. The guns were modern for their time and able to fire radar controlled at shipping and using a 'Predictor' for anti aircraft fire that worked out the 'lead' needed to hit aircraft travelling at speed. The predictor was in fact an early computer device developed in Canada during the war and given to the British people by the Canadians to aid their defence. Anyone who has been Duck or clay pigeon shooting will know that you don't shoot at the target, but lay the shot where the target will be when the shot gets there. That was the basic principle of how it worked.

The 3.7-inch 'Vickers Armstrong' anti aircraft guns fired a 28lb high explosive shell some 41,000 feet vertically or 20,600 yards horizontally and at a rate of 25 rounds per minute when automatically fed. These were backed up by 'Bofore' guns firing a smaller two-pound round with an effective range of 5000 feet at a rate of 120 rounds per minute.

Hitler gave the Luftwaffe the task of bombing the British people to their knees and into submission, destroying not only factories and buildings, but also their spirit. The predictor, like radar, was a great help in turning the tide of war and holding back Hitler's Luftwaffe from our shores. They even had reasonable success against Hitler's new terror weapon nick named 'Doodlebugs' the German VI and VII rockets, fired from the German occupied Dutch coast and capable of reaching most of the south east and London.

It is hard to believe or even imagine what Londoners were going through on one August day in 1940, at the height of the battle of Britain, the German bombers made 2000 sorties over London. It was known at the time that the Luftwaffe had 2400 operational aircraft, compared to Britain's 400 operational fighters that were charged with the task of stopping them. No wonder Churchill said of the RAF *"Never have so many owed so much to so few."*

When Guy Maunsell originally designed the forts, bizarrely no consideration was given to their re-supply. Of course it was absolutely essential that the forts were able to take on food, fuel and personnel, not to mention water, which presented the biggest problem of all. When we ventured onto the 'Sunk Head' forts for the first time, there were notices pinned on the walls reminding the crew that they had to be careful with the use of water, since there had been a crisis on a previous occasion when the supply tender could not get out for weather, and they had run perilously low. Maunsell hastily designed an add-on of a landing stage that was bolted to the tower. It was a last minute add-on. The landing stage had wooden legs, which the supply vessel could lay alongside, without hopefully doing too much damage to itself in the unpredictable weather of the North Sea. Most of these landing stages had collapsed and washed away into the tide by the 60s and the only one left was on the Knock John forts. This one leant over at a jaunty angle where it had half collapsed over the years under the pressure of weather and ships lying alongside it. It leant in towards the tower and somehow had dropped about twenty feet while still connected to the tower by bent and rusty bolts, although the once horizontal deck at the top of it was now sloping down almost vertical. As a boy when my father had the pirate radio station 'Radio Essex' on the 'Knock John' fort and later 'Britain's better music station' or 'BBMS' we used to lay the boat alongside it and climb the mussel and barnacle encrusted, bent and mangled ladder onto the landing stage that was by then at forty five degree angle. At one stage the only access from that up to the forts main deck was by being pulled up by hand with a rope tied around your waist. I have to say even though I wasn't very heavy in those days, the thought of half a dozen spotty pale teenage DJs, whose only physical exercise was dragging on a cigarette or opening a can of beans, hauling on a rope with my life depending on it was not my idea of fun.

It was the mid sixties that my father had the notion to get involved with pirate radio. The term 'Pirates' had been given to these independent sea borne stations by stuffy government officials, and was meant to have been a derogatory name to dismiss them like despicable criminals. It had the exact reverse effect. The public instantly loved it, and the press took to the exciting new phenomena with glee. Officialdom could not have dubbed them with a more exciting name if they had employed a team of public relations gurus to brand and promote them and their programming.

Looking back it is hardly surprising that my father wanted to get involved in this whole new medium that was unfolding in front of his very eyes as he went to work every day fishing. He had heard commercial and local stations in America and had been intrigued by them. We were at sea on the 'Mizzy Gel' an ex-admiralty harbour launch that had been converted to a fishing boat, when he suddenly said *"Lets go and have a look on the Knock John forts!"*

It was January 1965 and I was a mere 12 years old.

We steamed across to the distant fort that rose out of the water like some huge alien machine from outer space, casting a huge dark shadow on the calm sea. As we got closer and closer it just got bigger and bigger until it was towering above us blocking out the sunlight. An eerie wartime reminder of a bygone age.

The tide swirled between the towers like a mill race, making unsettling gurgling noises. There was an old wartime vintage ladder down the inner side of the tower under the cold foreboding shadow of the platform high above. My father grabbed a rope from the deck and tied the boat up to a rusty protruding bolt stabbing out of the concrete tower.
"Wait there while I climb the ladder and have a look around."
When he got to the top, not wanting to miss anything, I shouted up to him *"Come on Dad, I want to come and see what it was like up there."*
He looked down at me from above, a look of serious deliberation etched on his face. *"Come on up then,"* said the old man nervously, *"When you come up, bring the boat hook. Some of the ladder is not very good and we can hook it on some better rungs above to bridge the bad bits."*

Not very good!
My old man has always been the master of understatement!

As I carefully climbed, the sides of the manky old ladder became thinner and more dilapidated, where the wind and tide had been rusting away at them for twenty odd years. Pebble sized bits of rust were starting to fall on my head splashing loudly into the murky, muddy swirling water below. Suddenly, the wafer thin sides started to bend into an S shape as it wobbled from side to side. Small sheets of rust fell off them as I put my weight on the rungs.

At this point, my father bellowed those classic words *"Whatever you do son don't look down!"*

Until this moment, looking down hadn't even occurred to me. I had been far too busy clinging to the stupid thing and trying not to lacerate my hands on the razor sharp edges. As I tried to keep my weight close in to the tower and slither up it as weightlessly as possible to stave off what seemed like an inevitable fall when it all tumbled into the sea with me on it.

Well, what do you do when someone says that? Perhaps I should rephrase that; what does Michael do when told not to do something? Look down? I suppose its human nature! So down I looked!

Well, my legs went weak and turned to jelly, and I froze on the ladder unable to move up or down.

It seemed so high, maybe sixty feet. My knuckles had turned white gripping the ladder rungs. I knew I had to get moving again as no one could help me if I didn't. Just look in front I told myself. Look at the rungs, and climb.

Clinging onto a rusty, wobbly, bit of old ladder that was bending and just dying to snap off under my weight and the thought of it sending me hurtling into the sea or worse still, onto the foredeck of the boat. The boat with its bow rollers, bollards and rusty old anchor fluke pointing up into the air at me like something that Vlad the Impaler would have been proud to have in his toy box. All the while still clutching onto the bastard spiteful rusty thing I was climbing was enough to get me moving again!

I have to say I have never been too keen on heights, but I can't resist climbing up on things, if they are there. Now that doesn't even make sense does it? Oh well, I have carried that one around for all my life, and still find myself looking down uneasily from great heights now and again.

I got to the top of the ladder and crawled onto a small wooden decked landing stage with sturdy, thick planked decking. Hanging down was another short ladder, from there leading through a narrow dark tunnel of steel and concrete, about four foot long up to a heavy steel hatch red with rust, above our heads. My father climbed the ladder, put his shoulder against the hatch and pushed with all his might. It opened with a great creaking noise from the ancient wartime hinges, and thick rust started showering over our heads.
We clambered one behind the other, up into the bright sunlight of a beautiful summer's day onto the deck of the fortress, shaking small shards of rust out of our clothing and hair.

The Knock John fort had not been manned or seen visitors for many years. It did however seem to have a good thriving population of Cormorants. They sat with hunched shoulders and looking at us from under hooded eyes like the boatman from Hades that carried souls across the River Styx. Rows of them like the soldiers from hell. Eventually, one broke ranks and flopped lazily up into the air. Followed by the others one by one like ungainly grumpy old men. Annoyed at being disturbed from their perfect sanctuary. Leaving a thick layer of bird crap, the product of many years undisturbed solitude covering everything that they could have perched on. The dark painted rusty metal rails and building were streaked with white. Even the anti-aircraft guns, still in place and pointing aimlessly up into the sky for long past enemies, were covered in the stuff, dried and dripping off them in thick white streaks.

Walking from the hatch across the riveted steel deck, we went through the door into the main building and waited for our eyes to adjust to the windowless darkness. We were in the main corridor that was some fifty-foot long and ran from one end of the deck building to the other. As our eyes adjusted to the darkness, we could see heavy steel doors studded

24

with large round rivets on either side. We gingerly walked into the gloom and opened them one by one. Most of them stiff on their steel hinges had not been opened since the war.

It was like boyhood stories of the '*Marie Celeste*' an ancient ship found drifting and unmanned with all sails set in the vast oceans, with no explanation of what had happened to the crew. Each room had a small porthole made of brass, with thick bullet proof glass allowing daylight to stream in round shafts from outside, adding to the strangeness of the situation.

We were not sure what we would find as we put our shoulders to the doors pushed our way in one by one. The whole experience was surreal and very creepy, like entering a haunted house and expecting someone or something to jump out on us at any time. It had been left fairly tidy by what had clearly been an orderly evacuation by the post-war caretakers. There was nothing that could be classed as personal possessions left behind.

On one side of the hall were the officer's mess and the captain's cabin, which were lined with wooden panelling to insulate them from the cold riveted steel structure. On the other side were the toilets and washrooms. There were also some wartime pinups on many of the walls, looking very faded and old-fashioned; a reminder of bygone times and the previous inhabitants.

Some of the rooms were filled with rows of metal washbasins, and others contained a row of toilet cubicles. Each had a brown wooden sign on their identical heavy riveted steel door with individual hand-painted signs declaring their use marked either officers or crew.

At either end of the hallway was a hatch leading down to the towers with a foot high raised combing. Like you would find on a ship to stop the water running down the hatchway should the deck flood. There was a companionway descending down the tower to the next floor, like a heavy built ladder with wooden rungs covering the steelwork and handrails at either side, again like those on a ship.

Clutching the combing and then the sturdy railings, we lowered ourselves through the hatchway and down the steep stairs to the concrete landing some twelve feet below. At the foot of the stairs in front of us was a wooden framed door constructed of red steel mesh in a similarly built framework surrounding a lift shaft. We opened the door, lifted the hinged safety rail and gingerly looked down into the blackness; it was like looking down a mineshaft into a black, seemingly bottomless void. I kicked a small piece of rust down it but couldn't hear it hit the bottom.

We carefully shut the safety rail and closed the door in case some unfortunate adventurer should wander down there into the darkness and unwittingly step off the edge into oblivion.

To the left there was another hatchway and steep stairs leading down into the darkness of the tower to the floors below. To our right there was another door, this time made of wood and more like a house door. This opened easily into the machine room where the remains of two large wartime generators, used to power the wartime guns and lighting, stood on thick concrete stands to dampen down the noise and vibration while running. There was a heavy wooden workbench in the corner and the remains of old fashioned looking control panels to one side. It was quite dark and difficult to make things out. My father noticed a wooden air vent in front of the engines, like a sliding hatch set in the wall, allowing cool air from outside to the large cooling radiators on the front of the generator set engines. He squeezed himself around the front of the engine and turned the wooden latch. Allowing it to fall open with a bang, with this, shafts of hazy daylight suddenly streamed into the room.

On the workbench were several live rounds of heavy machine gun ammunition. The lethal debris of a bygone war, looking in a very sorry and dangerous state, the once shiny brass bullet cases discoloured with green amongst rusty old tins of nuts and bolts. My father picked them up one at a time between thumb and forefinger, and very gingerly threw them out the engine room window into the calm sea below.

I remember thinking, as all this was going on in the semi darkness, how creepy the whole situation was. If anywhere in the world should be haunted, this was the place. I kept imagining I could hear noises from out of the darkness; my skin crawled as the hairs on the back of my neck were raised. It was really not a very nice place to be.

I was relieved when Dad said, *"Come on"* and we went back up the companionway onto the deck and walked down the main corridor checking out the various rooms once again on the way past.

Coming outside into the daylight once again, there was another set of heavy metal ladders leading up through a hatch in the corner onto the roof above the main building. We climbed the ladder and separated from each other. We quickly looked into the different steel rooms above. Yet another level above accessed by a steel ladder was the main radar fire control room for the guns. There were some very faded and dog-eared blue and khaki coloured wartime books and message pads lying around on the floor. I picked them up and dusted them off, fascinated that they were still there and in good condition. Clutching this piece of history in my hand.
I looked up and could see bullet holes in the thick Perspex windows of the radar unit above my head, no doubt the legacy of a German strafing run years before. *Did the fort guns bring the plane down? Or did it get away?* Standing there alone in the silence, for a split moment I could hear the forts alarm bells urgently ringing out action stations, the thumping of heavy boots on steel decks as the gun crews ran pumped full of adrenaline to their prearranged stations. The tortured screaming of aircraft engines from the skies as the enemy planes came in to attack the little fortress below. The rattle of machine gun fire and thump, thump of heavy artillery from the forts main armament, hurling airbursts of flack up into the sky. Desperate to shoot down the attackers before they could get near enough to drop their lethal cargo of bombs on them.
This place was eerie. It was like being in a time warp.

The shrill scream of a seagull broke the spell.

I'd seen enough and was glad to regain the company of my father and return to the deck below. Once again, we squeezed through the hatch in the main deck and could see the faithful old Mizzy Gel bobbing around in the tide far below. There was a bit of a conflab as to who should go down the spiteful old ladder first. Until Dad decided it should be me as I was the lightest and if the ladder should collapse leaving him with no other way of getting off, he should be the one who would dive into the sea.

As it happened apart from a few minor cuts and having our hair filled with more rust particles, the descent was fairly uneventful. We clambered back onto the boat that was sitting tidily at the bottom of the ladder.

The old boats engine was still rumbling away as the old man didn't like stopping it at sea due to its uncannily reliable habit of not starting again. I cast off the rope and we motored away from the fortress's dark shadow. As we got up speed, we saw the local police launch go past, taking a keen interest in our activities with their binoculars. They must have been returning from the state funeral of the recently deceased wartime leader 'Winston Churchill' in London. Quite profound really I suppose in retrospect as it would have been him that ordered the building of the forts. They have even been referred to on occasion as 'Churchill Forts'.

I did hear later that somebody had tied up alongside the landing stage on the 'Knock John' fort several years before in an old ex-military landing craft and looted all the gunmetal and brass fittings they could find. They loaded so much copper wire and metal fittings onto the old thing that it sunk. They scrambled off the boat onto the fort as it disappeared beneath the waves.
Marooned with no prospect of alerting the world to their plight, their biggest problem was water. They nearly died of thirst before being rescued and at one point licked up puddles of rainwater and bird crap off the deck when by good fortune it rained.

The funny thing is there were 20,000 gallons of water in a large tank in the middle of the building. Had they actually tried to turn a tap on or flush a toilet they would have found some war time water!

With his reconnaissance done and having dropped the daily newspapers aboard at the nearby 'Mid Barrow' lightship, I asked my Dad why he had stopped off to deliver them. He said it was a lonely old life for the men that manned them. And it was only fair if nearby to give them whatever normal everyday small luxuries that most people ashore took for granted, if you were in a position to do so. *How many times over the ensuing years did that conversation spring to mind I wonder?*

We steamed the boat back to its mooring at Paglesham in the Essex backwaters and made our way home. The old man had been quiet most of the time, deep in thought over what he had seen and the possibilities that went with it.

When we got home, I could hear him talking to my mother about how he was going to get involved with this very exciting phenomena nicknamed by the press 'Pirate Radio'.

'Radio Caroline' was the first station to broadcast from a ship off the UK and did so from an Old Dutch coaster registered in Panama the ' Mi Amigo'. She was anchored in the 'Wallet,' an area of water north of the Gunfleet sands but over three miles offshore in international waters, the nearest point of land being Walton on the Naze on the Essex coast. The station had offices in a very prestigious address; Chesterfield gardens in London and was owned by Ronan O'Rahilly. Legend has it that Ronan's father had a shipyard in Ireland, and when he was approached to kit out a radio ship, Ronan got him to hold the job back until he could get a ship together himself and beat them to the post.
Ronan's ship was the first to broadcast and became known as 'Caroline South' and the original ship then anchored off the Isle of Man and became 'Caroline North'. Rumours abounded that the stations were called

Caroline in honour of John F Kennedy's daughter. It wasn't long before that that Kennedy had faced up to the Soviet Union and won the standoff over the Cuban missile crises. It was and probably still is the nearest the world has ever been to a nuclear war. A large cargo ship, shadowed by US hunter-killer submarines, her decks laden with nuclear missiles under canvas covers lay off the Cuban coast. Russian troops on the ground in Cuba had even been given permission to use tactical nuclear weapons if the Americans had landed. A Soviet nuclear submarine nearby had been given permission to use nuclear missiles at their discretion, if the captain and one other appointed officer both agreed to press the button. Many years later it came to light that the submarine commander wanted to push the button but the other assigned officer whose permission was required refused to fire. That unknown Russian officer possibly saved the world from a nuclear holocaust on an unprecedented scale, had the west responded, as they undoubtedly would have done. A year later Kennedy had fallen to an assassin's bullet in Dallas, Texas.

Like many people of a certain age, I can recall exactly and what I was doing when the world was told of the tragedy. I was on the beach opposite my Grandparents house on the seafront at Thorpe Bay in Essex, trying to drag a very heavy dinghy up the beach that I had found loose in the tide and had notions of salvaging. My grandfather would not come and help me because he was riveted to the news from America on the flickering black and white television in his back room. There was talk of financial involvement with the radio station, but I never heard anything concrete, and it might just have been a clever political move by O'Rahilly. Either way Kennedy did not live to see the results.

It was the first I had heard of my father's interest in radio, and it was to turn into a fascinating and very eventful era of our lives.

Unlike today, there were no off-the-shelf transmitters and studios or if there were it was extremely expensive kit, and almost impossible to find. Recording and studio equipment that can be bought in the local shop these days just wasn't there to be had.

So much had to be gathered together. My father commissioned a transmitter to be made. It turned out that it was made from an ex-USAF beacon transmitter built for guiding aircraft into land, and produced only 1000 watts of power.

My father then decided he had to place some men on the fortress to prepare for the transmitter's arrival.

When they arrived at the Knock John fort, they were dismayed to find it occupied by people from another radio station 'Radio City' who had occupied the nearby Shivering Sands army forts. They had it seems heard of my father's intentions and thought they would put a stop to his plans. Dad climbed up, introduced himself and they were asked to leave, they did so without too much persuasion.

My father then left his people on the fort while he returned to Southend to continue putting together his new commercial radio project.

While away, his people were in turn ejected again and landed in Whitstable on the Kent coast. My father by then was getting the hump with all this. He asked George Dell, a local blacksmith to the fishing industry and old friend of many years, to make him up a hook ladder. He had been told the new people had cut away anything he could have climbed up on the fort. When he got down to the boat on the next tide ready to return once again to the Knock John, there were George, Mike Todd and a couple of other old stalwarts sitting on the boat ready to give him a hand with his increasingly dangerous task.

It was October 1965 and the boat dropped the old man off on the landing stage. Dad looked up and saw two men peering over the rail from above. *"You can't come on here"* they shouted threateningly and started throwing lumps of wood and pieces of metal at him.

Using the short hook ladder he swarmed up the side of the forts decrepit landing stage and climbed an old derrick arm propped against the rail above that led up to the main deck above. As he got higher and higher the missiles stopped raining down on him and the men disappeared.

Cresting the rail and jumping down onto the deck nursing a few lumps and bruises, he was not a happy bunny!

After a considerable wait, the very sheepish defenders appeared from down the tower and he ejected the Radio City men once more!

One of them, then a very young 'Dick Dixon' whom I met forty-five years later at my father's wake, said he couldn't believe how having climbed up onto the landing stage my father proceeded to climb onto a loose derrick arm. He said it was just leaning there precariously, where it had fallen unsecured with nothing holding it in place. He decided at that point, if Dad wanted the fort that much, then perhaps he should let him have it. He said to Dad he would lose his job for letting him on the fort and Dad said don't worry you can come and work for me if you get fired. Which eventually, he did. The old man was by now getting himself a bit of a reputation as an unstoppable nutter, which under the circumstances, was quite a useful reputation.

He decided to stay there himself for a while until all the flack had quietened down and the threats gone away. He only wanted, after all, a bit of adventure. To set up his own commercial radio station which ended up being as the jingle proudly proclaimed, 'Radio Essex on 222 metres 24 hours a day.'

As I recall, there was no real violence in these incidents. Although Reg Calvert a former dance hall entrepreneur and talent agent who owned Radio City did make threats to my father. Very shortly afterwards during a fall out with his own partners, Calvert was himself killed. As I recall Calvert went to see Major Oliver Smedley, a distinguished war veteran who had won the military cross in Northern France after the D-day landings. Smedley had been around the radio business from the beginning, involved with Caroline North and South and various incestuous deals with Radio London and other offshore stations. There was some kind of financial involvement with Radio City. There was a dispute over the ownership of a rather large transmitter on the Shivering Sands forts, Radio City's base of operations that Smedley and his associates had bought and imported from the USA.

Smedley hired a boarding party of London dockers and took over the fortress by force. Failing to reach an agreement, Calvert went to Smedley's house in a sleepy Essex village, and a row broke out on Smedley's doorstep. Smedley grabbed a shotgun and killed Calvert.

Smedley was arrested on a charge of murder, but on going to court, he was found not guilty on the grounds of self-defence because Calvert had an offensive weapon on him. Apparently a small CS gas gun disguised as a pen.

Later having returned the fortress to Calvert's widow, Smedley again had designs on taking it over once more and approached my father to help. My father told him that despite his own run-ins with the now deceased Calvert. There was no way he would get involved in doing harm to a now defenceless widow. Further, should the fort be taken from her, he would make it his personal mission to retake it and hand it back to her.

It was a sad incident and didn't help the pirate radio cause. The British government were not slow to use the incident to discredit the radio stations and the people involved with them.

I was away at boarding school during much of this time and only got involved during school holidays.

I particularly remember spending one chilly Christmas on the Knock John in 1965 with the DJs and staff of the station. We all went out there: me, my parents, my sister Penny and Fruitcake our cat. We had a really good time!

I was somewhat perturbed at going into the studio in the early hours one morning. Finding one of the DJs, Chris Stewart, sitting at the microphone, unshaven, in his striped pyjamas babbling away to his devoted listeners with a hammer next to the turntables in front of him.

He was quick to explain that he was the only one up at that time of the night and was a bit concerned 'Joshua' might walk in.

"Joshua?" I questioned him. "Who the hell is Joshua?"

"You mean you haven't heard about Joshua? He's the ghost that lives in the North tower. No one goes there that's why we all sleep in the South tower." He said in a concerned and fearful voice. I noticed his eyes were starting to pop out of his head on stalks a little, in an ever so slightly demented fashion as he warmed to his subject. It was strange hearing this from his deep resonating BBC style voice. "Only the engineers go down there on sufferance to tend the generators when they really have to" he explained. Apparently there had been many strange things going on. Noises heard for no logical reason. Strange smells emanating from that tower. Generators had been known to stop for no apparent reason. The lights going dimmer and dimmer until plunged into darkness. Machinery stopped and the station would go silent and off the air, only to restart itself without human intervention. Tools also went missing and things were moved unexplainably.

On one occasion, voices were heard coming from the depths off the tower; with this, a posse of young, skinny, pale and spotty DJs was assembled armed with heavy spanners, knives and various improvised weapons to descend into the bowels of the tower to investigate, in case a rival faction had taken up residence there. They found nothing. They were all without exception convinced that things weren't quite right in the North tower.

'Hmm' I thought, that was the tower where months before Dad and I had thrown the ammunition out of the generator room window into the sea, and I had felt decidedly uneasy. Next day I took a torch and descended the seven floors to the bottom of the tower. It was dark and creepy, and the rooms were much as they would have been during the war when the sailors messed (ate their food) and slept in bunks built around the walls. Needless to say I didn't find anything other than the skeletons of some long dead cormorants that had found their way down there and had perished unable to escape, but no ghosts or human skeletons wearing rotting wartime uniforms.

Once again however the hackles rose on my neck, and I was happy, with heart pounding and aching legs from climbing the stairs as quickly as I could, to regain the main deck.

Improvisation was the order of the day. The old man it seemed had cornered the market in hospital beds and stiff, itchy red hospital blankets that he bought from the Red Cross. They had probably been rejected by the charity for being too uncomfortable to send to the victims of natural disasters such as famines and floods around the world. Apart from being used as bedding for the growing crew of DJs and engineers the blankets were nailed on the studio walls for soundproofing that was an improvement on his original suggestion of using grey cardboard egg trays.

A studio was knocked together out of wood, in what had originally been the fort captain's cabin in the middle of the main building. A long wire antenna suspended from scaffold poles was erected above the upper deck, with the transmitter ending up in the wartime fire control room in the middle. In the UK office (the front room of our home in Southend) the commercials were made using a gramophone (A large wooden cabinet the size of a big chest of drawers with a wooden lid that contained an old fashioned record player and an ancient valve driven radio) with an old tape recording machine on the floor.

There were no fancy studios, and mixers in those days were something talked about in hushed voices like the Holy Grail.

Something that other people had.

No, all we had was just a nudge or nod from the presenter who was clutching the microphone making the voiceover. To the guy that had to start the music by dropping the record onto the already revolving turntable using a mat that you guessed it, was cut out of the ubiquitous Red Cross blankets. Turning the music up or fading it away was done using the volume control of the ancient device. The tape was then spliced by cutting it with scissors and stuck back together with a special thin Scotch tape made for the job. No hard drives or MP3s in those days!

Over this Christmas stay my sister Penny got all gooey eyed over one of the DJs 'Graham Johns', a well built good looking fellow and my father forbade her to spend time with him. Needless to say that had very little impact on them and probably exasperated the problem culminating in him crashing his car into a ditch during a secret liaison with her and flying through the windscreen onto the bonnet.

Most of his injuries sustained, we were told afterwards, were caused by a very concerned Penny dragging him unconscious back over all the broken glass surrounding the window frame into the car. It makes me wince just thinking about it.

Having not bled to death but possibly in an attempt to avoid further injury the romance fizzled out.

When we first went on the air the station was powered by a generator that Radio City left behind and I believe was on rental. Dick Palmer, one of the more sensible lads out there, who Dad had appointed 'Fort Captain', then managed to get one of the old wartime generator sets up and running, and the hired set was returned to them with thanks.

The main fuel storage tanks were out of an aircraft and were constructed from aluminium and wing shaped. Not surprising as our main sponsor and advertising client was 'Channel Airways,' a small airline out of London Southend airport that ferried people and cars to Europe.

I remember at one point someone left the tap open on one of these tanks and about three hundred gallons of fuel ran out onto the deck, and through the building. The outside deck was made of steel but in the middle where one of the anti-aircraft guns stood there was a thick layer of asphalt or tar. The whole lot melted with the oil and became a sticky mess. It was impossible to clean it up, and it got walked through the whole fort on people's shoes.

It got everywhere and on everything it even melted the soles of my shoes. The smell of diesel and liquid tar was quite nauseating. Anyone who has stepped on tar washed up on the beach will appreciate the task of trying to get it off. Needless to say, the guy that left the tap open was not a very popular lad after that.

Water was another big problem and all of it had to be laboriously carried out in five-gallon drums. Back breaking work and soul destroying when you heard stories of the jocks pouring it down the toilet when the seawater cisterns were empty, because they were to idle to pull up a bucket of seawater with a block and tackle from the sea below.

On a visit one day the disc jockey on air tried to get me to speak to the listeners. I just clammed up and could say nothing. As much as he tried I wouldn't say a word.
God I must have been shy in those days.
He then put some music on and talked to me, trying to make me feel at ease about the incident he asked if I would like a request played later in the day when I got home. I thought for a moment and said, *"Yes, I would like 'They're Coming To Take Me Away' by a guy called Napoleon XIV"*. It was a really funny song about a fellow that becomes insane over his dog running away (or as he describes it, leaving him) and ends up being taken away to the funny farm by those nice young men in long white coats, the voice getting more and more demented.
Unfortunately, my father ran a very straight radio station and the time slot I had asked it to be played in was, unbeknown to me, right in the middle of a very serious big band programme for the likes of Glen Miller and Duke Ellington. I can still see the look of thunder on the old man's face now as the record played to its eventual screaming demented conclusion. The disc jockey cheerfully explaining it was unusual to slot it in for that time of day, but the boss's son had requested it.

The station was eventually closed down after my father was prosecuted under the 1949 Wireless Telegraphy act which was later to become the 1967 Marine Offences Act for broadcasting without a licence inside the UK. In fact, the Knock John was beyond the normal three miles territorial limits. But Britain, in their struggle to stop the so-called pirates, turned to some new laws that were being pushed about in the international legal communities. The three-mile territorial waters limit observed by most countries came about because that was the distance a cannon ball could be fired and still penetrate a foot of oak or the thick wooden side of a warship.

Britain brought in some rulings that were vaguely recognised by international law at the time. One was the bay closure line. This legality went along the lines of, it doesn't matter how wide a river mouth was a line could be drawn across the mouth of it and all inside belonged to that nation.

The other one was if a sand bank dried out at low water; the three-mile limit could go to that and then take another three miles from there. Both of which aided the demise of Radio Essex.

The British government hated pirate radio with a vengeance. I recall as a boy growing up in the 60s that there was no pop music on the radio, apart from DJ Alan Freeman doing the chart top 20 on a Sunday. Other than that the only way you could get anything but boring talk was by tuning into 'Radio Luxemburg' of a night time. Luxemburg's signal would fade in and out of the ether and sometimes be unlistenable.

The market was wide open and the public was certainly ready for the change. The youngsters worshipped the growing band of dashing piratical DJs who were taking over the airways with their ersatz mid-Atlantic accents.

At one point, there was a radio station on nearly every fortress in the Thames and at least three radio ships lying in the 'Wallet' off Clacton. Radio Caroline on the Mi Amigo, Radio London on an old converted American minesweeper the 'Galaxy' and the last one to turn up 'Radio England' and 'Britain Radio' two stations; very cleverly broadcasting from one antenna on a ship called the 'Laissez-faire' which had come from America.

On an impromptu visit to the Laissez-faire, I was awestruck by the opulence and comfort of her. Not to mention the vast store of American cigarettes (that they handed out like wartime GIs in France, flinging them from the back of a jeep) and the huge tin of ham the size of a gallon can that the chef opened for our lunch, the likes of which I had never seen before.

These ships had large steel hulled Dutch tenders that were contracted from the 'Weissmuller Shipping Company' that specialised in huge salvage tugs and took on daring salvage jobs around the world. They ferried stores, fuel and staff from Felixstowe, prior to the Marine Offences Act coming into force. After that the ships were tendered from Holland. However, the Dutch soon imposed their own Marine Offences Act, and that also became impossible.

There were none of those big comfortable tenders for us. I remember coming home from boarding school one day to see half a dozen of our disc jockeys collapsed in exhaustion on the concrete stairs that led up to our Southend flat. They explained to me in tired voices that on the way home from the radio station, the engine in our boat had failed. As ever, not wishing to ask anyone for help, my father had issued them with 'Sweeps' which are long heavy oars from a bygone age that he had with considerable foresight kept on the boat for just such an emergency. They explained that he had got them rowing the old boat back to its moorings at Paglesham like galley slaves. I think they had been at sea for two days!

It is strange how odd things like that stick in your mind.
I recall just before I left boarding school thinking, *'What will I remember of this ancient scholastic place of learning? This vast Gothic pile with its château-like towers, massive bronze statues of devil dogs with vicious studded collars on high sandstone plinths towering above my head and scenes depicting violent life and death struggle between savage eagles and their large prey. All this, set in hundreds of acres of walled estate, bordered by the river Dee in the wilds of North Wales near Ruabon.*
What will I recall when I am an old man?'

I considered the deprivation my parents had put themselves through that I might go there, in the faint and desperate hope that my academic side might prevail. When they had brought me there for my first term passing through the gates and past the sandstone gatekeepers' lodges either side of the entrance of the long straight driveway (So long in fact, that the school was still not even visible at that point). Then an hour later, they drove off back down the same driveway, the Bentley my dad was so proud of disappearing into the distance. I felt like Little Lord Fauntleroy, totally alone and abandoned in a strange and surreal world. It was the last time I was to see that car, as time went on the cars were to get smaller and older.

I looked down deep in thought into the toilet bowl I was urinating in. Written around the edge was proudly emblazoned *'Armitage Shanks'*!

I have looked down and seen that name since in the four corners of the world. It never fails to amuse and make me chuckle and sometimes get some very funny looks in far-flung places. Even Sealand had its share of that hallowed companies products dating back to the war. This was clearly one of the more useful memories I still harbour from my formative years.

Money well spent. Never let it be said I didn't remember anything from school!

There were several other radio ships around the UK. Both on the east and west coast but the jewel in the crown was to be able to get a signal into London and establish a share of the London market. That is why most of them were off the Essex coast.

The radio ships were never political but I think that was the government's biggest fear. They had such a massive following and if they did get political then government would have no control. They could make or break elections with their vast following. They never did and it didn't take a lot of working out that they would have been stopped had they broken the unspoken rules.

It was said that Radio London kept their board room telephone in a soundproof box on the board room table because they thought that it was being tapped and that it was live all of the time. Our telephone at home where we had our office was constantly making odd noises when picked up and on one occasion an urgent voice was heard saying, "*look out they are on*" or something similar. At the time, I was at boarding school in North Wales and having been told this story by my parents I took it upon myself to write to the GPO. They were the state-owned institution that provided telephone services in those days. Considering my mother was always complaining that I never wrote her letters, I suppose I must have thought this a seriously interesting exercise to warrant writing one to them.

As I recall, I wrote to the GPO in London a most indignant letter. Explaining my concern that the government were tapping my parents and other radio station operator's telephones and the effect it had on individual freedoms and abuse of power, etc. Big Brother was an interesting phrase myself and my contemporaries had started to bandy about in those days. It must have been a month or so later. I was sitting in a particularly boring maths class staring out of the window wondering if I could work out a way to dodge games and get down to the woods. I wanted to try my hand once again at tickling a trout that I had seen in the shade of the riverbank, in one of the slow moving pools of the river Dee. Suddenly the Headmasters secretary burst into the room and went to the front of the class.

"Bates would you please come to the headmaster's office with me?" she announced importantly.

All eyes turned to me. This was unheard of. No one was ever pulled out of lessons.

I looked around the classroom of now smirking and sniggering faces, and I

could tell what they were thinking: *What's Batesy been up to now?*
My mind was racing this could only be bad news *'What the bloody hell have I done now?'*
As much as I struggled with the thought I really couldn't think of anything bad, I mean really bad that I could have done to warrant what seemed to be happening now. Stomach churning and breaking into a mild sweat, I was marched off down the long ornate hall that we, as mere mortals, were never ever allowed to tread. No pupil apart from the head boy ever walked the hallowed ancient floor tiles that we had been told were so rare and valuable, except when being taken to the headmaster's office. I'd had the rare and unwanted honour in the past of being caned by the head. This also was unheard of as normally the head boy could use a slipper as they called it. In fact, it was a gym shoe or plimsoll on your backside or for worse crimes the housemaster could use a cane on you. Being given six of the best by the head was something that, in all the time I was at boarding school, only ever happened to me, and four of my friends at the same time, and concerning the same incident.

Whilst on the subject, why is it that the spiteful bastards would always almost without exception say as a prelude to the thrashing *"Bates I want you to know this is going to hurt me far more than its going to hurt you"?*
I mean how the fuck did they work that one out? Was it a standard line learnt at the sadist academy as a preparation for taking the job?

My first caning at prep school was by Mr. Fox and he really was a ginger haired, pale skinned, freckled faced sadistic bastard. He had called me up to his study. Meeting me in the hallway outside and wearing his long black robe and mortarboard hat, he swished his long tapered cane from side to side with a whistling noise, in a moment of what must have been pure ecstasy to him. He was really getting off on it, when suddenly the tip caught the wall and shattered splitting the end.
Thank Christ for that I thought.
He held it in front of his face examining it carefully with a look of abject disappointment on his horrible ginger face, then looked at me and said

"hmmm I will need to get a new one come back at the same time tomorrow Bates". If only I had known then what I found out years later, that the unpleasant ginger bastard was having an affair with my mother's married friend whose son was in my class.

My mind was racing, I couldn't remember having transgressed the austere rules of the school and if I had certainly nothing to warrant another beating by the 'Old Man' as we affectionately called the headmaster. The secretary opened the ornate heavy wood panelled door, and I was ushered into the office. There was Carrington, the head, a tall, fair-haired man in his forties wearing his customary smart charcoal suit, sitting in a huge leather chair behind his desk. On this side of the desk opposite him was a grey looking gentleman in a crumpled grey suit. *"Bateo"* said Carrington in the surprisingly disarming fashion that he and he alone had been known to address me, *"sit down old chap"*, pointing to a chair next to the visitor.

"Bateo this gentleman has been sent here from the GPO in London. They are very concerned about allegations you have penned in a letter to them".
A wry and amused look crossed his face as his sweeping open-handed gesture passed me across to the grey man, *"Please explain your concerns"* he offered.
I was stuck dumb. There I was expecting to be battered for something. I didn't know I had done by the head when in reality I was being confronted by this fellow especially dispatched all the way from London to North Wales to allay my concerns on phone tapping. The headmaster was totally bemused and somewhat proud that one of his charges had prodded the establishment and received results. I was asked to explain my letter and my misgivings about the GPO.

I would like to think I stated my case eloquently and explained all my misgivings about the GPO and the government that controlled it; but I don't suppose I did at all. I could hardly remember what I had even put in the letter I had written so long ago. It was such a shock that the grey man had just turned up out of the blue, although I have a sneaking suspicion that the head must have known all along he was coming.

The man in the grey suit listened intently until I finished. He was most sympathetic about my concerns. He assured me that the government would never let such a thing take place on British soil. Even if they wanted to tap phones, the GPO would never allow it to happen and they didn't even have the technology. Special branch, MI5 and clandestine phone tapping were all figments of spy thriller writer's imagination he assured me. The conversation finished with him promising my classmates and me a visit to the local telephone exchange at Wrexham to see how it all worked. He shook my hand with a limp pudgy grasp and left.
I suppose it was an early lesson to me. I had doubts we would ever get invited to see how the telephone exchange worked and I was right, the invitation never came.
But on the plus side I noticed a secret door behind the heads chair that I had heard rumours of. It was built into, and part of the bookshelf with shelves of books actually attached to it and it was open a crack. I made a mental note to try and get back in there when the room was empty and see what was behind it. Some good comes out of everything!
Maybe the head was a Russian spy, masquerading as a stuffy headmaster with secret radio transceivers linked to the Kremlin in his hidden room behind the bookshelf. As for the grey man, what a load of crap he had come out with!

The task of closing down the stations fell to the Postmaster General, Tony Benn, the head of the GPO. The UK government used all of its legal and political powers to bring in new laws making it illegal to work on a pirate station. It became illegal to supply them with food or fuel and most detrimental to us: illegal to advertise on them. Thus cutting the revenue stream and their life's blood.

In desperation, some of the stations turned to what we called plastic religion. Fiery American evangelists would take half hour slots in the evenings to pump out their brand of plastic religion. I have to say some of it was quite amusing and I was fascinated in how they asked the public for money. Some were interesting to listen to in a philosophical way. Some were homophobic and others just seemed to be happy to sell you a plastic St Christopher to stick on the dashboard that apparently would save you and your family from any impending car crash. Complete with testimony's from people whose life the little plastic icon had saved as they drove through storm lashed roads towards certain death.

It was a total eye-opener for a young Englishman with old-fashioned values, even though at the time my father thought it somewhat of an unethical way of getting revenue. Radio Caroline was the last station to stay on the air; they were supplied ostensibly by ship from Northern Spain. In reality fishing boats from the River Crouch, West Mersea and other Essex backwaters were paid very well to deliver several tonnes of diesel a day in the dead of night on their way to work, until one of them, Howard Beer, was caught and given a nine-month prison sentence. Now it was serious.

I think it's sad that eventually the pressure put on them by the Courts closed them down. The pioneers of commercial radio in the UK, such as my father, went unrecognised. All the radio licenses were given to local businessmen who didn't have a clue about the industry. The DJs were ok and went on to work for the BBC, commercial radio and Luxemburg. Some even made it into TV. Tony Blackburn was one of them. Much loved Tony, who has made a recent comeback, used to think he could sing, and now and again without too much prompting would sing and clank on a guitar while on air from Radio Caroline.

I think it is fair to say that just as my father was getting organised with his station and stood a chance of making an income from it, the government stepped in.

In an attempt to make wages for the staff and pay for the fuel and food, my father and some of the DJs embarked on the good old 'Mizzy Gel' once more and motored the ten or so miles to the Tongue forts off Margate, to remove some of the copper and brass for scrap value.

I went with my dad on this mission along with a small communications transceiver that the station engineer had made so they could keep in touch with the Knock John. It wasn't the most reliable thing in the world, but the mark two model, created a couple of weeks later, was a little better.

There was a hole in the tower below the high water mark, and I could never work out how it got there. As a young boy I could climb through it at low tide and up the rusty companionways to the deck above. I have heard many stories of how this hole appeared while the fort was being manned by a caretaker crew in the early fifties. It was the relatively small size of the hole; I suppose some two-foot across that confused me. Both the towers were leaning in opposite directions on the skew-whiff and the top of both concrete towers had flowered out under the platform like a rosette so the companionways to the first floor were S-shaped as they had buckled. Tremendous forces had obviously been in action, whether it was hit by a ship (which I believe is the main consensus of opinion) or a torpedo or shell. I just couldn't understand how, if it was a ship, it had punched such a small neat hole so low down in the tower.

There was also talk of it just having settled badly when it was sunk in position and under scoured leading to the concrete barge base breaking its back. Either way the deck had a massive list on it, walking from one side of the main deck to the other was like climbing a very steep hill. I do know the caretaker crew were taken off by lifeboat leaving all of their gear. Having been on every fort in the Thames, both Army and Navy, I can safely say the tongue had the most original kit on it including Naval message pads, logbooks and gun sights. The only parts missing off the 3.7-inch 'surface to air' guns were the breechblocks. One of these guns I was to learn later had fired a low round by mistake that had skipped across the water and killed a young lad in a coal yard in Margate a few miles away. The dreadful accident was covered up and put down to enemy action by the wartime Ministry of Information.

We left the small crew on the fort and went into Margate harbour where I remember being chuffed with a heavy navy-issue grey steel helmet I had found hanging behind one of the doors. As a young lad, this was a fascinating trophy.

While we were away, a local tripper boat full of tourists had motored out to the fort and on seeing our lads in residence on the derelict fort asked what they were doing there. The guy in charge, Dick Palmer, said they were from Radio Essex and were going to start another radio station for Kent. *"Great"* said the crew of the boat, *"what will it be called?"*
The young Dick Palmer struggling for a reply looked up to the sky where a seagull was flapping about. In a moment of inspiration, announced it was to be "*Radio Albatross*".

They started taking requests from the day-trippers to be played on Radio Essex, which were duly radioed across to the station, some twelve miles away. In return the boat would bring out fresh drinking water, bread and milk, much to the delight of our crew and the owner of the boat who advertised the fact.

Obviously the tower with a hole in it was flooded, as it was under water when the tide was up. What was left of the wartime generators was just a lump of red rust in the middle of the room. The other tower was dry and in original condition with its wartime bunks, cupboards for food and heavy pine dining table. There was however damage to the top floor. One dark, calm night this tower also flooded and our crew were taken off the fort by lifeboat. Clearly someone had opened one of the seacock valves, housed one floor from the bottom, that were designed to flood the ammunition magazine in the event of fire.

So ended the Radio Albatross saga.

In 1945 near the end of the war, the Tongue forts engaged a flotilla of 15 German E-boats (Fast torpedo boats). They had left Ijmuiden in Holland intent on a high-speed attack on shipping entering the Thames. These 30-metre craft, capable of some 43 knots, usually attacked out of the dark; launching their torpedoes at close quarters before racing off. On this occasion, they hadn't counted on the forts and their stable radar controlled guns, with which they sank one as they approached their targets and drove the others off back into the North Sea.

Collectively the forts in general were credited with shooting down some 22 German aircraft. Destroying 30 odd German V1 flying bombs or 'Doodlebugs' as they were nicknamed, an early version of our modern jet propelled missiles.

The so-called radio pirates changed the face and sound of radio in the UK and Holland where there were other radio ships. In the UK, we were always told that the BBC, who had until then a monopoly on radio broadcasting, couldn't play constant music because they couldn't afford to pay the punishing performing rights fees to the artists every time a record was played. Eventually, meetings were held between them and the way was found around it. This laid the groundwork for the issuing of licences for commercial radio stations throughout the UK, broadcasting the popular music the public wanted to hear.

In reality, the record companies would send the offshore stations hundreds of records a week as the more they were played on the radio the more they sold.

The government began making claims of interference to the emergency services radio frequencies and anything else they could think of. They took the stations on one by one, prosecuting them individually. My father's station Radio Essex later renamed *'Britain's Better Music Station'* or '*BBMS*' was taken to court on the 30th of November 1966. He pleaded guilty of breaching the Marine Offences Act and was fined £100 with the threat that if he did not close down he could be fined the same amount on a daily basis. In 1966, this was a considerable amount of money.

I was back at boarding school in North Wales at the time. I knew the court case was taking place that day, but there was no way I could find out what the results were. It was very worrying and extremely frustrating. Filled with anxiety, I tried to reach my father on the only pay phone in the school to find out if he had been fined or even committed to prison for giving the public what they craved. It was impossible to get through; his telephone was constantly engaged and I wasn't really meant to be using the school phone without special permission. The phone was located on the wall outside the headmaster's study; it was only a matter of time before I got into trouble for being there.

Eventually, I came to the conclusion that there was a problem with the school phone. With that, I bunked off lessons and walked across the bleak snow swept playing fields. Taking a short cut through the woods to a small shop that stood on its own a couple of miles away with a cold and windswept red phone box outside. Not surprisingly, I got the same results, a constant engaged tone. Disappointed that I had walked so far in such diabolical weather, only to find the same engaged tone from the stupid thing. I was freezing cold and desperate to know what had happened. In a moment of blinding inspiration, I had a brain wave!

I phoned the operator and explained the situation. She was unbelievably sympathetic bless her and broke into my father's phone call with a journalist and told him I was on the line, Halcyon days when you could actually talk to an operator. A real person, not a robot telling you to press this button and then that button as the expense racks up. Only to find someone comes in the door at the crucial moment and distracts you or worse getting to the last bloody digit and pressing the wrong one, or a distant voice from the other side of the world, with a thick accent that you can't quite understand. You know it's English, but it just isn't quite there. In those days, you never heard the words *"Please hold your call is important to us"*. Followed by ghastly piped music for twenty minutes before getting to speak to someone in a different time zone who doesn't really want to help you at all. What's that thing when they say these days? *"For security reasons please give me your date of birth and the first line of your address and postcode"*. Excuse me but if someone phones, up and wants to pay my gas bill for me, I don't care who they are. Take the money!

But I digress. My father explained what had happened and said the phone had not stopped ringing with journalists calling. Needless to say, he was in fighting spirit and intended to carry on broadcasting. In reality, financial pressures and the continued threat of further fines forced him to close the station down at four thirty in the afternoon Christmas day 1966.

The day before this, Christmas Eve, we left Southend on a calm sea in the old Mizzy Gel (My sister Penny's pet name for my mother from when she was small) to collect some disc jockeys from the radio station. We then steamed from the Knock John forts out into the North Sea and headed for what was then 'Roughs Tower', seven and a half miles off Harwich.

We arrived about nine or ten o'clock in the evening on an extremely black and bitterly cold night that would change my life forever. We approached the lowest point: a wartime landing stage bolted onto the south tower. It was constructed of steel with a solid timber deck. In the middle of it, the rusted remains of a diesel-powered cargo winch were visible in the gloom. Dangling down from this was a thin piece of ancient looking rope. It must have been high tide because standing on the wheelhouse roof it was just possible for one of the lads with us to reach the rope. With a leg up from the others, he shinned up and onto the landing stage. There he found a heavily made rope ladder, which he lowered down to us below. The other guys including myself started to climb it and then up a steel ladder to another smaller landing stage with another steel ladder to the deck above.

As we got to the top two men came out of the accommodation and confronted us. One had an air rifle. One of our blokes came up behind him as he looked down on us below and took the air rifle off the very shocked fellow. We swarmed up onto the deck and introduced ourselves. Hardly a word was spoken. We went inside with them and found that they had been preparing for Christmas. They had a Turkey, Christmas pudding and all the usual bits and bobs, including cigars to celebrate their Yuletide isolation. The only lighting they had was a few candles spluttering away and a one-burner bottled gas cooker. We told them to pack up their gear and we would take them ashore. We asked whom they worked for, to which they replied "*Radio Caroline*" which was broadcasting from a ship a few miles away.

They chatted away to me, and my father on the journey into the harbour. After we dropped them off at Harwich they told their boss that all these heavies had turned up with shotguns and pickaxe handles. It couldn't have been further from the case. We had no weapons and it was a handful of not very macho DJ's and a 14-year-old boy. My dad had to stay on the boat to handle it, as he was the only one of the motley crew capable.

A few years later my parents were on the Harwich-Hook of Holland ferry and one of the crew showed them a men's magazine. Amongst all the bums and tits there was an article about Sealand, which explained that my father turned up on a boat, with my mother disguised as heavily pregnant and sea sick. When the concerned occupants of the fort allowed them to land, my mother whipped out a sub-machinegun from under the bump and took them all prisoner at gunpoint. It never fails to amaze me the stories I continue to hear or read about us.

After dropping them off at Harwich, we sailed for Southend and home once more. It had been a long, very cold and uncomfortable journey. We were glad to get back to a warm bath and hot food.

A few days later we were at sea again unloading all the generator and transmitter parts from the Knock John forts, to take them to the Roughs Tower. As a boy, I can honestly say I never heard my father use a swear word stronger than '*Bloody*', but as he and I on the boat took aboard the vital parts of his radio station in ever decreasing weather conditions he was becoming more and more under pressure.

The wind and tide were such that we were having to make passes between the towers hooking a single load aboard with every pass, in extremely dangerous conditions.

As we made one such pass, the wooden transom (back of the boat) became snagged on a rusty bolt protruding from the concrete tower. With a crunching and cracking of tortured timber it ripped off half way down near water level, threatening to flood into the old ladies engine room and sink us in seconds. Fortunately with the foresight of the Navy, its original owners, copper tingles had been nailed around the shape of the transom: thin sheets of copper nailed on the sides and beaten to shape around the transom. As the water started to pour into the engine room with every roll of the boat, my father grabbed a broom and hooked the now flapping as if hinged wooden transom out of the sea pushing it back into place again. Legs astride to keep his balance on the heaving deck and clutching a large sledgehammer he bashed it home, driving the long nails back into the hull as he teetered precariously over the back of the boat. He ran back into the wheelhouse and brought the old boat back around to collect yet another important load in the worsening weather.

Two trays of eggs came down on a rope.

"I don't want fucking eggs! I want fucking transmitter parts and fucking generator parts!" roared the old man.

I was gobsmacked. I looked at him. I was fourteen years old and not once had I ever heard him use such language! Did I really just hear him shout those words? So my dad was human after all!

Mumbling and muttering under his breath Dad got the old boat underway and steamed off towards Sealand some three hours away and unloaded the transmitter kit and some DJs, along with the *F'ing eggs*.

A short time later, our crew abandoned the Roughs fort amid stories of running low of food and water. They were taken off by lifeboat. In those days, there were no mobile phones or radio communications. They had learnt from the guys we took off the fort that there was a prearranged distress signal for the passing pilot boats that went past to look out for if they had a problem. It consisted of hanging a bucket from the barrel of one of the 3.7 anti-aircraft guns. So this they did and somebody called the lifeboat out.

I recall an amusing incident from 1966. The radio station had closed and there was just no money at all. One of dad's old pals Bill Russell, a local car trader, gave him a Ford Anglia car. It was an old wreck that he had taken in part exchange but dad was very grateful for it.

We were parked outside my grandfather's house and had just gotten in the car to go home. This required climbing into the passenger side to get into the drivers seat as the drivers door didn't open. A police car pulled up behind with his blue light flashing. A young 'bobby' got out and walked around the old wreck with his nose in the air, and a look of disdain on his face.

"Would you mind getting out of the car please sir?"' he said pompously from under his pointy blue helmet. He reached down to pull the drivers door open and tugged on it.

"Don't do that!" shouted the old man anxiously. The policeman must have thought he had an escaped axe murderer in his sights and heaved on the door handle with all of his might to arrest him before he could escape.

"No! No!" shouted dad, *"Leave the door alone!"* With the sound of tortured metal and the squeal of seized hinges, the door came open and detached itself completely from the old car; landing on the policeman's foot. He wasn't very happy and dad got fined for a long list of offences including driving a dangerous vehicle.

My father had meetings with Ronan O'Rahilly, the managing director of Radio Caroline, and it was decided that perhaps they could work together. O'Rahilly sent my father a huge bouquet of flowers that he thought were for my mother but they were for him with a note saying *"Peace man"* or something very similar. My old man was horrified that a *'bloke'* had sent him a bunch of flowers. He quickly handed them to my mother seemingly worried holding them for too long might deprive him of his masculinity.

My father never quite got to grips with the fact that it was the 60s, and the Beatles and Rolling Stones topped the charts and flower power was appearing. To him this was all a bit suspect and unmanly, and the world was becoming a bit *Namby Pamby* as he put it.

Despite the flowers and O'Rahilly's fashionably long hair, talks were held at Caroline's offices in Chesterfield Gardens, London. It was agreed we would each put staff out there and start a joint venture together. Work was started to cut the radar, radar room and fire control rooms away from the top to make space for a helipad

The work completed and the helipad marked out with a smart 'H' clearly visible from the air. O'Rahilly went out in a helicopter, stayed overnight and talked to our man on site Tony Mandel. He told him that when he gave him the nod, he would cease working for us and come into his employ with double wages. Tony was good enough to tell me about this on our next visit as he wasn't happy with the situation. My father told him he was to go ashore and to get his gear packed. I offered to stay in his place with another guy called David Belasco who was on the boat with us. After some trepidation, my father agreed. This must have been in my Easter school holidays of 1967. I was 14 years old.

Belasco was a short scruffy man of 25, who had been helping around our Southend office some time. He was fascinated by the whole pirate radio phenomena. My father told me that Belasco had confessed to him that he had been in 'Borstal' (reform school) as a boy and had served some jail time for petty theft later in life. Dad said many of the troops serving under him in the army had been bad boys in civilian life but had served king and country with distinction when the war came along. He had promised himself that when the war was over he would always give someone a chance irrespective of their past.

In Belasco's case it was a decision my father lived to regret.

Holding The Fort

The following day Radio Caroline's tender came out. A fine steel Dutch fishing boat complete with clog wearing crew. They had come to collect some of the many empty oxygen bottles used in the burning gear that had been employed in the removing of the steel building where there was now a helipad.

At the north end of the main platform, there was a piece of steel channel bolted down to the deck and poking over the side with a rope and pulley block shackled to the end of it, at about waist level. This they had been using to lower the oxygen bottles and pull their stores up. It wasn't ideal as it was not possible to pull down on the rope using your body weight; it was more of a horizontal pull.

I had been talking to the two Radio Caroline guys the day before. One of them, an unshaven wiry looking lad with short dark hair, had only been there a day and was convinced that he really didn't like it on the fort. The other guy, a big lad with ginger hair was made of much sterner stuff and was happy to stay until relieved, as this is what he had agreed with his boss. They were lowering two oxygen bottles down between them to the boat below when they got into trouble holding the rope. I hastily ran across to help and got hold of the rope in front of the two struggling men and heaved. The boat had moved away, and we were having trouble holding the weight.

"Take a turn!" I barked over my shoulder.

"Got it" came the reply.

"Are you sure you have a good turn?"

" Yes got it" was the reply.

I let go of the rope and couldn't believe what happened next. The rope whistled out and the bottles crashed into the sea with an enormous plash narrowly missing the boat. I looked behind me and the big lad had collapsed to his knees staring down at his hands in horror. He had it seems taken two turns around his hand with the rope and not around something solid as any seaman will tell you the term '*Take a turn*' means. As the bottles plummeted into the sea, the rope had whistled through his fingers and in a fraction of a second the bones were exposed on all the fingers of one hand in furrows an inch wide. I felt sick to my stomach. It happened so quickly, and I suppose with such burning friction from the rope they didn't even seem to be bleeding as if cauterized by the heat. Just the white exposed bone. Then the blood started to well out from the edges of the wound and pump onto the deck. I ran to get a towel and we bound up his hand tightly, the agony contorting his face.

He was bravely prepared to stay and await relief but I convinced him to leave and get to the hospital. We put a rope around him, he half lowered and half climbed down the rope ladder. In reality, he was in a very bad way and did need to get some help. The place was so dirty he would have got an infection in no time and I am sure the Dutch skipper would have had to give him some morphine from his medical box for the trip home.

So there we were, myself and this other chap in full command of the fortress. We had no way of informing my father what had happened. We just had to wait for him to return, whenever that might be.

Belasco in the meantime had run out of cigarettes. Being quite a serious smoker, this caused him some problems. He was constantly agitated and looking for every reason to try and cadge a lift ashore on a passing yacht at the same time trying to talk me into going with him. He was becoming a bloody nuisance. I was getting more and more pissed off with his mood swings because of his addictions to tobacco when I noticed him smoking a cigarette.
"*I thought you had run out of tobacco?*" I asked warily.
"*I had*" he replied with a smirk. Explaining he had solved the problem by reaching down behind the built in wooden bunk beds that were fitted around the inside of the tower rooms when the fort was built. Extricating hundreds of wartime dog ends that sailors had put out and thrown down

behind their bunks. These cigarette butts he happily pulled to pieces and rolled into new cigarettes, some thirty years after the original owners had put them out. He worked his way industriously around all the bunks and any likely places a sailor might think to put out an illicit cigarette.

The Caroline tender returned the next day with more people, but I told them sternly they couldn't land. With that, they went away somewhat bemused. That night the sea was like a millpond, absolutely flat calm. Belasco messing around and always playing the idiot shouted into the night *"We know you are out there! We can see you!"*
To our shock an aggressive voice bellowed back out of the darkness *"Never mind you bastards! We'll be back and next time you won't see us!"* As I strained my eyes into the darkness, I could just make out the silhouette of a small wooden fishing boat with no lights on.

Hmm, I thought, not so good.
Sitting out here with no backup. The reality of the situation saturated my thoughts. No one to call on for help and no way to tell my family what was going on. My dad didn't even know we were fighting people off. As far as he was concerned we were still out there with the Radio Caroline staff.
"Right let's make some defences!"
Armed with a new sense of urgency, we gathered up all the heavy oxygen bottles we could find and balanced them on the flat narrow rail ready to launch over the side onto any invaders. We also wired the ends where the regulator was meant to screw on together with fencing wire. If a grapnel were thrown up, they would all get pulled down in a massive bundle on the person throwing it. Each bottle weighed some 70 or 80 kilos.
We wrote, *'DANGER ELECTRIC FENCE 10,000 VOLTS'* down the outside of the rail in large white letters. In a government report I read years later, this was a major consideration and concern in a plan by the services to forcibly take the fort over. Since we didn't even have a generator and only had candles and hurricane lamps at the time, that simple message went a long way!
I found a couple of gallons of petrol in one of the big ammunition boxes on

the deck, used to service the 3.7s, that must have been stored there to power a welder or something. We made up some Molotov cocktails and put them in milk crates so we could move them around quickly to any defensive position. Having only read about how they were made by the Russians to hurl down from buildings on the advancing German tanks during the war and chatting to my father about them in conversation, I thought perhaps I should try one out to ensure I had assembled them correctly.

We lit the fuse with trepidation on one, half expecting it to explode in our hands before it could be thrown. Hurling it onto the corner of the steel deck, where with a shattering of glass, and a whoosh, it covered an impressive area of the steelwork with flickering yellow flames. Success!

My finest effort was a homemade shotgun that I fashioned out of electrical conduit with, profoundly, a firing pin made from something I had unscrewed from the anti-aircraft gun. I fixed it on a wooden board, inserted a 12 gauge shotgun cartridge, screwed down the home made breech and arranged it so a heavy switch box slid down the board and struck the firing pin. I pulled the string and ducked around the corner of the building. Much to my surprise it went off with an almighty boom and more importantly didn't blow itself to bits. Delighted with my ingenuity and success, I looked about for more defensive projects. We now had the means to defend ourselves if we came under attack and I was feeling a lot more confident about everything. We also had quite a good quality .22 calibre air pistol that I had found on the 'Sunk Head Tower' some ten miles away. We had visited the Sunk on the way to the fort a few days before. It was interesting to us because it was the only other fortress outside UK territorial limits.

This fortress had been the site of a proposed television station a year before: 'Tower TV' but this project came to nothing, the occupants abandoning it by lifeboat, leaving a rope ladder hanging down. My old man said, *"Go on son, get on it"* as we swept past.

It was lucky my father had trained me at a very early age in the art of climbing or at least hanging on. As a boy, my grandparents lived in a very imposing house on the seafront at Thorpe Bay in Essex. They had a beautifully kept garden with several large, imposing trees. While climbing one of them several feet above the ground, I missed my step and fell to the grass below. As I staggered to my feet, nursing a sore arm, my father ran across and gave me a totally unexpected clump.

"What was that for" I wailed, *"you said I could climb the tree?"*

"Yes" said the old man in a gruff voice, *"but I didn't tell you could fall out of it!"* and so ended my first climbing lesson!

So there I was on the foredeck of the boat. I recall prematurely getting hold of the bottom rung of the ancient looking ladder. Its weathered and rotting wooden rungs that had clearly seen far better days. I was unable to pull myself up further to get my foot in the bottom rung. I looked down at the gurgling water a few feet below me. By now my arm muscles were screaming with pain, thinking I might have to let go and swim to the boat if it couldn't make it back to me in time. I was horrified to see whirlpools of swirling muddy water as the tide ebbed out through the razor sharp barnacle and limpet encrusted towers at a fair old rate. I tried to work out in my mind if they would be strong enough to suck me down to oblivion if I let go. They certainly looked horrifying to my young eyes. This unanswered dilemma gave me the strength to hang on longer.

I knew I had to hang on. Dangling helplessly like a ripe apple on a tree ready to drop off, thinking my arms were going to leave their sockets. Just feet above the swirling water, watching my father bring the old Mizzy Gel back around with its infamous no-reverse gearbox. Ever so slowly it seemed, right around the fort and back into the tide to the ladder, so that I could get back on it. The thought carving through my mind that I couldn't hold on much longer and if the old man missed me and had to go around again I was in for a swim in the murky swirling waters below my feet. He didn't miss and I launched myself with pounding heart and aching arms back onto the boat.

After regaining my composure, I was able to have a fresh attempt. This time from the wheelhouse roof, giving me a better start to throw myself a little further up the tired old rope ladder and to get my foot firmly on the bottom rung. Once on the ladder I scampered up to the top before the tired old thing had a chance to give up on me.

On the Sunk Forts we found an air pistol hidden and forgotten under a mattress, as well as some old tank transmitters and a generator. Interestingly, the fortress had been placed in somewhat deep water and on a big tide I doubt there was twenty feet separating the sea and the deck. Because of this, seas had swept over the top of it and filled both towers with water. It must have been a frightening place to be with the seas breaking onto the deck in storms that's without the Germans trying to bomb it and shoot it up.

Once we had gathered all we could make use of, we made our way back to the Mizzy Gel.

The Mizzy Gel, what can I say? Everything about the poor old boat was a floating nightmare! It constantly leaked and needed pumping out daily, even on the mooring where it spent much time dried out on the tide. If the pump were to fail at sea, the poor old thing would have sunk in a relatively short time. But that's why the old man always had a bucket handy for just such occasions. I can see him bailing the thing out now to *'get the level down a bit'* so he could work on the pump.

The engine never wanted to start and when it did the batteries invariably wouldn't charge with the ancient dynamo system, so we constantly had to drag massive 50-kilo batteries ashore to charge them. This also, of course, was done the hard way. Needless to say, they were the biggest and heaviest batteries I have ever seen then or since, they were originally made to power electric milk floats and were half the size of a dining room table!

My father's mooring, where he mostly kept the boat, at Paglesham was a quarter of a mile down the river from the hard path where you could get a vehicle near. The batteries had to be dragged out of the engine room, loaded into a skiff (no easy feat on its own) and rowed to the hard path.

From there they were dragged up the hard path and over the five-foot sea wall, to the car and taken home. After charging them, the arduous process would start all over again in reverse. I hated the bloody things!

The bloody gearbox, when it worked at all, would overheat and slip. Putting the boat in astern to go backwards was a lottery and invariably didn't work at all, which made for a lot of very interesting times!

The pump was the most important part of the whole setup, as it had to be running almost constantly while at sea. It was belt driven from a spinning pulley wheel on the end of a shaft that protruded through the engine room bulkhead into the fish hold. It seldom worked and when it did the belt was always flying off. I can see my father now risking his fingers several times a day to feed the V belts back on to the spinning pulleys before priming it with a bucket of putrid water from the bilge. All this machinery was meticulously serviced with a rusty adjustable spanner, a pair of half seized grips and most importantly a club hammer and cold chisel for 'undoing things'.

On one specific and very memorable occasion, battling head on into a southwesterly on our way home, under deteriorating weather conditions the bilge water began to rise. The pump was playing up and the belts washed off the spinning pulleys prompted by the rising water level in the hold. You could see it rising by looking back from the forward wheelhouse door, my father decided to issue the ships safety equipment. He pulled back the throttle levers (which had originally graced the dashboard of a wartime Mosquito bomber), set the wheel and ducked into the cabin. He emerged a moment later with two canvas World War Two German airman's life jackets, proudly displaying the German eagle and I imagine a few swastikas under the grime. Explaining as he did so, that someone down the pub had given them to him a few years ago. *"Put that on!"* he said with the same tone of voice I would imagine the captain of the Titanic used to give the abandon ship command. At the same time shoving the rotting and mildewed thing in my direction. Fortunately, as I struggled into it, the wind and seas took pity on us and started to drop.

Many years later, while advising on the forts and other structures in the Thames and North Sea for a BBC television series, I met a gentleman who, while now old and in a wheelchair, had been stationed by the Navy on the Sunk Head Forts when he was a young lad.

He told me that the Marines were issued with billhooks (like a lance with a sharpened hooked blade on the end) to fend off any attacking German marines that might try to board them. These things were what they used in Drake and Nelsons time to fend off the Spanish and French boarding parties, when the crew would throw grappling hooks into the others rigging pulling the ships together and charging onto her decks. Fascinating stuff I didn't know such things were still in use during the Second World War, but it made sense I suppose. Let's face it, my dad had been issued a broom handle with a bayonet lashed to the end of it. Not the most modern of weapons to patrol Romney marshes for invading Germans during basic training at the beginning of the war.

The old gentleman recalled witnessing a man during his time on the forts, fold his clothes up, lay them out neatly on his bunk and then climb the companionway to the main deck. He then proceeded to commit suicide by jumping over the side in the dead of night. He couldn't understand why the man rather selfishly took his ration of cigarettes with him.

A new term was added to the navy's medical phrase book: 'Fort madness' and apparently there was a good bit of it about in the crews that manned them.

He also told me a nice story of how they saw a parachute mine floating down towards them on the tide. They informed the Marines who blasted away at it with their .303 rifles. It was too close to get their big guns to bear down on it so there was nothing else they could do.

They all put on life jackets and the officers were in two minds whether to launch the boats (they had a 27 foot whaler under each side) or whether to just lay on the deck with their fingers pushed firmly in their ears and think of England. They decided to do the later and he swore they could hear the mine scrape past the towers as they sweated above. When it had gone, they radioed a nearby Destroyer, which opened fire with their big guns, blowing it up and resulting in much ribbing from the destroyer crew as the marines on the fort had failed to hit it.

The original idea of these Navy forts placed across the mouth of the Thames was to stop German bombers using the river as a navigational aid to find London. During the night the German bombers were dropping parachute mines in the River Thames and its approaches, resulting in a lot of damage to the vital convoys that were the lifeblood of the UK and its war effort. It's not necessary to physically hit a mine for a ship to detonate them and do damage to its self. Some of the devices were acoustic mines detonated from some distance by the sound of engine noises that travel through the water. Magnetic mines could detect the magnetic field of a ship and its wiring machinery. The shock waves from the massive explosions buckled ships plates, bent their propeller shafts and wrecked the propulsion machinery, turning it into useless junk.

HH90

The next uninvited guests to turn up were on an old black wooden fishing boat with a stern wheelhouse in broad daylight. We spotted it a long way off, as we had been carefully watching the horizon to the southwest almost willing my father to appear and bring us a relief crew or at least some much-needed stores. He also needed to know what was going on out there. We were running dangerously low on everything!

This boat coming from the direction of Southend-on-Sea surely had to be him and we were getting quite excited at the prospect. Even when it was near enough to see clearly through the binoculars I thought it must be a boat my dad had chartered for the trip as it was coming straight for us. After what seemed an age, the old wooden trawler arrived, slowed down and stopped under the fort. There were three scruffily dressed men on deck in an assortment of denim and donkey jackets. One of them, presumably the leader, cupped his hands to his mouth and shouted up in a friendly voice. *"Your father has sent us to relieve you. Put the ladder down mate so we can come up."*

Belasco, delighted with the news and the prospect of getting ashore to his family and not to mention cigarettes, said in an upbeat tone *"Great we can go home now".*

I pulled him away from the rail so as not to be seen from below and said *"Look I know most of the local boats in Southend and this isn't one of them. Besides, you don't have to be an Einstein to see that the fishing registration HH90 is a local Harwich one".* Most local boats from our part of the Thames were LO or London registered.

After a considerable amount of arguing, I managed to convince him that these were not friends at all. As much as we both wanted to go ashore and a few luxuries like sugar and tobacco would be nice this was not the way. I bent down and selected one of the petrol bombs that I had made from the milk crate on the deck. Still not quite sure it wasn't going to blow up in

64

my hand. I tilted it so the rag fuse became doused in petrol, brought it back upright, lit it and threw it onto the landing stage as hard as I could (the lowest point of the fortress). With a shattering of glass it went up with a very impressive '*Wuumpf*' and enveloped an old piece of machinery in yellow flames.

"*Now shove off!*" I shouted, "*or the next one goes on the boat!*"

The would-be invaders hastily retreated to what they considered a safe distance and stopped the boat again. They then had an '*I'm tougher than you and I've been in harder prisons than you*' shouting match with Belasco in which they exchanged much swearing and death threats.

I watched all this somewhat bemused as the boat eventually headed off, this time in the direction of Harwich. I was sure this was the same old fishing boat that we had inadvertently stumbled across in the darkness a few nights before.

We decided that the lower landing stage, which hung on girders about 15 feet below the main platform, was just too low and near to the sea affording too easy access to the deck. It was, after all, how we had climbed up onto the fort in the first place. With that, we carefully climbed down onto the landing stage with burning gear and cut it away at the front. It fell away as if hinged where it was still attached at one end to the tower. Belasco, who could climb like a monkey, then climbed underneath and standing on the tower fixing brackets gingerly proceeded to cut away the last remaining attached twisted metal and bolts. Dropping it into the sea with an almighty crash and plume of white water.

It was starting to concern me that if the same people and boatmen kept coming at us again and again they would strike lucky eventually, catch us unawares and get aboard. I decided we should become more proactive and shift to a more offensive posture. These people had to be shaken up so that they would not feel inclined to return for another go. Right now we had no control and the attacks were coming whenever and however it suited them, day and night, and on their terms. Two people keeping 24 hour a day watches, three hours on and three hours off through the night was becoming totally exhausting and extremely stressful for us. So things had to change.

To this end, we left a 40-foot rope ladder hanging over the side as bait and attached it to a lever. If anyone got onto it we would have the option of pulling the lever, allowing it to drop some ten-foot, sending the attacker into the ice-cold North Sea. It didn't take long.

In no time at all, the 'Offshore 2' tender turned up and put a rather large man on the ladder. It is not until recently I found out that Ronan O'Rahilly, Caroline's boss, was on the tender along with some radio station staff. A chap called Percy Scadden, who I remember introducing himself to my father months before in the Pier hotel Harwich as Bill Scadden: ex-flying squad. It seems he preferred Bill to Percy, so adopted the name. Scadden lived at nearby Frinton and was a licensed radio amateur. He kept communications between the radio ship and the office in Chesterfield gardens London. Also onboard was Jimmy Houlihan, who I was told was Ronan's bodyguard and had previously been the minder of notorious London landlord Peter Rachman. Rachman had owned hundreds of slum properties in London in the 50s and 60s, mostly let out to immigrants. He had an incredibly bad name as a bullying and threatening landlord. He would send his rent collectors around with German Shepherd Dogs to intimidate the tenants into paying the rent, to such an extent that a new word was to come into the English vocabulary to describe such people: 'Rachmanism'.

The large chap on the ladder stopped climbing when I appeared from under the rail and I told him to stay where he was. The crew of the boat looked up horrified as our first Molotov cocktail came spinning through the air onto the deck of the steel boat, followed by various missiles we had amassed for just such an occasion. *It pulled away at full speed!*

Bill Scadden ran down the deck, his jacket ablaze, he had quite a good turn of speed for a large and not so young man! The Dutch crew rushed out of the wheelhouse with a clattering of clogs on the steel deck. Waving fire extinguishers around as they chased him down the deck to put the flames out and then proceeded to douse the mast and superstructure with foam, quelling the fire quickly.

After not very long the man on the ladder started saying his arms were getting tired and he could hold on no longer. We called to the offshore tender to come and collect him, happy that he wouldn't be part of any more attacks against us in the future. The captain refused to come near us. Feeling sorry for the very dejected man hanging from the ladder, we lowered our wooden stores crate that we used to winch supplies up from our tender and told him to get in it. This he happily did and sat there safe, if a bit cramped, awaiting events. As time went by and it got dark we lowered him down some food and a Tilley lamp and bantered with him. He made it very clear that we definitely wouldn't be seeing him again if he ever got out of this mess he had gotten himself into.

We were chatting away to him suspended in the box as you would to a canary in a cage when the sound of powerful engines and urgent voices broke the stillness of the very dark and calm night.

Here we go again. Snatching up the milk crate of Molotov cocktails, I ran to the other side of the fortress, from where the engine noises were coming. I could see bright navigation lights coming towards us out of the darkness at quite a speed. Hunkering down under the rail so as not to be a target from the new threat I fumbled the box of matches out of my pocket with adrenaline shaking hands. This was not good. Only two of us and we were now being attacked from all sides.

A searchlight stabbed out through the darkness and a loud hailer crackled into life with a tinny, amplified voice. "*Attention this is Walton lifeboat we are the neutral party, we have come to take the man off the ladder*"
This was repeated several times followed by "*Do we have your permission?*"
Shit I had nearly bombed the RNLI!
I mean they are the good guys and regularly risk their lives on a voluntary

basis to save lives at sea!

"Of course" I shouted, *"pick him up."*

The old wooden Watson class lifeboat came into view close underneath, manoeuvring to get near the ladder and the unfortunate man. At one point it got jammed between the two towers of Sealand fore and aft, and only managed to get free with much pushing and shoving, not to mention cursing from the crew. The man in the crate couldn't move. His limbs had frozen up with inactivity and he was unable to help himself. His lifejacket wouldn't allow him to move in such a confined space. Belasco had to climb down the ladder and cut him out of his lifejacket with a knife and help him down onto the lifeboat where many willing hands reached out to pull him to safety.

Walton lifeboat crew gave us a wave and steamed off into the darkness. It was also the last time we would see the Offshore Two tender.

It was the 27th June 1967 and I was nearly 15 years old.

I was starting to get a sixth sense about these things and when I mentioned to my father about it, he said *"Well if you feel under threat and feel that an attack is imminent you should listen to your inner thoughts. It is quite possible that if nothing matures of your thoughts, it could well be that people are thinking and planning bad thoughts about you. Just because nothing happens when you expect it, it doesn't mean people weren't planning and wishing you bad but just couldn't fulfil their wishes."*

Future events in my life have convinced me that there is some merit in this way of thinking.

One particular chilly early spring evening I was convinced there would be an attack that night. I couldn't sleep and paced about all night in the dark looking, listening and waiting for something to happen. I stripped my powerful .22 air pistol, cleaned and oiled it.

I was convinced that something would happen that night.

I checked the milk crates of Molotov cocktails and made sure there were matches to ignite them. I was absolutely convinced there was something afoot and we would see action that night. As dawn broke, I could hear an engine running slowly nearby on tick over. It was flat calm and high water on a beautiful clear spring morning. Out of the breaking light came a white boat. She had no wheelhouse as such, just an open steering position on deck and several men running about launching an inflatable dingy. Two very fit and serious looking men climbed into it and started to paddle towards me with stealthy controlled strokes of the paddles. The nearer they got, I could see they had an outboard engine on the back, rope ladders, grappling hooks and ropes in the boat. These guys clearly meant business, and they had all the kit to execute their plan.

As they silently paddled across, I watched them through a hole in the rail. I slithered across the deck into the main building and woke up Belasco. I returned to find them almost under the platform and preparing to launch a grappling hook attached to a climbing rope in my direction. I got some matches out of my pocket and tried lighting a petrol bomb. The bloody matches were damp and refused to light; the ends were crumbling off them and falling to the deck.

I was starting to get worried now. I got down to the last two when suddenly the red phosphorus end of the last one spluttered and spat for a second, allowing me to light the fuse on the Molotov cocktail. I leant over the side with my arm extended straight out and let it drop straight down into the open boat below.

It was a perfect shot!

The bomb exploded in the middle of the boat, hurling them into the sea. As the inflatable boat drifted away in flames, the two hard cases swam as best they could in their lifejackets to the nearest barnacle-encrusted tower and clung on.

They shouted some abuse at us, which was followed from above by some lumps of wood we had assembled for such an occasion. Their tone soon became more conciliatory and polite.

Followed eventually by "*no more governor...please...no more guv*" in whimpering tones.

The guys on the larger boat decided they had to come in and pick up their fallen comrades in arms. The boat came steaming across at speed but unfortunately for them the wheel was exposed and I clattered away at the helmsman with the air pistol. The many hours as a boy spent sitting on the bow of my father's fishing boats with air rifles and air pistols, firing off some 250 slugs a day at targets of driftwood and flotsam proved good in my favour. Not to mention hours of pistol shooting on the local police range with small-bore weapons while my father taught small arms combat shooting to the local constabulary. Whenever they got close, I kept driving the helmsman from the wheel with ease. I can see one of them to this day with blood running down his rage contorted face, holding his hands up in a strangling gesture, indicating what he wanted to do to me given the chance. This pissed me off even more and he became my primary target until he gave up and ran below, having been discouraged by a few well aimed .22 slugs. *What did they expect?* They hadn't exactly turned up with a bunch of flowers and I had no reason to believe they would have treated us any better had they managed to board us.

To their credit, they put up a very brave front in what was a very difficult situation for them. There was quite a bit of blood about on the boat and I was being sworn at rather profusely and threatened with all sorts of violence. They tried several times to come in close and eventually had to give up and retire to a safe distance defeated.

It was clear the guys in the water had had enough and the cold was getting to them. The crew on the larger boat were as equally exhausted and dejected. I told them they could collect their friends and not to come back or it would be worse for them. They came in near, not wanting to get right underneath. Threw a rope and towed the first desperate man at speed to safety; pulling his cold, rigid, half-drowned from being dragged through the water body over the rail. They then came in and collected the other man the same way. They were as stiff as boards but because they both had lifejackets on I had considered it safe to leave them in the water for some time to discourage them from coming back again.

I was told later that one of them on the boat was O'Rahilly's minder, and the guys in the water were famous London gangsters later to be indicted and jailed for torturing other villains. They looked like they might have been brothers.

Whoever they were, they didn't come back!

With the constant pressure on us from the Customs and Excise, we often became low on food. Rationing was a way of life to us. At one point we had nothing but tins of corned beef and tins of peas. Not the most exciting diet. There was one tin of steak and kidney pudding that I had been saving as a special treat.

The big day came when we decided to spoil ourselves with it. It was getting dark and due to a lack of paraffin, we had been reduced to using candles for lighting. I fired up the single burner gas ring and reverently put the tin into boiling water. We sat watching, mouths watering as the pot bubbled for the 45 minutes instructed on the tin. The moment arrived to take it out of the water. I lifted it out carefully and put it on the table in the half-light. Opening the tin and sharing out the fabled pudding with a generous portion of tinned peas each. We started to eat. *Hmmm...* it didn't taste quite how I had imagined it would. Maybe my taste buds had been wrecked by a constant diet of corned beef and pale green soggy peas out of a tin?

I took another mouth full.

No, it definitely wasn't meant to taste like this. In fact, it was disgusting. I got a torch and examined it. It was green and black. It had white mould on the green mould and a rainbow of other colours around the edges; it was rotten! Retching, I pulled the tin out of the bin and found a small hole in the lid. God knows how long it had been maturing on the shelf for this moment? *Yuck!*

My only solace was that the hunger had gone away!

Operation Gallows

August 1967

It must have been about this time that my mother and sister started to stay on the fort with me and became very involved. My father was having a very difficult time financially with the government legislation closing Radio Essex down and all the staff had left. My mother and Penny, pretty with her striking long auburn hair and just seventeen, were helping him with his project.

I have to say at this point, with Dad, it was just expected of you. There was absolutely no consideration that you might want to get a job or go to university and lead what most would consider a normal life. He had plans, and everyone else was expected to back him up.

They were very hard times, with many hindrances from the Customs and Excise and other officials intent on thwarting my father's project. We had no vehicle at the time and had to take several five-gallon drums of paraffin for heating along with boxes of food stores and any other life sustaining supplies on the bus. We would travel from Southend where we lived to Paglesham, a sleepy little Essex port steeped in a history of smugglers and oyster fishing, set in the marshes on the River Roach where our boat was moored. It must have been a good hour on the bus. We then had to drag it all down the unmade road, along the seawall, load it into a rickety dinghy and row it out to the old boat.

When we got to the fortress, some four and a half hours later, we would unload the stores into a wooden crate that we had made from wartime bunk beds we had scavenged from one of the mess rooms in the towers. This was nailed together and a lifting strop was made up from lengths of winch wire held in place around the outside of it with a few bent nails, and a shackle in the top to hook onto the winch. In the first instance, the winch consisted of what I would now consider being a rather large trailer winch which the old man had got from somewhere. We would turn a handle manually and lift people or stores painfully slowly up onto the landing stage platform below the main deck. We would then put the ratchet on to lock the device while we climbed down onto the lower landing stage. Then lean over the side to take the stores out of it or in the case of my mother who wasn't strong enough to climb the rope ladder I would have to help her out of the box.

The winch itself was only held on with two loose bolts and wobbled about all over the place as you wound it in. Frequently the solid bearing on the end of the shaft that had been replaced with a bit of copper plumbers pipe would wear through, allowing the cogs to jump and the whole thing to run out, causing whatever precious cargo being lifted to crash into the sea. On one particular occasion as I was turning the handle and winching my mother up, one of the wire strops holding the stores box broke with a ping and just missed her face. This left three, not very healthy looking, rusty wire strops of the same vintage to hold the box with her in it some sixty foot above the raging sea.

I can see her face now as white as a sheet; she was absolutely horrified and told me to keep winding as fast as I could. My arms were nearly leaving their sockets with the effort and strain.

Eventually, the box came level with the landing stage platform. I ran down the steel ladder to help her out of the box. For someone who hates heights, can't swim and has the strength of a louse, I sometimes wonder looking back how she coped. On top of all that, she couldn't deal with the cold. Not just she didn't like it; I mean she would pass out while hanging out the washing on the clothesline in the winter at home in England. Sealand was hell for her. In the early days with a lack of heating and the forts design that allowed the cold, bleak easterly and northerly winds driving across the North Sea to strike the structure from every conceivable direction. During the bitter weather of November 1967 we had no heating oil for over three weeks. The boat hadn't turned up and all we could do was wrap up in blankets to try and keep warm. I was able to make my mother the odd hot water bottle using our gas stove to boil a kettle but mum suffered greatly with it.

Sometimes the water tanks would freeze completely solid for days on end, to get drinking water we would have to smash chunks of ice out of them with a club hammer to put in the kettle.

I guess if you have never known extreme cold it would be hard to understand how you can look at your hands pulling on a wet cold rope or anchor chain in sub-zero conditions and not being able to get a grip on it. Willing your hands to tighten around it so you can pull on it, as your life might depend on it and often it did. You eventually resort to trying to command each individual finger to grip and it still doesn't happen. You then put them under your armpits to warm them up. The cold is replaced with the agonies and aches of the circulation trying to return to your fingers, even though there can only be a small difference in temperature. I have to say I am no great lover of the cold myself, I suppose I get that from my mother and the years of having no choice on the subject.

We also had two rope ladders that everyone else, including normally my sister, used. One of them was a ships ladder and was designed as it sounds for use alongside a ship. It had oblong, flat rungs and was meant to hang alongside a ship's hull so that the boarding pilot or crewman could climb up the face of it. However it was so ungainly to use the way we needed, it hanging free. If you climbed the side of it the sharp cornered rungs would dig at you and drag on your clothing with every painful step. So instead we favoured an old wartime ladder that had originally been attached to a mast on the fort in 1943, made from steel hawser with hard wood rungs a bit thicker than a broom handle, that wasn't quite long enough. So we had tied another ladder, of unknown origin, made out of rope and wooden rungs to the bottom of it. This made it long enough to use at low tide when the distance to the deck was another eighteen foot or so more to climb. Needless to say, it always seemed to be low tide when the boat arrived. Mainly because we would take the fast running ebb tide down from our Essex moorings some forty miles away and the flood tide going the other way landing at Paglesham on the next high tide. On one bright and sunny afternoon I had climbed the ladder up onto the fort from the old Mizzy Gel, leaving my father on the boat to load the stores box and hook it on. It was quite a calm day and my mother stood at the rail looking down on the boat, her face frowning with concentration, giving me instructions when to start winching up. I forgot to mention but apart from all the other dangerous deficits this old hand hoist had, you couldn't see the boat from where it was bolted on to the chassis of the old 3.7-inch anti-aircraft gun. To be fair, it was bolted there because there were some holes in the gun that matched two of the holes in the winch. We didn't have anything in the way of a drill to cut through steel to make more.

My mother instructed me to start winding it up. So off I went, turning the handle as fast as I could to get the crate clear of the boat as quickly as possible, in case it fouled something and caused damage. This was always the most dangerous moment of unloading. The boat being pushed about by wind and tide, rolling and pitching in the weather and usually not in a position to be manoeuvred when unloading. If the hook that was attached to the solid fort snagged something on the rolling boat, only extremely good luck could avoid disaster. We learnt very early on that the only way to deal with it was to unhook the stores box once it was lowered. Move the boat away from the hanging hook and winch wire. Fill the box with the stores, return under the fort to hook it on again and then get it clear of the boat and its rigging as quickly as possible. My mother turned and looked at me with a face of sheer horror, wavering desperately for me to come over. I flicked the ratchet onto the cogs to stop it running out and ran to the side. Sixty foot below me was my father clinging to the box as it swung like a pendulum on the wire, with him half submerged in the water.

He explained afterwards in his usual understated fashion. He had got the boat into position and hooked the box on but the wind and tide had pushed the boat away and left him the wrong side of the box. As the wire tightened he had been swept over the side by the box itself, grabbing it before going in the water.

I ran across to the other side of the deck where the rope ladder was dangling down and flung myself on it and shimmied down it hand over hand. As I did so the old boat, to my amazement, was turning in a full circle on tick over and passed by underneath me. At the last minute, I launched myself off the ladder, landing with a thud on the wooden deck. I ran into the forward wheelhouse and brought the boat around to retrieve my father, who by then had managed to haul himself out of the water onto the box. It was an unbelievable stroke of luck that brought the boat over to the ladder, but as usual not a lot was said. Dad soaking wet took over the controls on the boat and I climbed back up the ladder to get back to winching up the stores as if nothing had happened. In hindsight it could have all gone so dreadfully wrong.

It was such a different world. No mobile phones, no emergency radios or marine VHF. We never wore life jackets. I don't think we even had any flares, *what are they?* Life rafts were for big ships! Depth sounder? It's hard to believe in these days of echo sounders and fish finders, that in those days a lot of boats still carried a lead line, which a man would launch with a splosh in front of the moving boat. By the time the weight hit the bottom, the line was straight up and down. Allowing him to either read marks on the line, or measure as he pulled it in arm over arm one fathom or six foot being the distance between outstretched arms. Apart from judging the depth with it, in fog they would attach a bit of tallow to the weight to get a bottom sample that would stick to it to help judge where they were. Radar? Don't be ludicrous, that required lots of money and banks of batteries that needed charging up. GPS hadn't been invented. In fact, the only thing we did have was a compass and in fairness my father did get it swung by a compass swinger when he thought it due. The guy would have you move the boat about while he screwed little magnets to the dashboard near the compass until it read true. He would then give you a hand written deviation card showing where it was out, if at all, and by how many degrees. Clever old fashioned stuff but still used on boats and ships today. When all the fuses go on the high-tech GPS and navigational plotter and its blowing a gale of wind in the dark; you should always be able to turn to your compass and paper charts, get back to basics and more importantly be able to believe what they tell you.

In a communication marked confidential from P.D. Nairn at the Ministry of Defence on the 2nd August 1967 (coincidently my fifteenth birthday) that was copied to around twenty people including the army, navy, air force and the pipe smoking Prime Minister Harold Wilson:

"If we were to take over the fort, sufficient forces would be needed to guarantee success. Her Majesties Government could be made to look silly if we failed.

I suggest a frigate and two helicopters be used and if the fort does not surrender we should be prepared to land men or 'Shell it'. With a fifteen year old boy on the fort this is an impossible option.
I cannot imagine the idea of middle-aged policemen sliding down ropes from a helicopter is a viable option so the first down would need to be Marines. A lucky shot from the fort could bring down the helicopter with considerable loss of life.
CDS does not believe military personnel should be used in such an operation and it has been decided that the police have no authority to act and if anyone was killed there would be little chance on either side of prosecution.

Prime Minister to be kept informed."

Wow...they considered shelling us from a 372-foot, 2450-ton Frigates 4.5 inch main armament! Whilst I sat there on the fort blissfully unaware on my 15th birthday that these communications had even taken place, and we weren't to find out for another 30 years!

One day not long after, a naval ship 'HMS Bembridge' with its immaculate shiny black hull and blue upper works, came over the horizon and chugged slowly across the flat calm sea towards us. She was built on the lines of a large trawler with an aft wheelhouse. An admiralty MFV built for their good sea keeping qualities and used by the British navy around the world for doing some of its more mundane tasks. With the bronze colours of the summer sun twinkling off the afternoon sea, she heaved too underneath the fortress.

On the deck of the ship were marines, sailors and two police officers shading their eyes against the bright afternoon sun as they stared guardedly up at us. In those days, ordinary British police wore silly pointy hats but the more senior ranks had a more military style flat peaked hat. These guys were the latter, so we surmised they must be reasonably important types.

The skipper manoeuvred the well-maintained steel ship underneath with skill and the sailors ran about with fenders made of woven rope and some that appeared to be made from woven cane like long cane baskets. They looked like they had come out of a museum. They pushed them between the ship and the tower to stop the paint being scuffed off the hull against the thick layer of limpets and barnacles that surrounded it.

One of the policemen shouted up importantly from under his peaked cap, claiming they had a very urgent message for us from my father and could they come aboard.

My mother and I stepped back out of sight and had a quick conference. Not sure what to do, we concluded that since they were obviously genuine police officers and since they were being conveyed out to us by the Royal navy on a ship very well known to us, it would be ok to let them land. *After all if you can't trust a British Bobby whom can you trust?* I told them it was ok for them to come up. Launching the rolled up rope ladder shackled to the rail over the side with a practiced flourish, allowing it to swing back and forth until it steadied above the boat.

We were unaware at the time that the Ministry of Defence had been in negotiation with my father in an attempt to purchase the fort back from him. They had sent several different people to see him at his flat in

Southend and there were rumours that they had taken over an office at Southend police station from which to orchestrate the mission.

They first of all offered him a derisory amount of money to vacate the fortress (Government papers seen since, indicate that the Minister of Defence instructed only a small amount should be offered). They also threatened that if he didn't take it then we would be removed by force, probably not the best way of dealing with someone like my old man.

My father was concerned for our welfare on the fort as we still had no means of communication and were oblivious to the political jousting taking place on the mainland.
When he refused, they arranged further meetings with him to ensure he stayed ashore, and staked out his house in Southend day and night, logging all of his movements and whereabouts. They reported their progress to the ministry and the war office several times a day. As negotiations broke down with my father, they sanctioned *'Plan B: Operation Gallows'*. As the Navy ship approached Sealand, the airwaves were thick with coded messages between the ships and Whitehall.

"The Football team is in position and ready to go".
The Onsite commander was *'Boss'*, all radio stations taking part were *'Cricket Bag'*, the command navy ship *'Big Brother'*, the Royal engineers ship from Chatham *'Little Brother'*, the Royal marines *'Royals'*, the demolition team *'Bouncer'* and the navy communications centre at Chatham *'Bull Nose'*.
Unknown to us, at HMS Ganges naval base, not eight miles away, there were two Wessex helicopters on the ground with engines roaring and rotors thundering round. Carrying twelve Royal Marine Commandos and a demolition team ready to fast rope down on us at a moment's notice. This would be put into action on command from the ship that was now laying alongside our fortress home.
A team of Royal engineers was also on standby with helicopters and support ship ready to destroy the fortress when the Marines had overrun

it. This was proper cloak and dagger secret service stuff with the two uniformed policemen at the forefront of the subterfuge. The airwaves were crackling with coded messages and orders .*We hadn't got a bloody clue it was all going on around us!* We knew nothing of all of this as we innocently and naively invited the two policemen, key to the operation, up and into our midst.

It was a well thought out plan, made with the military precision that the British armed forces excel in and originally involved all three armed services. The two 'James Bonds' came forwards to the front of the ship and the first one launched himself very inelegantly onto the rope ladder. He was wearing a huge orange, Board of Trade approved, kapok-filled life jacket. Of the sort, they issued to the passengers on sinking cruise liners and it wouldn't have looked out of place on the Titanic. This fellow had clearly never seen a rope ladder before in his life, let alone climbed one. With his colleague below champing at the bit to follow him up and sailors dragging at the ladder to hold it in place, he gamely put his foot in the first rung. Now there is only one way to climb a free hanging rope ladder and that is up the side, holding one of the side ropes and inserting your foot sideways onto the rungs alternatively from either side, quite a task; even without sporting an oversized lifejacket. If you try to climb the front of it like a conventional ladder, your feet and the ladder below, disappear out from under you. So you end up in a sitting position with your legs out straight, all your weight and that of the ladder (which is considerable) goes on your arms and you just can't move. After kicking and struggling about for a few minutes like a fish being landed, one of the sailors catching his flying hat in the process, the embarrassed fellow was plucked off the ladder by the sailors at about shoulder height; he had only managed to achieve a couple of rungs in height, one leg still tangled up in the rungs; he ended up laying on the deck exhausted by his efforts. His colleague, keen to have a go, shot him a contemptuous look for putting in such a useless effort. Stepping forwards into the breach, he launched himself onto the ladder. This chap had more enthusiasm but he too couldn't work out what the problem was. He wanted to show his pal how it was done, but instead had the ladder dancing around like a puppeteer's strings and before long he too was back on the deck gasping for air and looking very dejected and somewhat stupid.

All the while we are looking down incredulously at the scene some sixty-foot below. It had never occurred to me that a simple skill that I had learnt could be such a hard thing to do for the uninitiated.

Now you would have thought with all the effort and planning involved, not to mention Marines, Ships and helicopters, they would have made sure that the front line troops so to speak, were up to the job.

Well, I thought, *if it was such an important message they had to convey I had better go down to them and see what they had to say.* I handed my mother the Walther P38 pistol (A wartime trophy that my dad had recently added to our armaments) and she placed it on the floor under the rail so it could not be seen from below.

"*I'm coming down*" I shouted, stifling a laugh and trying not to grin. Clutching the edge of the rail, I climbed over the side of the girder rail onto the ladder. I was very young and fit, having only just had my 15th birthday a few days before and had been practicing climbing down the ladder using only my hands. This was a perfect time to show off my new found talent in front of the Royal Navy, not to mention the would be 007s.

I shimmied down hand over hand jumping the last few feet onto the deck; still not realising I was unwittingly entering the lion's den.

"*Come this way, please sir*" said the policeman very formally, as he turned on his heels and led me aft to the accommodation at the stern of the ship, below the bridge. The two police officers gave me their rank and names before introducing me to the skipper who shook my hand with an amused look on his kindly weathered face.

"*It's like this*," said the first policeman in a matter of fact sort of way, "*your father has sold the fort back to the British Government and since tax payer's money has changed hands it is imperative that you allow some marines to stay on the fortress with you until your father comes out to explain. Only two marines and they would do all the cooking and washing up and this, and that".*

The other policeman was nodding vigorously in agreement with his colleague's words.

I wondered what they were going on about, but they were doing their best over a cup of tea to convince me of the value of their help. I had already had to get over my disappointment that the hot cocoa drink, I had read about in books of the navy Atlantic convoys, scraped from large blocks of cocoa in the galley no longer existed. What was the British Navy coming to? Now I had these two buffoons extolling the virtues of Her Majesty's finest washing up and dusting skills.

I was starting to get bored now, and the policemen were getting more and more insistent and agitated. I could see the frustration in their faces and was starting to feel a little intimidated and threatened in their company. Some seventy-foot from the ladder at the other end of the ship was what had become my home and sanctuary above. I didn't want to be there anymore and looked about me for an escape.

While this conversation had been going on. The skipper had been out on the deck chatting happily with my mother and asking her if he came back with the papers, could she get me to sign them and join the Navy.

I said to the policemen if they brought my father out the next day I would be happy to comply but until I had spoken to him, there was no way I would allow access to the marines. Besides which, we were quite capable of doing our own washing up. It was explained again that public funds had been given to my father, they had a duty to protect government interests and the marines were essential to making sure no other party took it from us. The skipper had by this time come back inside the accommodation where we had been talking. I said to them in what I hoped was a confident tone. *"If you are that worried go and get my father now. Bring him out here tonight and we can resolve the situation. The weather is fine and the forecast good. I am sure he would be only too happy to oblige if what you*

say is true."
One of the policemen turned to the skipper and said no doubt with a wink *"You can't get the ship in underneath the fortress in the dark can you skipper?"* The skipper somewhat embarrassed by being put on the spot by a landlubber nodded in agreement with him.

At this point I was starting to smell a rat and announced that if he couldn't manoeuvre the boat underneath in the dark he should change his job and perhaps let me do it as it was not that difficult a thing to do. The skipper gave a chuckle and went off to have another chat with my mother.

By now I had had enough and knew I needed to get away. Turning my back on the two policemen, I stepped over the high combing of the doorway and walked out onto the steel deck heading towards the ladder my heart pounding in my chest. I was feeling very uncomfortable; I could feel the policeman's eyes burning into my back, raising the hackles on my neck. I could hear them following me through the doorway and outside. I expected them to grab hold of me at any minute.
The ladder looked so far away.
Time seemed to stand still and the air was buzzing with electric tension. As I moved as quickly as I could down the deck, the policeman whom I am sure was racked with indecision of what to do next, suddenly shouted forward to the officer of Marines to put two Marines on the ladder.
"Marines on the ladder" came the barked command from the smartly uniformed officer. Two very professional looking marines, obviously pre-warned, stepped forward. The first one got hold of the ladder readying to climb it.
I looked up at my mother above and said with a firm a voice as I could muster *"Mother if they come up the ladder shoot them!"*
My mother, stunning with her model looks and blond hair glistening in the sunshine, without uttering a word, reached down to the deck and held up the Walther P38 pistol for them to see and then replaced it out of sight on the deck again.
"Get those men off that bloody ladder shouted the skipper" in a

commanding voice.

The young men only too happily jumped off, back onto the steel deck looking somewhat relieved.

I walked through the silent sailors and marines who after all were only being asked to do their duty, unsure as to whether I would be grabbed by them or the policemen following closely behind me. They all took a step back to let me through, pointedly standing well back so as to not be threatening, having considered the danger from my mother above. The skipper, now at the front of the ship stepped forward grabbed the bottom of the rope ladder. With a wink and an old fashioned look, he handed it to me saying quietly *"It has been a pleasure meeting you sir"*.

With a sense of relief, I gratefully accepted it. Jumping onto the side of the ladder, I ascended as swiftly as I could. Climbing over the rail onto the deck, I turned back looking down at the ship and the upturned faces. I reached as far as I could down the ladder and briskly hauled it up and away from my nemeses.

Christ was I glad to be out of that devil's kitchen! The Bembridges' engines rumbled into life as she backed off from under the fort and headed for Harwich. Still unaware of the greater picture around us we kept a very special vigil that night.

Government papers now reveal that had the policemen, who turned out to be military policemen, or the marines gained access from the ship, we were to have been subdued and the helicopters were to be called in from HMS Ganges followed by the Royal Engineer's demolition crew.

After the debriefing the next day conducted by the Captain of HMS Ganges, a written report was sent to the Directorate of Operations and the Prime Minister.

It stated that our morale was extremely high and that my mother supported strongly everything that I had said to the policemen. It subsequently noted that she considered it a holiday to be out there; bless her, if only they knew!

Also, from the conversation, they suspected we were not alone on the fort. It was observed that the fort was very well protected, including stocks of various 'missiles'. Backed up with a good supply of gas cylinders hanging down from the perimeter. These could be released on to any target underneath. Others could be apparently rolled over the edge.

They reported that Bates' son stated they had already beaten off seven attempts by rival pirate radio factions and was cheerfully confident of beating off others that might wish to try their luck. He described my manner as very friendly and talkative.

No mention was made of the fact the police had tried to climb the ladder, or the marines had been ordered to climb it. In fact the reverse, they said I made it clear from the start that they would not be allowed to come aboard the fort, that I climbed half way down it and spoke to them from there. It was a totally different version of events! I know exactly what happened as I was there but official reports on many of the incidents over this period of time are not as they really were. I guess people had to protect their jobs and future pensions. A lot of papers have been pulled from the files in the interest of 'National Security'; destroyed with a note inserted telling of their destruction and date of destruction mainly in the 90s but without explanation of their contents. I would have loved to have sight of them.

These events in August 1967 were the culmination of a huge amount of UK government activity in the previous months. Harold Wilson the then Prime Minister had asked for the situation with the fortress to be resolved. He had called a meeting at his offices at 10 Downing Street involving the government Treasury solicitors, the Ministry of Defence, the Home Office and various other official bodies that thought they might have an interest. These included the Post Office as at the time they were in charge of radio and television broadcast licensing, as well as the mail.

The Law Office department at the Royal Courts of Justice had written and rewritten legal opinion after legal opinion to try to bring the fortress into the UK jurisdiction. They quoted from the continental shelf act that was brought in to deal solely with oil, gas and mineral extraction in the North Sea and surrounding waters. It was never intended for it to be used in such a manner. They claimed in some of their opinions that because the UK military had built the fortress, it belonged to them. They also advised that if the UK ever built in international waters again they should destroy the facility when they had abandoned or finished with it. They feared that the pirate stations, that they had so successfully managed to close down, could start rebroadcasting from this fortress.

Despite all of this, the vast amount of man hours involved, and the not unexpected convincing arguments that you would expect from the Treasury solicitors for their masters. They obviously did not find them strong enough to act upon.
So more meetings were called in earnest and it was decided that of all the services, the Navy should be used and that the situation should be resolved by force.

However, the initial plan to storm the fortress by helicopter and ship were rejected by the Prime Minister. When it was explained to him by the Admiralty that any attempt to attack our position would undoubtedly be met by considerable resistance and there was every possibility of loss of life or injury to service personnel or the Bates family. It was after all a fortress and as far as they knew protected by an electric fence not to mention some very determined people. Harold Wilson, bless him, rejected the plan as he didn't want to see military personnel or even my family injured or killed. It made me very proud to be an Englishman as well as a Sealander when in later years I read the minutes of this meeting. There are not many, if any, world leaders that would have the fortitude to take that stance under such pressure from their cabinet to resolve the situation.

It seems after this period we made new friends with the Navy, specifically from HMS Ganges the shore base nearby. They would come out most days and give us newspapers, the odd bottle of navy rum and other goodies. Two smartly painted inshore minesweepers the '*Flintham*' and the '*Dittisham*' would suffer all sorts of weather to see if we were ok. Several years later I met the lieutenant commander that skippered one of them when they visited my hometown of Southend-on-Sea for the 'Nore Race'. I was invited aboard the ships one by one at the end of Southend pier and shown the greatest of hospitality. They told me it was tradition not to allow a guest to buy a drink or a cigarette while on a British naval ship. I don't know if that is true or not but they certainly showed me generosity of the highest order and a fantastic evening!

Independence Day

My father was in two minds as to how he was going to use the fortress. Originally he had planned to restart his radio station 'Radio Essex' but the more he thought about it, the more he thought he could find a better use for it. There was also talk of a health farm. Let's face it; if you needed to get away from drink, drugs or even food, you couldn't get much further than that. There would be no sneaking over the wall of a night time to the local pub or having contraband smuggled in but in the end that was not what he decided.

He was having a drink one night with his old friend Lionel Conway, a retired City of London lawyer who had downsized his practice and opened offices nearer home in Southend. Lionel had been a childhood friend of my father and had represented him and my grandfather for years. I even went to school with his children and our families had grown up near each other.

As they chatted away, my father explained that he had come back from the fort and said to my mother *"Well darling, you now have your own island"*
To which she replied *"Yes, but it's a pity it doesn't have palm trees and a bit of sunshine and maybe its own flag".*
My father had dwelled on this and put forward to Lionel *"Supposing I want to make it my own country? You know, declare independence? Who could stop me?"*
Lionel suited with grey thinning hair and gold-rimmed spectacles, as you would expect from a City of London lawyer, ruminated deep in thought, making cathedrals out of his hands. He then announced in a confident and studious voice *"I don't think anyone can stop you but of course you can't do it"*
"Why not?" asked my father in an enquiring tone.
"Well, because you just can't!" said Lionel. He thought some more. *"They*

would lock you in the Tower of London and throw the key away; it would be treason. They will take you through Traitor's Gate to the block and chop your head off like Walter Raleigh" his tone becoming more dismissive.
"But it's in international waters," persisted the old man, *"and Britain have abandoned it and relinquished all claims to it."*
"They will send the marines in. You can't do it. It wouldn't be allowed to happen" insisted Lionel lucidly.

So the old man went away his mind buzzing with the challenge. He could see flags, passports, coats of arms, company registration, stamps and coins. *The possibilities were endless!*

With that, we set about designing a flag. My father concluded that the simplest way of creating an independent state would be to make it a principality. His reasoning was that we didn't have the manpower, infrastructure, time or money to create law books not to mention the social and political structure required for a nation. In a principality however it would be simplified and the Prince's word would be the law. It also, and probably more importantly to him, gave him the opportunity to make my mother his Princess. She had always been his Princess but now he was going to tell the world.
On my mother's birthday, 2nd September 1967, a small party of us gathered under the flagpole for a simple ceremony, raising the flag for the first time. A fine red, white and black design and declared the new nation of Sealand. My father described the flag: Red for Roy, Black for our days in pirate radio and the white stripe for a path of purity that we would endeavour to walk (slightly tongue in cheek).

An invited journalist witnessed our Declaration of Independence and an exclusive story was subsequently published in one of the Sunday newspapers in England.
As it was an exclusive, the newspaper in question was happy to pay handsomely for such a fun and interesting story. My father being out of contact and away on Sealand; Belasco somehow got hold of the payment

and issued himself with what he considered his fair share of the payment and bought himself an old vintage Buick car with the proceeds. My father was furious as we were in dire financial straits and needed the cash to buy stores. It resulted in a fight on Sealand; Belasco tried several times to push my father over the side whilst my mother, sister, several others and myself watched on. With a drop of over 60 feet into the swirling tide, Dad would have been in serious trouble if he'd gone over.

Eventually dad picked him up in a bear hug and squeezed him until he collapsed gasping for air and retching on the deck. Everyone, including my mother left, leaving me, and my father on Sealand.

Within days, unknown to us isolated on Sealand, our boat was set adrift from its moorings and ended on a breakwater. Grinding paste had also been put in the engine to destroy the machinery if it was started. My mother had to deal with all this on her own.

On arriving home from Sealand a few weeks later, one of the wheels came off of our car as we drove down the road; it had been sabotaged in the boatyard car park. A wreath was delivered to the house. Things were getting seriously unpleasant.

I have no idea who approached who but come the end of October, the Customs and Excise sent a man to see Belasco at his home in Southend. Belasco suggested he might like to take part in an unofficial raid on the fort and hand it over to HMG.

Returning a few days later, the Customs and Excise official explained *"There are two gentlemen in the car who would like a word with you."* Belasco recognised one of the men, from a meeting with my father, as a Mr. Sweby from the Ministry of Defence and the other remained nameless. Belasco was given a phone number to call if stopped by the police while going about his nefarious deed and another 01-9307022 extension 6105 for the Duty Commander at the Ministry of Defence in Whitehall if he needed any help or to report a successful take over. The Ministry of Defence named it 'Operation Dictation'.

I was on Sealand with my sister while this was going on, blissfully unaware. Belasco had tried unsuccessfully to steal a fishing boat from Harwich and was intending to climb up onto the fort at night with some associates. He had a bag containing homemade black balaclavas, black gloves, several torches, gaffer tape, chloroform (enough to kill fifty people in the wrong hands we were later told) and some rag to sprinkle it on to hold over my face to render me unconscious. His plan was to chloroform me, bind me up with the tape and lower me down to the fishing boat below. Then cast it adrift in the tide while he signaled a waiting naval ship to come and take over from him.

I don't know how my father learnt of all of this but he confronted Belasco who handed him the bag and went with him to a lawyer's office to give a sworn affidavit of the whole skullduggery going on. Dad went to see Paul Channon, our local Member of Parliament, who wrote to the Minister of Defence, Dennis Healy, demanding an explanation. Not surprisingly denials were made and most of it was swept under the carpet.

Papers released 30 years later confirm the majority of this and Belasco's involvement.

Our declaration of independence prompted the UK government into pulling out all the stops to put an end to the fledgling nation before it could gain any credibility. They had only just come to terms with Rhodesia issuing a unilateral declaration of independence a couple of years before. They were in no mood to have a new state emerge just seven and a half miles off the east coast.

Their first action was to inform my father that if he was going to run stores out to Sealand on the old Mizzy Gel. She would require a load line certificate and would need to have a 'Plimsoll Line' on the side of her hull, showing how deep she could be loaded. This would require a survey designed for the big cargo carrying ships that plied the seven seas and clearly the tired old Mizzy Gel would never pass it in a million years. He was told that whenever he went to Sealand he would have to clear Customs at Harwich and have all his paperwork checked; including the load line certificate that everyone knew he could never achieve. My father protested that taking out some bags of shopping and a few gallons of paraffin to feed his family and keep them warm hardly represented the movement of cargo. He was however encouraged by the fact that having tweaked the tiger's tail in declaring independence, they now considered his taking out the groceries to his family as international trade that needed to be cleared through Customs every time. We steamed the old boat from Paglesham to Harwich and after tying up the boat on the town quay; Dad went up the road to the Customs offices to speak to the officials. They gave him some forms to fill in to apply for the fabled load line certificate that they again insisted he needed and sent some Customs officers down to the boat to inspect the 'cargo'.

They stomped about the boat looking presumably for illicit contraband. Eventually coming across our meagre 'cargo', which consisted of tins of baked beans, corned beef, dried milk and other such exotic delicacies required to sustain life on the North Sea. They took to their task with enthusiasm and started opening the tins to make sure as they explained the contents were really as labelled. My protests fell on deaf ears as they rummaged through our exports. It was reminiscent of old gangster films in the USA during prohibition but this was Harwich; certainly not New York, and these were tins of Spam, not whisky!

My father returned from his meeting with the Customs and Excise, clutching a hand full of forms they had given him, with steam coming out of his ears. The sight of the spoiled stores and the departing blue uniforms clambering across the quay did absolutely nothing to improve his demeanour. He was, to say the least, furious. We marched up the road and using the last of the money he had on him, which wasn't a lot, replaced as much of the spoiled stores as we could.
Getting back to the boat, he disappeared down the splintered wooden

hatch to the engine room to start the old engine. This entailed shorting out the starter with a flash, a bang and shower of sparks, using a half melted rusty screwdriver kept especially for the job. The ancient diesel engine that had started its life powering a tractor clattered into life in a cloud of smoke, the old man appeared from the depths of the engine room with a face like thunder.

Throwing the ropes off the quay and mumbling under his breath about *"bloody uniformed bureaucrats sitting in nice warm offices. Who go home to their families and centrally heated warm houses of a night-time after making decisions that would stop him looking after his own family? Let them try and bloody stop me."*

We steamed off into the fading light in a freshening easterly breeze. An hour and a half later we arrived at Sealand. After circling the fortress a couple of times in the dark shouting and whistling to attract their attention, we spotted the dull glow of a hurricane lamp above. The stores box was lowered with Penny winding the winch handle and my mother giving her shouted instructions from the rail. We unhooked the box and filled it with the much-needed stores. Bringing the boat around again, I hooked the box on and shouted for it to be lifted off the now heaving deck, in the swell that was getting up with the increasing easterly breeze. Unloading finished I climbed the rope ladder up into the winter darkness and clambered over the cold steel rail, some sixty foot above, to join my mother and sister. Having given her a hug, I lowered my mother, shivering with cold, down to the boat in the stores box, to go back to Southend with my dad.

It was late February and a very cold night. It goes without saying that the boat didn't have any heating or even a wheelhouse door that shut properly. My mother was frozen and the boat broke down twice on the way back; my father no doubt fixing it with his trusty tool kit.

Because of the breakdowns they were late on the tide arriving off Southend and were close to missing the tide into Leigh-on-Sea, their final destination. At this stage they were confronted by the police boat, which asked them to stop that they might board them. Having been on the boat some two days in the freezing cold and with my mother verging on hyperthermia, my father refused to stop.

With that the police boat roared up alongside and a policeman jumped on the deck commanding the old man heave to. Giving the *'Bobby'* one of his best menacing glares. My father told him to keep out of his bloody wheelhouse and carried on into Leigh creek where the police boat was unable to follow with its deeper draft on a rapidly falling tide. Much relieved at getting alongside, tied to the wall on the very last of the dropping tide and all achieved with the help of his new blue-uniformed crewman. Mum and Dad left the policeman standing next to the boat, clutching his notebook, probably wondering what he was supposed to do next. They then climbed exhausted, cold and hungry up the nearby, very steep and cobbled church steps to get to the bus stop at the top to make the final leg of their epic journey home.

In the mean time, Penny and I were on Sealand and unknown to us, Dad was getting more and more flack from the Customs and was being threatened with prosecution if he didn't clear Customs every time when visiting Sealand. On reading government papers released under the thirty-year ruling, it was clear that officialdom had been tasked with stopping us. They had considered prosecuting my father for allowing me to leave school so early at 14 but decided this would look petty and decided to ignore it. They chose instead the angle of cutting off our supply of food, water and fuel, using any regulations available. Following several weeks of no contact with home and staring forlornly at the horizon for hours every day looking for the supply boat that never came, Penny, and I were running very low on food and water.

We were reduced to making hard tack biscuits from flour and water. Using a huge sack of flour that we had in our storeroom and distilling seawater to make drinking water using a big old kettle on the gas stove, some metal sheeting and pipe as a condenser. It was a very slow process that didn't produce much water and it certainly didn't taste very nice, but it gave us just enough to survive on and I was chuffed with the simple achievement of making it work.

I can honestly say we never considered the idea of giving up or calling for help. It was never even discussed; it just wasn't the way we had been brought up.

My father was horrified by the situation and struggling to deal with the bureaucratic hurdles they flung at him one after the other he decided to go to the press. On the 9th of March 1968, a small plane flew over. Alerted by the sound of the engine, Penny and I ran outside and waved to the smiling faces looking down at us from above. It buzzed about for ten minutes or so, with someone taking pictures until, with a saluting waggle of its wings, it disappeared off into the distance. It was nice to see some supportive friendly faces but we couldn't work out why they were taking pictures of us.

The very next day the 'Daily Telegraph' published a photo of Penny and I waving at the plane and the headline was "*Look at their starving faces*". It went on to explain how HMG were trying to blockade our small family by fair means or foul, putting two young lives at risk in the process.

That day the elegant old steam tug '*Ocean Cock'* from Felixstowe turned up with a blast from its whistle and a cloud of steam. It dropped its anchor with a loud splash and a clattering of chain so that it lay underneath the south end of Sealand with the ebb tide. On the aft deck were my father and some journalists from the Daily Mail, who had chartered the fine old ship, complete with an all important load line certificate and the magic Plimsoll line. But more importantly there was a seemingly vast amount of food, fuel and barrels of drinking water purchased by the Daily Mail.

The resultant story published the next day was to the British public akin to the relief of Mafeking. Meetings were held in Whitehall to work out the next move. It was decided they were to stop persecuting us with the

Customs and other officialdom as it was making HMG look foolish and in the process giving my father a somewhat local hero status as he slithered in and out of the Essex marshes with his old boat.

It was a great lesson to me regarding the power of the press, as well as the liberties a free press helps sustain.

HMS Egeria Incident

November 13th 1967 at 14.50

On a very calm and slightly misty cold winters day, my mother and I watched the minesweeper HMS Egeria approach the fortress from the west. The watery winter sun reflecting off of her immaculately white painted hull and green decks. My father had made it very clear to me that he did not wish any naval forces anywhere near our newly declared nation. He saw them as a serious physical threat, combined with the fact that he had heard the naval hydro graphics squadron had been tasked to try and find an area of sand bank, however small, between Sealand and the shore that might dry out on very big tides. This would allow the UK to take another three-mile hop from it bringing Sealand into the UK three-mile territorial limits.

As the ship approached I waved it away, but it continued steadily on its course towards us. As it got nearer I shouted *"clear off"* and indicated with waving arms that they were not welcome. It seemed they were oblivious to my remonstrations.

So I fired two warning shots into the air from a nine-millimeter Berretta pistol, which also seemed to have little effect on their resolve to get close to the fort. I fired two shots a hundred foot across the bow of the ship in true warning fashion and they still kept on coming at me.

The ship was now not much more than fifty foot away, I changed magazines and let rip a full clip; rapid fire into the water six foot in front of her bow.

There were shouts and the jangling of engine room telegraphs from the open bridge, clouds of black smoke erupted from the ships funnel as the skipper threw her into astern and she backed off at a good speed.

She stopped a quarter of a mile away and lay still in the water for half an hour. Whilst, I assume, the skipper described the incident to the admiralty in Whitehall and asked advice. She then got underway in the direction of

Harwich.

I saw no mention of the incident in the press or of any kind until I read government papers nearly fifty years later. Statements had been taken from the Skipper Lieutenant Commander Robinson and two of the crew who described the incident. They told of a youth of fourteen wearing jeans and an anorak, and had a dark 'Beatle' crop of hair, no doubt referring to the long haired 60s band. The Director of Public Prosecutions, Sir Norman Skelhorn, in London informed the Southend police but instructed them not to react. The Ministry of Defence was told to keep the matter confidential until they had taken legal advice.

The advice given was that even if the UK was within its rights to invade (which it was not), the task would be difficult, full of risk to the occupants and the services, and would tarnish the governments image.

The Prime Minister ordered further investigation.

So it comes as somewhat of a surprise to learn that less than four years later, in documents marked confidential, the Admiralty were discussing the idea of coming alongside the fort using the same ship or one from the same squadron to attach a piece of equipment to it. A 'Hifix', which would allow them to get an exact daily position to work from while surveying the approaches to Harwich and Felixstowe harbor. Essential to the 'National Economy of a maritime nation' and save them some twenty thousand pounds a week on other methods of survey, this all before the days of GPS.

The Minister of State writing to the head of Naval Home Division informs him however that absolutely no approach should be made to Roy Bates asking his permission as this could be construed as recognition of Sealand. It is then suggested that an article could be placed in the press in the hope that my father would see it and allow them to proceed unhindered. They soon realized this was unrealistic, so it was decided the only options they had were to either invade or not use the fort at all for the survey.

Another option was that 'Flag Officer Medway' had contingency plans

'Operation Proclaim' and 'Operation Proclaim Alpha', which involved a full time armed naval escort and an armed party, which would involve considerable expense.

Whatever happened there were to be no discussions with Roy Bates, as from experience confrontation would involve danger to life and embarrassing publicity. Political considerations were overriding.

German Friends

It was 1968 and Pathe News made a film about Sealand (which is now available through our YouTube channel). Pathe News programs were shown in the cinemas across Europe and around the world before the main film came on the screen. The footage shows me as a very young and innocent looking lad, my parents and two German boys: Walter, 19 and Roland, 18.

Walter and Roland were members of some German scouting organisation and had planned to hitchhike to Namibia. They planned to travel around the Dark Continent with rucksacks on their backs, before returning home to the real world and a life of work, marriage and family.

Walter, a tall skinny lad with long hair and a thin wispy moustache, had done an apprenticeship as an electrician. Roland, more powerfully built with shorter hair and an apprenticeship as a metalworker and locksmith.

Travelling from Germany and stopping off at Tilbury, hoping to get a ship to Africa, they found themselves short of money. At this point they found a newspaper left in a pub, containing an article about Sealand and the troubles we were having defending the fortress from attacks by various factions, government and others. They immediately changed the destination of their adventures and hitchhiked to Felixstowe.

They had no idea how to find us, so they made their way to Felixstowe in Suffolk, the nearest point of land, and camped on the beach. They asked locals how to contact us but with no success. Eventually, in frustration, they decided to 'borrow' a rowing boat and try to make their own way to Sealand that they could see invitingly and deceptively near on the horizon some seven miles away. They 'borrowed' anchors, oars, spare oars, ropes and anything else they could find on the beach or in nearby boats to help them with their quest.

And off they set!
Well, the fast flowing tides of the River Deben, their departure point, are well known on the east coast of England to sailors. The treacherous and very shallow bar at the entrance of the river made the seas kick up and had claimed many a life over the years.

They were lucky! They managed to get back ashore onto the beach, freezing cold and soaking wet, narrowly avoiding drowning.

They were taken in by a local fire fighter, who came across them while walking his dog on the beach and felt sorry for the two despondent looking young men.
Dejected and dismayed at not being able to contact us. They used the last of their meagre resources to take the train up to London and go to the Daily Mail offices in Fleet Street, where one of the journalists gave them our UK address in Southend.

Returning from the fort one day I came home to find Walter trying to arm wrestle my sister Penny and as I recall she was thrashing him, pushing his arm to the table, delighted with the result.

Walter wasn't very impressed, as he saw himself as quite a macho man, complete with the wispy moustache thing happening on his top lip. His English was somewhat better than Roland's and improved over the years they stayed with us, but he adopted *(deliberately I'm sure)* a cross between the American and a Cockney accent. He thought this was very cool. My mother would send him around the corner to get a loaf of bread from the baker and say to him ask for *"one large loaf"*. He would return bemused because by the time he had finished with it he was asking for one large love and it certainly made the girls in the shop laugh.

These boys were born in East Germany during the cold war and their parents smuggled them and their family into West Germany. This caused a problem when my father asked me to take the 'Mizzy Gel' from Paglesham to Southend for repairs. It was my first lone command of the old lady without my father being there and I made a total hash of it. Having said that, I was only fifteen or sixteen and the gods if not the machinery were certainly not with me. The passage required going through a lifting road bridge at Havengore on Foulness Island ranges, where the army tested artillery shells rockets and bombs, and had done so for hundreds of years.

As we approached the bridge, I shouted up to the watchman to open it and the famous 'no astern' gearbox didn't fail to let us down. That combined to my youth and lack of experience culminated in the boat crashing into the bridge and getting pinned against it with the fast flowing ebb tide. A large piece of RSJ girder pierced the side of the wooden hull above the waterline with a sickening crunching noise. I was beside myself; I had totally stuffed up and had to think what to do next to extricate myself from the situation.
Walter volunteered to jump over the side up to his neck in water dragging the heavy anchor up tide away from us. As the tide dropped, we managed to pull the shallow drafted vessel free.

The bridge operators who had been watching this carry on with bemused interest then opened the bridge and we trundled through only to run aground on a shallow bank on the other side.

An hour or so later my father appeared on the seawall a few hundred yards away with two military policemen who were waving to us to go to them when the tide dropped away.
We trudged over the mud to them and were asked for identification. We had nothing on us but told them who we were and that my friends were German and then in devilment, explained that they were from East

Germany. It had the desired effect; we were rushed off the island and out of the military area.

That night we were back and continued on our journey.
It was during this trip that Walter told me a story that I have reminded myself of many times in life when confronted with a seemingly simple problem diagnosed by others:

Not long after he finished his electrician's training he was asked by his parents to help an old lady in the apartment upstairs to sort out her wiring problems.

Up he went and banged on the door. The frail old lady explained to him that none of her lights worked in the lounge, that she had changed the bulbs but still no lights. He went to the fuse box and tested it. Everything seemed fine. He unscrewed the switch from the wall, tested it and found it ok. He unscrewed the light fitting and it seemed ok.
He then proceeded to pull all the cable out of the wall and ceiling, taking all the plaster and paint with it. Nothing seemed wrong. He then had a blinding flash of inspiration and decided to try the bulbs himself, and *hey presto*, in amongst this scene of devastation cable and plaster in the old ladies living room there was light.

Roland was the quieter of the two, a very steady and reliable man.

When we eventually got them out to Sealand, they were in their element and got stuck into making things work that had not been used since the war. My father and I had rebuilt one of the old 'Gardner' engines that powered the generators. Walter and Roland set to stripping the generator down and cleaning all the contacts, so that when we got it all running it would produce power.

It was Christmas and my father had acquired an old black and white television from somewhere. He managed to get it out there without breaking or drowning it. We thought if we could just get this generator running, we will have electric and be able to watch some Christmas TV. Walter ran some rescued wartime cables about the place. When he ran out of insulation tape he used sticky tape and when he ran out of sticky tape he tied carrier bags around the joints. No health and safety checks here!

We had also brought a fully charged battery out with us to start the diesel engine with. You have to bear in mind that if the battery went flat before we got the engine going we would have no way of charging it.

We laboured over the machinery under the light of hissing paraffin Tilley lamps. They gave off a good light but needed to have their pressure pumped up every few minutes. This was done with a piston pump much like a bicycle pump but made of brass and screwed into the paraffin tank in the base. This gave maximum light. They also got very hot. You could actually boil a kettle or warm up food on them if you had nothing else as a stove. Something that came in useful at times in my years of being on Sealand. Burns on the arms were obligatory from where they were carried up and down the many ladders and companionways in the towers above our heads or holding them out in front in a effort not to damage them. They were very delicate and if you were in the middle of a job and banged or dropped them one piece or the entire brittle glowing element would break off, either reducing the light or plunging you into darkness. Despite the constant effort of maintaining them, lighting them with methylated spirits and then changing over to paraffin and pumping them, they were an excellent and much appreciated source of heat and light. Far better than the hurricane lamps that we started with, which were smelly and exuded only a miserable dull light.

So as you can imagine, the simple thought of having electricity, that we all take for granted in our normal everyday lives at home in England, was something very special out there.

It was a few days before Christmas when we decided that the ancient
'*Gardner 4LW*' engine was ready to start for the first time since the war.
We cranked it over with the battery and nothing; it didn't even attempt to
start. My father did some more tinkering and priming of the fuel system
and we tried again.
Nothing!
I guess since the poor old thing had been lying around for nearly 30 years
without being started; it was somewhat of a miracle and accolade to
British wartime engineering that it even turned over. We removed the air
filter and held a piece of diesel soaked burning rag on the end of a
screwdriver over the air intake and tried again. As the engine spun over
the flames were drawn down the bores. The battery was starting to fail
along with our hopes of electric fires, lights and television for Christmas.
It was heart-breaking after all the work put in.
We connected up the old hand cranking handle to the front of the ancient
engine and pulled out the decompression levers, allowing the engine to
spin freely. My father, back arched, spun the handle as I engaged the
failing starter and all the while holding the flame over the air intake.
When it was spinning as fast as my father could manage I engaged the
decompression levers and the old lady ever so slowly rumbled into life.
First one cylinder fired and picked up, then the next one, until all four
were doing what they had been designed to do some thirty years earlier.
The oil pressure gauge climbed up to 45 psi and it sounded like a Rolls
Royce. We hovered around it tightening oil and water leaks in
wonderment of our achievement; a true symphony to our ears! There
however were still no lights. Walter and Roland unscrewed the covers
and tinkered with the generator and the gubbins inside but one thing was
for sure, it wasn't producing the electricity that we so wanted.

We stopped the engine and Walter with a concerned look on his face
investigated further. We all crowded around behind him, looking over his
shoulder eager to learn from his magic. An argument started because I
told him that I was sure when I was helping him clean up the terminals
inside it, that he had put a wire back on the wrong contact. He wouldn't

have it. He had checked the wires and was one hundred per cent sure that this was not the problem.

We went upstairs and sat down with my mother and sister, very despondent while they consoled us and did womanly things like produce cups of tea and food. Walter then leapt out of his chair and exclaimed that he had the answer. He remembered from his textbooks that if a generator was unused for a period of time it needed 'exciting' to re-magnetize it. After all the jokes of tickling it with a feather we trooped back down one flight of stairs with real purpose to the generator room and restarted the engine. Walter cloaked in concentration then took some wires, connected them to the battery and poked them in the side of the generator. *Bingo!* The lights all came on. The only problem was when he removed the wires the lights went off again. Following the initial elation there was despondency again.

You wouldn't think such a stupid thing as a little electricity could bring out such emotions in people. Several day later our morale in tatters, after some quite heated arguments, Walter agreed under duress to try swapping the wires around that I was so sure he had put back on the wrong contacts.

Bingo again! The lights all came on. But it didn't end there.

As we walked around the huge fortress in wonderment of the lights that we'd wired up. Glowing brightly, one by one the bulbs started popping as we looked on in horror. They did look very bright, even though the voltmeter said we were only generating 220 volts. Once again our 'all things electrical expert' was called upon to diagnose the problem. It soon became clear that the light bulbs we had were 110 volts and were being overloaded with voltage. That was it. We didn't have any other bulbs; there were no shops to buy more and no way to get any. We still had our fume free electric fires giving out a nice dry heat and a TV to watch, so it wasn't all bad news.

With the help of Walter and Roland we eventually got all three of the original wartime generator sets going. I have to say they really knew how to make engines in those days. I wrote to 'Gardner Diesels' asking for a manual. They very kindly sent me the original wartime maintenance books for the whole setup, including generators and control panels. These things had lain around for thirty odd years and we still managed to bring them back to life. Most of the old Scottish fishing boats had Gardner engines, whose motto was, "*a Gardner will always get you home!*"

When it became time to rebuild the last engine there were so many bits missing from it, even the sump plate, that we thought it might be easier to venture out to one of the abandoned Army forts off Whitstable and issue ourselves a complete one.

We were taken out to the Shivering Sands Forts by Fred Plappert, a big man with a thick mop of grey curly hair and a bushy beard. He looked in every way the archetypal fisherman with his trusty old boat '*Unity*'. She was a solid old thing built at Shuttlewoods boatyard in Paglesham at the turn of the twentieth century. Pictures of her launch can still be seen on the wall of the Plough and Sail Pub just down the road. Originally built for sail, she had brass hand pumps fitted in the deck about the boat. These were of a design going back to Nelsons time, comprising of a large brass plunger that you would pull and push up and down out of the deck. She was now fitted with a Ford diesel engine. The downside of Fred's boat was that it always had a nauseous smell of last year's sprats, diesel and bilge about it, that seemed to even taint the tea we made in the wheel house. But then again, most wooden fishing boats in those days were the same and I suppose my stomach was more sensitive then.

Fred as a boy had served an apprenticeship as a shipwright. He could do really clever things with wood, even though he had fingers the size of thick Irish sausages. He would steam and bend wood into amazing shapes to make his own skiffs and small boats. When he left his mooring, on an old boat he had, in the morning the wheelhouse was at the back of the boat and when he returned in the evening it was at the front. He got bored with fishing and decided to have a change around at sea.

Fred had recently broken his leg attempting to drive the ten or so miles home from the Plough and Sail pub after a particularly heavy drinking session. His big BSA motorbike and sidecar had failed to negotiate a particularly nasty bend. I mean, it was the same bend he went round two times a day, every day of the week on his way to and from work, on this occasion probably financed by a good landing of fish the day before. The 'Gold Watch' as he called Scotch, with beer chasers, must have taken a heavier toll than he realised on his driving skills. Fred was a solid old boy and even with his leg in plaster didn't want to let us down. We left Paglesham early in the morning, as daylight was breaking.

There is nothing quite like watching the sun come up in the East over a calm summer sea. Those who have never seen this have not lived. Hours later, the Shivering Sands forts appeared on the horizon. These were army forts and set out in groups of seven individual towers with catwalks or walkways joining them together. There were originally 3.7-inch anti-aircraft guns on each one with a search light and generator tower to one side. They were like huge boxes the size of a very large house on tall tripod stilts. The gun and searchlights set out textbook style, as they would be in a field on land but in this case on their roofs. From a distance, they carved a war of the world's style silhouette. We got alongside the tall wood-covered concrete piles underneath and tied the Unity up to some ironwork, dragging coils of rope and chain hoists over our shoulders. Large toolboxes in hand, we climbed up the rusty ladder to the intermediate platforms high above.

Once more ascending, this time through a thick, ten-foot or more concrete hatchway, almost like a tunnel right in the middle of the structure itself. Then up onto the deck inside the box shaped steel building above. It was a nice calm day, and the sun was shining, a welcome change walking out of the open doorway into the bright sunlight. Lugging my kit over to the rail, I looked down at the Unity. For a forty-foot boat, she looked so very small. I could just make out steam coming from the little wheelhouse as Fred made himself a cup of tea. When he couldn't get a glass of beer he did like his tea. We walked across the rickety swinging catwalk to the adjoining tower and had a look around. It was fascinating; there were washrooms, toilets and living rooms that must have originally been crew quarters. We went up the metal stairs to the roof. Unlike the navy forts, these ones were exceptionally high and as I leant on the rail a section of it fell off and tumbled into the sea below nearly taking me with it. We found a very heavy crane hook that had been taken off one of the huge wartime winches and with much huffing and puffing dragged it back across the catwalk to the generator tower. A few years later we visited the same forts and found the long precarious catwalks had all fallen into the sea. Needless to say, they were not the most psychologically comfortable things to walk across, swaying and flexing as you crossed them.

We then set about dismantling the engine we had chosen from the generator. This was no easy feat; most of the bolts had not been touched since the war and the threads were red with rust. Also, we had never had to separate an engine from generator before so it was new ground. After struggling with it all day, we finally had the engine laying on the deck, free of its beds and all three of us as black as rooks from thirty years of oil and grease. Dragging it to the side with the chain hoist was relatively easy but the chain hoist was not long enough to lower it all the way down to the boat. We had three long ropes and attached them to various parts of the engine.

I looked over the side to see Fred, leg in a plaster cast, sunning himself like a Walrus on deck.

"Oi Fred move the boat" I shouted.

Fred mumbled back with *"it will be ok where it is"*

"No move the boat we are going to lower the engine" I insisted.

"Well, you have it tied on don't you" he shouted back in a patronizing tone.

"Of course, it's bloody tied on," I replied with growing impatience *"move the fucking boat Fred. It's the right thing to do"*

Grumbling and mumbling obscenities to himself, Fred dragged his plastered leg up to the front of the boat and started to pay away the rope, allowing the boat to drift away down tide.

"Let more rope out" I shouted insistently.

"It's all the bloody rope I have" retorted a very grumpy Fred.

It didn't look like he had moved far enough to my mind, but that was obviously as far as the old salt could be bothered to move it.

On the fort above using levers and a lot of brute force, we dragged and lifted the engine over the side with the help of the chain hoist. Dangling in the air, we unhooked the chain hoist taking the strain on the two thick ropes, with the other thinner rope lying at my feet as I directed operations from the edge looking down over the side. Walter and Roland had several turns with the ropes around some sturdy stair railings welded to the deck. All looked well as they proceeded to lower it gently down, a few feet at a time.

Suddenly one of the ropes snapped with a loud twang and crack, followed in quick succession by another loud twang as the second rope parted!

The engine was hurtling through the air towards the sea and boat; at that moment I felt the third rope still attached to the falling engine, whistling past my calf. I looked down horrified to see I was standing in the middle of coils of it and was set to get dragged over the side with it!

"Shit!" I leaped up in the air. I swear to this day that I hovered like some Tweetie Bird cartoon character until the rope had all disappeared over the side, before landing back down with a thud on the steel deck where it had been.

Meanwhile the heavy old engine, now at terminal velocity, exploded into the sea not six foot in front of the Unity, putting up an almighty column of water.

Fred, who had been standing at the bow sucking on a cup of tea, took a step back in horror, fell over the old wooden capstan winch that ran diagonally across the bow and was now lying on the deck like an upturned crab soaked in seawater and tea, cursing and swearing with pain and the indignity of it all.

We looked at the severed rope ends and found they had been clean cut on the sharp edges of the engine.

Lessons learnt? Always move the boat, tie the ropes myself and never EVER stand in coils of rope

I had been very lucky to have not gone over the side with a turn around my foot attached to the engine. I don't think there would have been a lot of surviving that one!

When we got back ashore somewhat crestfallen from our wasted efforts and with nothing to show for the day apart from a bloody great crane hook that we were never going to use. Fred had to go back to the hospital to have his plaster removed and his broken leg reset. He was justifiably not a happy man. I liked Fred!

It couldn't have been long after this on a warm summer's day and the wind was blowing a storm force ten. The Sunk Pilot Service had been suspended and the pilot vessel 'Pathfinder' along with most of the shipping had run for shelter. The sea was white with foam. The violent wind was tearing the wave tops off, throwing spray high into the air. Walter appeared from down the south tower soaking wet and looking very pleased with himself.

"Where the hell have you been?" I asked inquisitively.

"I have just climbed out of the generator room air vent in the north tower and climbed underneath the platform along an RSJ and back in through the air vent in the opposite tower" he proudly announced, his voice thick with adrenaline.

It was a bet he had with Roland and as we spoke Roland was doing the same thing as his side of the wager.

Roland soon appeared somewhat wet and with the same look of glee on his face as Walter. They looked at me as if to say *the Germans have more balls than the Brits*. I pushed them out the way, went down to the generator room, slid the air vent hatch open and climbed out onto the rusty service rail that encircled the tower.

The wind was unbelievably strong, clawing at my clothes and making my eyes water as it whistled through the towers under the platform above my head. Huge seas rolled by underneath me, hammering the towers with awesome force. The air was thick with stinging salt spray. I climbed around the rail and reached up to the big RSJ girder that joined the two towers. Pulling myself to it with shaking hands, knowing one wrong move and I would perish in the raging North Sea below. Forcing that notion out of my head, I climbed very gingerly hand over hand, with just my toes on the bottom edge of the girder and my fingers gripping the top of it. I crossed precariously, ducking under the cross members going in the opposite direction every few feet as I went until I reached the service ring around the opposite tower. Clambering carefully around it and into the air vent of the opposite generator room back to safety.

Now it was my turn for a smug look. *Bloody Germans who do they think they are?* I suppose did some stupid things out there as a young lad. One time alone and bored, I watched a program on mountaineering. They were abseiling down a large rock face. I recalled seeing the mountaineering club giving a display of it at boarding school during parent's open day and being fascinated how these guys came flying down the side of a building in great bounds. I dug out an old webbing belt, a shackle and the only decent bit of rope we had. (Coincidently the same piece of rope that had nearly killed me as I stood in its coils during the falling engine incident on the Shivering Sand forts not long before). I put it all together in the way I thought it must work and abseiled down one of the tower lift shafts some seventy-foot below. Perhaps not the cleverest thing to do when you are on your own, miles out at sea!

During another bored moment and having read the classic assassination book 'The Day of the Jackal', I was fascinated when Fredrick Forsythe described how the assassin drilled out a bullet and filled it with mercury. He then fired it at a pumpkin. As the bullet struck and slowed down, the mercury flew out the hollow end and destroyed the pumpkin. *'Got to try this one'* I thought. Taking a .22 bullet I carefully removed the lead from the brass case with a pair of pliers and drilled it out. I filled the hollow with mercury from an old thermometer and sealed it in with some candle wax. Before I put it back together, I tipped some extra gunpowder in the cartridge case just for good measure. Being a bit short on pumpkins; I placed a pile of books fifty foot away down one end of the main hallway and climbed down a few steps of the companionway, down the tower. With my head poking out of the hatch, pulling the bolt back to collect the round and snapping it forwards into position, I loaded and aimed the ancient old BSA rifle and fired at the pile of books.

BANG! Powder and god knows what flew out of the breach in a cloud of smoke and debris some of it hitting me on the forehead. Somewhat dazed I thought Christ I've blinded myself.

Gradually my blurred vision came back to normal, which was a result! I had all black bits embedded deep under my skin just missing my eyes. I then remembered being taught that if you got mercury under the skin or in the blood stream you died of poisoning. I nervously convinced myself that this was not the case and it was only gunpowder that had blown out of the breech. I didn't die so I assume I was right, either that or my chemistry teacher was talking crap, which wouldn't have surprised me either. The books didn't look a lot different than being hit by an ordinary bullet, so experiment over.

Regina V Bates

It was May 1968 and I was 15.

The bitter winter had yielded to spring and early summer. Penny and I were sitting on the wartime ammunition boxes outside on the deck, enjoying the first warmth of the sun, allowing it to warm through to our bones. It had been a long and cold winter. To the North West, a ship appeared on the horizon growing bigger and bigger with each minute as it steamed towards us with purpose.

As it approached, its immaculate black and white paintwork gleamed in the morning sunlight. A large old-fashioned yellow funnel, sporting a coat of arms and the name '*Vestal*' emblazoned proudly on the bow. We watched through the binoculars as the ship slowed down and came to a stop about a quarter of a mile away. Before dropping her anchor with a loud splash and rattling of chain, as it ran out through the hawser pipe. Shouted orders echoed across the calm sea. We spotted, in the distance, a motorboat being lowered over the side with four or five men in it. The boat, with its noisy puttering engine and a white bow wave, sped across the calm sea in our direction. As they passed close underneath, the men on board were leering and making obscene gestures at my sister and shouting over the loud engine to each other, crassly describing what they would like to do to her. They headed for the buoy to the southeast of us. They then climbed aboard it and replaced some of the mechanism, before re-boarding the motorboat and heading back in our direction. They slowed down as they passed underneath the platform and shouted that they were going to come back in a few days with shotguns and throw us off.

Whether these guys were prompted by the authorities to cause a scene or just being foolish I don't know, but they got their reaction. With my sister shaking and in tears, I went inside, snatched up a nine millimetre automatic pistol. Snapping the slide back to cock and load it, I took careful aim and fired two warning shots across their bows. Telling them in no uncertain terms, to shove off and not come back. I think they got the message!

A few days later the same Trinity House ship returned and lowered a boat. As it got nearer I could see my father in it. We lowered the rope ladder and he climbed up to the deck. Giving us both a big hug, he said he had brought a policeman out who wanted to speak with us about the incident. The policeman wearing a grey suit introduced himself as Detective Chief Inspector Ronald Sewell. He showed me his warrant card and started to caution me. My father stopped him in his tracks and said in a commanding voice *"I have allowed you to come here today to speak to my children on the understanding that you are here as our guest and that you realise you are outside of your jurisdiction and have no right to give a caution. Do you understand?"*
The policeman nodding apologised and then explained there had been a complaint and asked us to explain exactly what had happened. Having taken notes in his book. He wished us well and departed with my father waving to us from the bridge of the ship as it sailed off into the distance.

September of that year, I was walking down the road near our house in Southend when an unmarked police car pulled up next to me. Two uniformed policemen got out, put their hats on and walked over to me. *"Michael Bates?"* They asked in an official manner. I had never been stopped by the police before in my life and was more than a little surprised that they should even know my name.
"Yes" came my cautious reply.
"Could you get in the car please sir? We have been sent to take you as quickly as possible to Harwich magistrate's court".
I complied and before long the Ford Cortina was headed for the motorway as the driver pushed it up to speeds in excess of a hundred miles an hour. I was fascinated, I could see the speedometer over the driver's shoulder and was mesmerised by it. Now and again they would switch on the blue

flashing lights and siren to clear the road in front. I really had no idea what to expect. I hadn't been told I was due in court and at the age of nearly sixteen it was all somewhat new to me.

We arrived at Harwich in record time, and I was rushed into the courthouse where I was surprised to see my father. Apparently because he had been unable to get back from Sealand to attend court, the magistrate had asked that Trinity House send a ship out to collect him. My father didn't argue with the request and went with them on the condition they brought him back to Sealand afterwards.

A portly beady-eyed court official read the charges.

"Count 1. That Paddy Roy Bates on a day unknown between the 1st January 1967 and 6th May 1968 at Roughs Tower within the jurisdiction of Harwich magistrate's court had in his possession a .22 pistol and ammunition to enable Michael Roy Bates by means thereof to endanger life. That is laid as an offence contrary to section 22 of the firearms act 1937.

Count 2. The offence is laid contrary to by means section 1 of the firearms act 1937, Michael Roy Bates on the 6th of May 1968 at Roughs Tower within the jurisdiction of Harwich magistrate's court had in his possession a .22 pistol without holding a firearms Certificate in respect of the same in force on said day.

Count 3. Is laid as contrary to section 22 of the firearms act 1937, Michael Roy Bates on the 6th May 1968 at Roughs Tower within the jurisdiction of Harwich magistrates court had in his possession a .22 pistol and ammunition with intent by means thereof to endanger life. How do you plead?"

We pleaded not guilty.

The magistrate took advice and declared himself not qualified to hear the case. It should be transferred to a higher court at Chelmsford Assizes, where it would be heard in front of a jury.

I wasn't sure what all this meant to me, and my young life, but it was something I was sure I could have done without.

Two days later, my sister Penny decided she didn't want to live on Sealand anymore which obviously meant I would need to spend more time out there with my mother. We were extremely thin on the ground in terms of manpower and money. Looking back, I can't blame her, what teenage girl would want to spend so much time cold, hungry and in isolation.

It didn't seem long before the big day of our court appearance came along.

The 21st of October 1968, my father and I standing on the cold winter steps of the Shire Hall Chelmsford; dressed impeccably in polished shoes, suits and ties. We were introduced to our QC (Queen's Council) Mr. Eastman. Whose job it was to defend us. With him was his assistant Mr. Turl, who was struggling under the weight of a pile of very large and ancient looking law books. Each of them had pieces of paper containing scribbled notes poking out of them in various places.

Our lawyer had already briefed the QC and after a conferring for a few minutes we entered the large, very imposing courthouse.

We were ushered into the court, and my father and I were told to stand in the dock, flanked by a policeman either side of us.

It was all very daunting with the enquiring eyes of the jury upon us. This feeling was augmented when the judge came in wearing his red robes and powdered wig. I never had seen such a sight in my life.
"The court will stand" came the announcement as the old judge Justice

Chapman shuffled across the marble floor to his seat at the head of the court.

The charges were read again, and we were prompted to plead guilty or not guilty?

"My clients plead not guilty to the charges", announced Mr Eastman in a confident and assertive voice.

Mr. Boreham QC assisted by John Newey, both seasoned and successful prosecutors of the pirate radio stations, opening up with a long diatribe of why we were there and the magnitude of the situation. You would think listening to him we were mass murderers seeking potential victims, as venom seeped from his mouth. When he concluded his monologue, it was the turn of our QC to speak. He put forward confidently to the court that, despite the assertions by the prosecution, the use at sea of a bang and a flash from a gun, or other such device were standard and much used international maritime signals to warn a vessel it was standing into danger. Moreover and more importantly, he asserted the court did not have the jurisdiction or authority to pass judgment on an incident that had clearly taken place in international waters.

Justice Chapman calmly called him to the bench. He then called the prosecuting QC to the bench. With their heads close together, they argued and jousted backwards and forwards in subdued tones. The prosecuting QC becoming more and more animated flailing his arms about, his long black gown flowing through the air as he did so. Clearly things were not going his way. Eventually, the judge put his hand up in a dismissive and silencing action, directing them to return to their seats at the front of the court.

He then announced to the court and jury very concisely that there was an issue of jurisdiction and before going any further with the case this must be resolved.

The prosecution stated that since the fortress was originally built by the UK it was owned by the UK. Further that the Admiralty had jurisdiction over ships at sea and there was no reason to believe that this did not include forts. It was asked that if two swimmers were crossing the English Channel and one drowned the other midway in international waters, in which court the case could be heard, if any. Ancient laws dating back to 1536 including *'The offences at sea act'* were mentioned. A case was quoted of a smuggler on a beach between the high and low water mark, shooting a sailor on a sandbank standing in shallow water in Hong Kong harbour. The sailor was then picked up by a long boat and died in the boat. Where was the crime committed on the shore? On the water covered sandbank? In the British boat where the sailor died? Should the case be tried in an Admiralty court or a county court?

Similar cases that had occurred abroad in France, Portugal and ships on the high seas were brought up.

The old judge listened intently as both QCs fought it out, citing laws dating back hundreds of years. It seemed bizarre from where we sat in the dock.

Justice Chapman called for an adjournment for the important business of lunch. We all stood as he and his staff trooped out.

My father and I were ushered to the cells located below the court in the bowels of the building to await their return. The steel door crashed shut behind us. In the ancient and well-used cell, we sat next to each other on the cold concrete bench. The lunch break seemed to take forever, while we sat in an underground cell with nothing but our thoughts, discussing the day's events. I asked my father what he thought of the old judge. He said he seemed a fair man and was pleased that the case was being fought on jurisdiction. He just hoped the judge wouldn't have too much port and brandy with his lunch and send us to the Bloody Tower to be executed for treason!

At some point, we were offered lunch but neither of us had an appetite so we both declined.

Eventually, after what seemed a lifetime, footsteps could be heard coming down the corridor outside the cell. Then a scraping noise as the steel peephole was opened to see what we were doing inside the cell. Followed by the rattle of keys as the heavy steel door was opened with a creaking of heavy metal hinges. We were escorted, once more by two policemen back up the steep stone steps into the courtroom above.

The jury was ushered in and, on the command of the clerk, we all stood as the judge once more entered the courtroom and took his seat in the ornate chair in the centre of the bench. The usher told the court to be seated and the judge started his summing up. He first of all instructed the jury that they would not be needed to give a verdict on the case. As it had been fought on whether the court had the jurisdiction to try the case and not on whether a crime had been committed.

Looking down at his notes, he commenced his summing up, while looking up now and again and peering over the top of his half-moon glasses at the full courtroom. He said with an element of amusement in his voice *"This is a case with a swashbuckling element that would perhaps have been more appropriate to the reign of the first Queen Elizabeth."*

He mulled over all the arguments for and against. As he spoke his voice getting quieter and tapering away until we could not hear him at the back of the court. It did not seem from where we sat that things were going very well. The old boy was taking what seemed an inordinate amount of time to go over each individual item and his voice kept running out of steam.

Eventually, he gave his verdict as we struggled to hear him. *"What did he say?"* I asked my dad nervously.

"It's gone against us son" was his dejected reply.

"What now?" I asked my voice now thick with trepidation.

"We will just have to appeal" he said dejectedly.

Suddenly it seemed the whole court was on its feet, opposing QCs and lawyers were shaking hands and noisily congratulating each other on their cleverly fought case. They then came over to us extending their hands. We were nonplussed. They were reaching into the dock giving their congratulations.

"What now?" asked my father irritated that everyone was so pleased with our demise.

"Nothing!" said our lawyer *"Could you not hear the judge? You have won the day, and there is no possibility that the government can appeal the decision. Sealand is outside UK jurisdiction! 'Terra Nullius' No man's land!"*

Except, of course, now it was ours! I looked at my father as relief and then joy flooded across his face, shaking hands furiously; even the police guards offered their congratulations.

While we were in court, my mother had been alone on Sealand. She had no idea how the case was going. She was worrying herself sick until hearing a report on the BBC radio news that evening. She had been visited no less than five times during the day by navy minesweepers that were keen to know if we had left the fort unattended during the court case.

The very next morning before my father and I could get back, my mother was visited by a very well known female war correspondent and gave her an interview.

It had been suggested by government that perhaps it would be a good time to overrun the fort while we were in court, but on hearing my mother was alone on the fortress, it was considered by the powers that be that to do such a thing would be 'bad form'.

On the 23rd, the Navy minesweepers turned up and the crew gave us a hearty cheer and waved to us. A short while later, the Evening News turned up on a small fishing boat. The journalist managed to get his feet wet getting onto the rope ladder. We dried his shoes for him while he conducted his interview, but on departure he managed to get them wet again jumping onto the boat, a neat little Cornish crabber, owned by Ken Craighill. He and his crewman, Alex, became regular visitors and would often drop us off some fish or fresh bread on the way past going to work. Sadly a year or so later Ken was to lose his life while returning from a fishing trip in foul weather. When his boat swamped, and broke up one night on the notoriously dangerous River Deben sandbar, in a gale of wind. The sandbar was massive, towering out of the water and only had a small entrance through it. At low tide you could not get through it even with a small boat and the seas would build up into a confused frenzy with any easterly wind on an ebb tide. There were two posts on the shore that in daylight you would line up, one in front of the other to make the entrance with leading lights in the dark. Luckily for Alex he was no longer working on the boat. Ken was a hard worker and would be seen out in all manner of weather long lining for cod nearby. The fishing industry had claimed another life!

Next a rather large tug turned up with more eager reporters. For the next few days, they came in droves to talk to us about our plans for the future.

Following the court case, officialdom was not slow to react to the new situation. On the 25th November, only four days later, a certain Mr. Bamfield wrote to a Mr. Ellis-Rees head of C.2 at the Ministry of Defence in Whitehall. It read as follows:

"The legal background from the Customs side is that section 52(1) of the Customs and Excise act 1952 requires that, save as permitted by the Commissioners, no ship shall depart from any port from which it commences a voyage to an eventual destination outside the United Kingdom until clearance of that ship for departure has been obtained from this department. The penalty for failure to comply with this provision is £100.

Following his acquittal at Essex Assizes earlier this week Bates has I understand, stated his intention of going to the fortress on his boat Mizzy Gel and if he does so, I think there is a high probability that he will make no attempt to obtain clearance from us; and the same applies for any subsequent voyages he may make.

Although we might have no doubt in our minds that Bates is using the Mizzy Gel to make 'Unauthorised' trips to the Roughs Tower, this does not, of course mean that you would necessarily have sufficient evidence to institute proceedings with a reasonable prospect of success: Even if we could prove that he had left port, we would still have to establish (with evidence that a court would accept) that he had actually gone to Roughs Tower. But assuming that we could do that on at least one occasion, I am very doubtful it would be viable to institute proceedings. It would be contrary to the practice we normally follow when a ship fails to obtain clearance outwards (we normally send the Master a warning letter) and the offence would be regarded merely as a technical one. I think it very likely that the court would impose a nominal penalty or even none at all. This would undoubtedly be claimed by Bates as a further triumph over officialdom, it would be used by him to obtain even more publicity and I have little doubt that our role would be made to appear as little more than petty victimisation.

In these circumstances, my view is that until such time as there has been an opportunity to formulate a generally agreed policy for dealing with Bates continued occupation of the Towers, we in Customs should not go out of our way to bring charges against Bates merely for failure on his part to clear outwards: but it would, of course, be a different matter if we were to have reason to believe that he was, for example attempting to evade export prohibitions. I hope this course will be acceptable to you, and to Lawrence-Wilson (Cabinet Office), Hart and Trevelyan (Home Office), Hetherington (Law Officers Department) Lovell (Post Office) and Ware (Treasury Solicitor), to whom I am copying this letter"

On the 12th of November, Trinity House once again decided to service the nearby navigational buoys. Whether this was of necessity or more likely I would think, as a test of our reactions after the court case. Either way it made for another rather interesting day.

It was reported in the Daily Express the next day with the headline 'Nervous Invaders Call In The Navy'.

The story told how the Navy sent in a gunboat in traditional style. The 120-ton minesweeper HMS Dittisham, with armed ratings, wearing combat helmets, and carrying automatic weapons, had instructions to only fire if fired upon and were in extreme danger.

The reality is the Dittisham appeared first and hove to below the fortress, and within our earshot. As they did so, the order was given to uncover the ominously business like 20mm Oerlikon cannon on the foredeck. The canvas cover was pulled off with some showmanship just yards away from where we stood looking down on them. The gun was dramatically loaded with a drum magazine by the gun crew, who were standing by, ready to engage. My mother and I watched with bemused interest just a few feet above them. A splendidly uniformed Officer on the open bridge, some thirty feet below us, then unfurled with a flourish what looked like a scroll in a very flamboyant and theatrical fashion. He then started to read from it in as loud a voice as he could muster. Its wording was to the effect that if we fired on the buoy workers the navy would then return our fire. I asked him to repeat, as I couldn't hear, which he started to do again until he realised we were laughing at him reading out some anti-piracy version of the riot act.

With that, he promptly screwed it up and threw it to one side. The ship moved away and as it steamed off towards the buoy maintenance ship we could see three sailors in combat gear and steel helmets. Out of sight of the officers on the bridge and tucked in behind the accommodation hatch with outstretched arms, they were vigorously waving white handkerchiefs in surrender. It was a very funny moment and I wish I could have captured it on film.

I recall coming ashore from our boat at Paglesham one day and walking around the seawall with my father. I was surprised when he lunged out, down into the long grass and dragged the wriggling figure of a man in a blue uniform out of it by the scruff of the neck.

"How dare you spy on me?" boomed the old man as the skinny little man with a rather large pair of binoculars hanging around his neck tried to wriggle free. *"How bloody dare you skulk around spying on me?"* he repeated his voice rife with anger. *"If you want to know something, bloody well ask me! Where do you come from and who are your superiors?"* he demanded of the struggling fellow.

"Southend airport sir," said the fellow in a pleading voice.

"I will see you there with your superior in half an hour" barked my father releasing his grip on him.

The shaken little man half fell and half scampered off down the seawall to his waiting motor bike, kick started it into life and looking over his shoulder at my father in terror, Dad's eyes must have been burning into his back, puttered off as fast as he could towards the airport.

We arrived at the airport long before him, although I don't recall passing him on the road and had a rather fiery meeting with the fellow's superior. It was explained to him that a few gallons of heating oil, tins of beans and sacks of potatoes to feed his family were hardly the makings of an international smuggling operation. With further heated protest my father stated that he hadn't fought a war for King and country to be spied upon by one of its employees.

I have to say we never noticed any Customs lurking around Paglesham after that.

The old Mizzy Gel (bless her) was well past her sell by date and was a constant liability. I can remember my dad coming out to Sealand and staying; while myself and a guy who had been helping out called Jim, were charged with the task of taking the boat back to Paglesham.

Jim knew absolutely nothing about boats so the decision making was left to me. The old lady broke down off Clacton and we couldn't sort out what was wrong. I decided that the only option was to sail her to safety, however that wasn't so simple as she didn't have a mast to attach a sail to or any sails for that matter!

Solution? Pull the long hold floorboards up, nail them onto the back of the wheelhouse at the front and nail some of the famous itchy red blankets between them. The old girl limped along quite well in a stiff easterly breeze and we sailed to safety far up the River Blackwater to St Lawrence Bay. There we left her on the anchor and walked ashore when the tide dropped on the ebb. Mike Todd and his brother Steve towed us back with the 'Venture' to Paglesham the next day.

Such incidents were repeated several times before my father decided the old girl needed to be pensioned off and got rid of her.

Gone Fishing

Since we arrived on Sealand there had always been substantial pressure to maintain enough food and water for survival. The most obvious way to alleviate the food problem was to start catching fish. I had very little experience in this department but took to the task with enthusiasm. We didn't have a fishing rod, or line or hooks. Thinking about it we didn't even have bait. It was reminiscent of mans early attempts at fishing with a bit of modern man thrown in. I looked about the place and found some synthetic rope from the radio station. This I unravelled and joined together for the line. The hook was a bent nail sharpened on the concrete floor with as much of a barb as I could make on it with a hack saw blade. The weight was a small switch box. The next problem was the bait. We tried all sorts: tinned corned beef, cheese and eventually settled on bacon as the most successful. We caught some nice cod with this improvised lash up until the arrival of our first fishing rod and decent bait.

Having the right gear was, of course, far more successful and we were soon catching several fish a day, some of which were in turn used as bait. It was self-perpetuating. The funniest fishing story was when we caught our first tope. For the uninitiated, Tope are small sharks. Looking just like the classic images we have all seen on television. The biggest ones we caught were four or five foot long and must have weighed 50 odd pounds.

The problem was getting them up the sixty or so feet from sea level to the platform. We were using 55 lb breaking strain fishing line, with a wire trace made from piano wire to stop them biting through the line. But the line would still break if we tried to lift them clear of the water. Simple, I thought. I took an old galvanised bread basket the kind bakers used to use in those days to cart their loaves about. Like a galvanised mesh tray; it must have been about three foot by two foot. I fashioned some strops, tied them to each corner of the basket and attached them to a rope so we could lower it down. The first attempt failed because, trying to be clever, we threaded the rod and line through the strops before lowering it. With the idea, the fish could be pulled into the basket when it rose to sea level. This ended up a real buggers muddle; the basket started to spin on the way down, and we lost the fish as it thrashed about and became hopelessly entangled. The next time I caught one we decided to lower the basket to one side of it and try to manoeuvre the fish in at the appropriate moment. This also ended in a massive frap up.

The problem was clear. Being members of the shark family, they behaved in a real shark like fashion. We have all seen how sharks behave on the films; they go round in circles with their fins out the water, looking mean and threatening. Well, these mean looking monsters we were catching were not a lot different. When you got one on the hook and began reeling it in, it would charge about from side to side and around in circles until you could get it in close. It was as much as I could do on some occasions, to keep them from swimming around the tower and breaking the line. They certainly put up a very spirited fight. But we had another plan! After much deliberation, we decided to shoot the next one we caught to stop all that Jaws like circling carry on and get the bugger in the basket.

The moment arrived. I had a monster on the line; it battled like hell as I struggled to reel it in. It broke the surface a hundred feet away and, before sounding like Moby Dick, had disappeared below the waves. I strained and dragged on the rod with aching arms until it was underneath the fort, churning around in small but powerful circles. My mother ran inside as arranged and came out with the 9mm pistol. With the rod in one hand and the pistol in the other I leant over the side and pulled the trigger.

Boom! The water erupted near the fish, but I had missed it.

Boom! I got it right between the eyes.

I was dead chuffed, for a big fish it was quite a small target some sixty-foot away and it wasn't exactly sitting still. I made safe the gun and put it down on the deck. This should be easy now I thought. But no, there was to be another disappointment. Being a shark it had no air bladder. It sunk like a bloody stone; we must have struggled for an hour to get the thing that was now hanging vertically under water into the basket, until the line broke. Eventually, with practice, we did manage to land some of them and of course we ate them.

In the early years the North Sea was alive with fish, which made a good supplement to the tinned food that was the mainstay of our diet. They would hardly be out of the water before being sizzling in the pan. In those days, there was a small fleet of open lobster boats that would come and fish very close by. I suppose there were some ten boats only about 20ft long with small inboard diesel engines that would come out of Harwich and fish right underneath as well as nearby. The method they employed was ancient. They would arrive just before low water and launch dozens of ring nets made from old-fashioned metal barrel hoops with a net bag suspended from the heavy hoop. Tied in the middle of the hoop on a piece of horizontal tarred string was some salted and putrefied fish heads that they kept a ready supply of in a barrel on the boat; fresh bait for crab, and stinking bait for the much prized and more valuable lobster. There was a three-part strop connecting the hoop to the hauling line that was also of tarred rope, and then there was the clever part. When threatened, lobsters flick their tail and scoot backwards with extraordinary speed, to counteract this and stop them escaping, the line to the ring net from the surface had to be kept tight at all times. Along the hauling rope every couple of foot or so was an egg sized cork float, also treated with the old fashioned tar. The fisherman would leave them on the seabed half an hour or so. When the net was on the bottom, the slack end of the hauling line would lay horizontally on the surface of the sea. In such a fashion that the fisherman could lean over the back of his small boat and reach the cork nearest where the line disappeared below the surface. He would then have a good yank on it throwing the lobster into the bottom of the net, before he had a chance to flick its tail and get away. Following that he would then keep a steady pull arm over arm on the rope until it came out of the water. This was one of mans earliest methods of fishing and was still being used in the 20th century. Sadly as the old fishermen died off, the fishery that had been around for generations was depleted and the fleet disappeared. Fishermen mostly use traps these days, which can be left at sea for days and then retrieved in the next spell of good weather.

We lacked barrel hoops. So I improvised and made dozens of ring nets and traps from metal cable conduit and anything else I could find and bend into a hoop. Lashing some old trawl net into the centre of it. Fishing from the down tide end of the platform, we caught quite a few lobsters and crabs. The joke at the time was *"Oh, not lobster for dinner again!"*

September 1969 saw the printing of our first set of stamps as well as a letter from President Pompidou of France congratulating us on the issue and wishing us every success. It seemed that interesting things were starting to happen for Sealand.

The stamps featured pictures of famous seamen from history, explorers including Sir Walter Raleigh, Vasco Da Gamma and Sir Frances Drake.

These were printed in Belgium and First Cover letters were sent around the world from Sealand via arrangement with the Belgium post office on a well-publicised helicopter flight from Sealand to Belgium. Our Postmaster General Christian Hache, a cheerful little man in a light grey suit and glasses, arrived on a helicopter to collect the bright red mailbag. It was my first experience of a helicopter as the noisy *'Jet Ranger'* landed with an enormous downdraft on our helipad. I was more fascinated with the helicopter than the inaugurating flight for our first stamps. I managed to convince the reluctant pilot to take me up for a spin around our country. It seemed so strange. I had spent the last two years defending this fort and taking care not to fall over the side, particularly from the helipad, which had no rails around the edge. Now I was sitting in the front of this machine as it lifted not more than a foot or so into the air and just drifted, it seemed, over the side suspended in thin air. I was convinced we were going to plummet into the sea. It was a surreal experience and despite the many hours since I have spent in them and the fact I have lost friends in helicopter crashes since, I still thoroughly enjoy flying in them.
One of the conditions I would insist upon for future helicopter companies ferrying journalists out was that they would have dual controls, enabling me to practice my dubious flying skills. One particularly brave pilot would

let me hold the dual controls as he landed the machine on the helipad. That takes some trust, as every movement one set of controls makes is duplicated by the other. Usually, I would just fly the machine over the sea or along the coast while the pilot looked on. It was a real buzz for me.

I think one of the funniest incidents that occurred was after Captain John Crewdson had been alone with me in his Aleut flying back along the Essex coast.

He said *"Do you know what happens to these things when the engine stops?"* I had read up on Auto rotation but had never seen it done. John coolly flicked some switches; the engine noise died and the machine started to plummet out of the sky. I could see a tractor hundreds of feet below pulling a plough across a field. It was getting bigger and bigger at an alarming rate. The method is to put pitch back on the engineless spinning rotor blades just before impact thus making a really hard, but hopefully not fatal, skidding landing without power. As the ploughed furrows in the field got bigger and bigger the guy driving the tractor could now be made out clearly from the cockpit of our plummeting aircraft. I wonder what was going through his mind. I know mine had gone into overdrive.

John put the pitch back on the blades and the shuddering machine slowed down. Then just before the impact of a forced landing he brought the engine back into life and powered the machine back up high into the clear blue sky. I found this fascinating and kind of cool. So a few weeks later while flying a Brazilian TV crew across the Dengie marshes on our way from Southend Airport to Sealand, I said to John in devilment *"That was really cool doing the Auto rotate thing the other day. Why don't we show the journalists how it's done?"*

With that, John flicked the switches, the engine died and the helicopter started to plunge out of the sky towards the ground. At the same time, he calmly announced over our headsets that there is nothing to worry about and this is only a practice drill. Immediately the headsets were full of very loud panic-stricken Portuguese voices shrieking in our ears. I turned to see our passengers with eyes bulging out on stalks and furiously crossing themselves as they prepared to meet their maker in a foreign land. Then it clicked, unusually for journalists they hardly spoke a word of English so had not understood that we were only fooling around and were convinced we were going down for real.

Then on another occasion there was a female journalist who was absolutely beside herself with indignation when she discovered from the pilot that someone without a pilot's licence had been at the controls over the North Sea. Furthermore, had actually landed the machine on Sealand as the pilot talked me through it. I had loads of practice and it was great fun!

It was around this time that we had a visit from a journalist who was based in Monaco.

He met over dinner with our family lawyer Lionel Conway, in the Boston Hall Hotel on Southend seafront. The man, Lionel said, wore an expensive suit and ordered different wines with each course. Lionel was rather impressed with him. After dinner, he came straight to the point. I represent an interested party who wishes to buy Sealand lock, stock and barrel for £250k. At current values that would equate to some £2.57 million, an awful lot of money, but my father turned it down.

To this day I don't know why he did considering our situation at the time.

He never did divulge who he represented but indicated it was Aristotle Onassis the mega rich Greek shipping tycoon, who was one of the wealthiest men in the world at the time and had married President Kennedy's Widow Jackie.

Tiger

1972 saw us issuing our first Sealand coins. We did this in association with an American banker from Houston Texas, named George Garner. I never met him but my parents took several trips to the United States to see him. They also had some stop offs in Florida, Mexico and the Caribbean on the way home. Life was improving and the coins sold well. Garner proved to be honest and there was a trickle of money coming out of our project. It was about this time we employed Gordon Wilkinson or Willy, as we affectionately knew him. He was to become a great friend to my family and me as we embarked on many adventures together.

We decided to buy a RIB (rigid inflatable boat) to make our life on Sealand easier, as well as improve communication and accessibility with the UK. It was early days for these boats; we decided on an orange and grey four-meter Avon Sea Rider and named it Tiger. It was a fine thing in its day. It had two side-by-side seats in the front and a forty-horse power hand start engine on the back. The fibreglass V-shaped hull design allowed the water to run between hull and deck through two small holes in the front when stationary. The theory being this would give stability when stopped and this section would empty out of a drainer at the back when at speed. We stored it at Suttons Boatyard in Wakering, housed in a specially built shed at the top of the slipway on the seaward side of the seawall. It sat on an agonizingly heavy, homemade steel trailer that, of course, could only be pulled up the slipway by hand. It could then be launched day or night in an emergency without the need to involve others. The boatyard built us a wooden box that fitted in the back of the little craft that we jokingly nick named the coffin, for obvious reasons. The coffin contained a small 5hp *Get you home* outboard engine, some tools an anchor and rope. We soon found that the 40hp engine was somewhat underpowered. When it had problems starting, which seemed often in spite of it being brand new, we would end up exhausted with skinned fingers and blistered hands from yanking on the bloody string. On reflection, we pushed the poor little boat to the limit. We had lifting eyes fore and aft fitted to it. When we arrived at Sealand we would unload the stores into our lifting pallet and swing them up onto Sealand using one hoist. We would then attach the two electric winches we had together. One large hook with another one, shackled to the top of it and lift the boat complete with two crew up sixty odd feet into the air and swing it onto the deck. Another problem with the hand start engine was not being able to start it out of the water for fear of damaging the delicate cooling pump impeller. If you unhooked and let it go in any swell, you could end up crashing into the tower while you were still pulling on the bastard string and of course you never quite knew if the bloody thing was going to start at all!

We soon learnt to unhook it on the top of a swell. But to remain attached to the hook by a long rope. That allowed us to drift clear of the fort. But gave us the possibility, if the weather wasn't too bad or the tide too strong to pull ourselves back to the hook and lift the boat out again if it didn't start. Combine all that with winter weather; the cold, rough seas, fog, snow and everything else nature could throw at us (It was more than a bit of a recipe for disaster). Then there were the winches we used to lift the little boat. They were the old lift shaft ammunition hoists from the Tongue and Knock John forts, in conjunction with the ancient greased wartime winch wires that we still used.

Willy and I had made the trip especially to retrieve the winch from the Tongue forts.

Getting underway in the early hours of a chilly November morning from Barling Creek in the Essex marshes, our friend Mike Todd at the helm of the *'Saltash'*. Mike, a handsome man in his forties with a strong Essex accent and a face permanently tanned from a lifetime at sea, was in good spirits. He had worked with us for many years and his fifty-foot fast and powerful ex Belgian beam trawler made good time, arriving late morning. We didn't know how we were going to get up on the fort but as we approached, we were relieved to see a rope ladder hanging down.

Mike shouted, *"don't be too long we have the tide to catch back up the river."*

One at a time Willy and I stepped off the high bow of the boat and climbed the manky old ladder to the steel deck above. Pulling up after us a bag of tools on a rope I had carried up on my shoulders.

These three phase electric winches were mounted inside the main building above the lift shaft runners that ran down one side of the towers. Allowing the gun crews to get the ammunition from the magazine six floors below up to the deck level to feed the guns. We bashed away furiously at the bolts with a club hammer and cold chisel trying to split the nuts, taking it in turns with painfully aching arms. Things like burning gear to cut them off in seconds were the stuff of engineering shops and big ships. My old man always thought you could achieve most things mechanically with a hammer (the bigger, the better) and a cold chisel. If that failed he would try and get a hacksaw, which of course he had in various sizes, onto the job along with an assortment of rusty blades. We somehow got the winch down off its trestle, where it had been fitted above the seventy-foot lift shaft, without dropping it. Only to find it wouldn't quite fit past this metal stanchion post made from a piece of four inch steel tube. The post holding the corner of the roof up and the bloody thing was welded top and bottom. Mike in the meantime was getting agitated and shouting up to us to get on with it or he would be leaving without us.

Looking back we must have gotten quite good at dealing with the most diabolical 30-year-old wartime nuts and bolts that had been in one of the harshest environments in the world. All carried out with crap tools. But having got the thing down on the deck without it or us plummeting down the seventy-foot lift shaft (quite an achievement in itself) we were now stumped. Mike was moaning and we couldn't get it out the bloody door to finish the job.

We needed it to lift the RIB and knew that if we left without it we would never return again to pick it up as there was so much cost and effort involved for everyone. We started to attack it with a hacksaw, but it was too thick and eventually we snapped our last blade. We sat there crestfallen, staring at this half ton of machinery that we really needed but couldn't get out. My dejected thoughts were broken by a moment of inspiration. We called Mike over who, thinking we were coming back down to the boat, was getting all excited about the idea of getting underway and going home.

"We are not quite ready," I told him *"we need the 'Turfer' sent up on a rope."* This is an incredibly powerful and extremely slow hand winch that has a thick steel hawser running through the centre of it. The operator hooks one end of the three-foot long flat machine onto something solid. The other end of the hawser onto whatever needs lifting or dragging. You then pump the lever on the side furiously to make it creep in ever so slowly. Well the bloody thing with all its wire was heavy enough for the two of us to pull up by hand. Mike wasn't very impressed when we told him we were not quite ready to lower the machinery down on it.

We hooked it on the huge RSJ girder that surrounded the platform and hooked the other end on the middle of the bastard upright that was causing us so much grief. The wire creaked and groaned. There were shuddering noises coming from both ends of the wire and I had visions of it breaking and whipping back at us with lethal force. When suddenly the middle of the stanchion started to buckle. Then with a loud bang the weld at the bottom snapped away from the deck. We were able to bend it clear and drag the machinery victoriously out onto the deck.

The story doesn't end there because as the weather was cutting up and the Turfer that we would now be lowering the machinery down with was frighteningly slow. It was decided we would attach the load on a rope strop that could be quickly cut on the top of a swell when it was in the right position over Mike's aft deck. The heavy weight of it could have wrecked the boat swinging about as they tried to unhook it as we were unable to lower it at more than a snail's pace. We had it lowered just right, *"You got the knife ready Ian?"* I shouted to the crewman.

"Yep" he shouted up, proudly waving the glinting blade of a knife firmly clenched in his rubber-gloved hand for me to see.

Mike manoeuvred the Saltash in; underneath just right so it would land on a pile of nets he had placed to absorb the impact. Ian Hodges, his young crewman, leapt forward with the razor sharp gutting knife he had been honing all afternoon for this critical job and sloshed at the rope.

Bang! It landed on the deck perfectly.

"Oh fuck!" came Ian's voice as he looked down in horror *"Oh fuck, fuck, I think I've cut my fucking finger off!"* he wailed as blood pumped out of his lacerated glove on to the deck.

Now Willy and I had to wait to climb down, the boat drifting away while Mike bandaged him up, as we unsuccessfully tried to keep straight and concerned faces.

"Come on Mike, we've had enough and want to go home".

A few days later we delivered the hoist to Sealand ready for fitting. We had to bolt it to the deck, on any other firm would have been simple enough task but electric drills were just things you read about in books. My old man surpassed himself as usual. Producing a big hand drill with an ominous looking shoulder butt, similar to a rifle butt, which you were meant to lean on as you worked up a sweat. Achieving not much more than polishing the metal you were trying to cut through. It had been given to me very proudly by my father with a couple of new drill bits and a sort of *'look after this carefully son'* expression. Thinking about it they probably weren't new and the drill looked like a bigger version of the kind of things kids have in their toy toolboxes. Willy and I had no way of sharpening the drill bits. Besides which, by the time we had managed to basically wear our way through the thick steel deck in a couple of places, we decided two bolts would be plenty to hold the bastard thing down. Oh and then there were the brakes! Originally the winches were fitted with electronic brakes that use a kind of inverted solenoid device but we could not work out how to wire them in. So we ended up with a metal lever pivoting on a thin bolt with a lump of wood bolted on it that pressed on the spinning flywheel acting as a brake shoe that could be replaced when it wore out.

With the new winches in place, we soon replaced the RIB engine with a new electric start 55hp model. No more skinned fingers pulling a starting cord! We would load up the boat with bottles of gas. Fifteen gallons of petrol for the engine, twenty-five or thirty gallons of diesel, ten or fifteen gallons of paraffin, boxes of food, our kit bags and usually two people. We would blast off down the river and out to sea, a journey of some thirty-five miles with only a compass and a watch to navigate through the many sand banks of the outer Thames Estuary. Fully loaded it would take about an hour and a half on a fine day. When the weather was bad, it could take forever. One calm spring day the fog came down so thick we didn't see a single buoy or navigational mark after leaving the river. We had to keep the throttle wide open once in the open sea to work out our speed. As when we slowed we had no way of calculating what speed we were doing and when to change course through the Wallet Spit way and down the Wallet to Sealand. Constantly looking at our compass and watches. When we arrived near Sealand we would turn the engine off, sound a hand held gas horn, whoever was on Sealand would bang on an oxygen bottle in return which made a terrific din and we would head towards the noise. The trick is to believe in your compass and not think you know better, which is not so easy to do in such a disorientating environment, something which we have all done at one stage or another.

The boat had no radio or electronic navigation equipment. One time my father turned up on a rough day and something sharp flying about in the back of the boat had pierced the sponson leaving one side totally deflated. He couldn't slow the engine for fear of the boat swamping. He had to circle at speed, keeping up on the plane until we had lowered the winch gear and hooked into the boats lifting strop. Whisking it out of the water as it filled up and half sunk. It was a great little boat but we were pushing it well beyond what it was designed for. We broke the fibreglass hull twice at sea, once ending up swamped on Clacton beach. The makers on the Isle of Wight were most helpful; they couldn't believe we had managed to break chunks out of the hull. They said bulletproof vests were made with the same material. They had dropped these boats from cranes high above the water to test their water impact qualities. Whether we were coming down hard on floating debris in the dark and damaging the hulls or just sea impact I don't know but I know we managed, without even trying, to break two hulls.

The bigger electric start outboard made things easier and safer, but that too came with its dramas. One calm as a sheet of glass day, flying down the River Roach on the start of our journey the engine note changed. The revs screamed as the load came off of it and the boat fell dead in the water. I pulled back on the throttle and tried again to engage the ahead gears. Nothing! There wasn't any drive. Willy cracked out the little emergency outboard from the coffin and we limped back to Wakering to investigate the now useless engine. After a couple of days, the engineers working for the company where we bought it told us they had repaired it and that the drive shaft between the engine and the propeller had snapped. They had never even seen this before!

Willy and I made ready for sea. We had promised to relieve my father so that he could attend a meeting in the UK and although the weather was a little fresh we decided it should be workable. It was freezing cold and we were glad of the crash helmets we had just started wearing on the RIB, not just for safety but also mainly to keep our heads warm! The bright fluorescent oilskins we wore over our warm clothes sheltered us from the wind; however the material they were made of was hard and uncomfortable in the cold. We would wear a small towel around our necks to stop the chafing but they were far from the most comfortable thing to wear in a fast open boat for a couple of hours being banged about as we flew from wave top to wave top.

We blasted down the River Roach and came out into the wider River Crouch and into the open sea. The chill easterly breeze kicked up the swell and it became more and more uncomfortable. We were accustomed to this and knew it was only for an hour and a half or so, and we would be sitting by a warm fire on Sealand. We made a course change to the North West, through the Wallet Spit way, a narrow and shallow gap between the Buxey and Gunfleet Sands that dried out at low water. The going got easier, with the seas on our aft quarter, but the pounding picked up again as we changed course again, once more to the North East and thundered down the Wallet. Walton on the Naze appeared about four miles away to the North. Then it happened for no apparent reason; the engine revs screamed away and the boat fell dead in the water. *'The same bloody thing!'* We looked at each other stunned. We tilted the heavy outboard out of the water, leant over the transom and tried turning the propeller with the engine stopped and in gear. It just spun. There were no two ways about it; exactly the same bloody thing had happened again (The manufacturers later told us we were running at a critical rev range, have you ever heard so much cobblers? There was nothing in the instruction manual about it).

We were soon in a right muddle.

The wind turned the boat stern on to the swells. The freezing cold waves were breaking over the stern and sloshing into the boat as we tried to work on the motor, struggling about in our wet weather gear and boots amongst loaves of bread and tins of food floating about in the fast swamping boat.

We very quickly decided that the best plan of action was to get the small outboard out of the coffin and get underway to somewhere or other; we hadn't had time to work out the finer details. We hooked the small emergency motor on the back and started to yank on the cord. *The useless thing didn't want to know!*

It had now started snowing but far from being cold; we were both covered in sweat as we continued to manufacture blisters on our hands with the starting cord. There was too much water sloshing about inside and outside the boat to do anything with the engine and it had been drowned by the breaking waves. We decided to chuck the anchor out to allow the boat to swing head into the weather. The anchor held well and Willy bailed the water out of the boat while I stripped the fuel system on the little engine and cleaned the spark plug. Small outboards have a reputation for always working on the garden gate but being a waste of time when you got them near a boat or any marine environment. This one was no exception; I don't suppose it was helped by the continual bashing it got while laying dormant in the coffin waiting for its next outing.

It soon became clear that despite every effort to sort it out; the bastard thing was as dead as a doornail and wasn't taking us anywhere. I have to say at this point that I hate outboard motors with a vengeance. They are the most wonderful things when working right, but they are absolute bastards when they are not. In those days despite it being all new kit they were a constant liability.

So there we were, thankfully the wind had dropped a little, it was getting dark and it was snowing heavily. The sweat we had worked up over the outboards was starting to chill inside our oilskins. We were in an open boat with no power, no communications equipment and not another boat or ship in sight. We did however have some parachute flares in a waterproof container we could fire off should we decide the situation had become desperate and untenable. In daylight we would be able to see the coast guard station on the shore at Walton on the Naze just a few miles away but in these conditions of zero visibility in the snow, it may as well have been on the moon. Willy and I had a chat and decided we would wait to see what the morning brought. Perhaps if the weather was better we could at least beat the crap out of the outboards with a spanner in daylight. We pulled our stiff oilskin hoods up and hunkered down in our seats and went to sleep.

I woke up a few times during the night freezing cold and covered in a thick layer of snow that had settled in the boat. I have always prided myself I can sleep anywhere but this was perhaps pushing it a bit far. It's lucky really that Willy and I didn't consider hypothermia or being run down by a ship otherwise it might have interfered with our slumbers!

The next day as darkness turned to light, it was a different world. The snow had stopped during the night and the sea was flat calm, however to our dismay it was absolutely dense fog, as thick as you get; just a few yards visibility if there was something to see. The trouble with fog at sea is, you never quite know how far you can see until there is something ahead of you to see, by which time it's usually too late.

The tide was ebbing away towards where Sealand must have been, some ten or twelve miles away, so we decided to pull the anchor up and see if we could drift down on it with the tide. This like everything else on this trip became a problem. The anchor had become fouled on some wreckage on the seabed. Without the engine to manoeuvre against the strong pull of the tide and tip it out of the ground, I had to cut the rope to get free of it. This was the last thing I wanted to do as without power or an anchor we were totally at the mercy of the freezing cold sea. We worked out a bearing for Sealand on the compass and broke out the emergency paddles to try and paddle across the tide. Because of the boats design, where it flooded between the hulls when off the plane and settled down in the water, it was like trying to paddle a log. If nothing else, we warmed up with the effort.

We drifted all day in the fog and just before dark we heard the engine of a fast lobster boat passing nearby. We knew who it was because this guy used to take his large 'Collie' dog to sea and it would sit in the prow of the boat barking. I mean, it never seemed to stop when the boat was underway on the many occasions I had seen and heard them. It was helpful because even though there was no way we could attract his attention in the fog over the engine noise, we knew where he had been working and what route he normally took. This put us to the North East of Sealand; we must have passed it during the day. I knew that the odds were he was steaming his usual route back from retrieving his pots. He would be using a navigator and watching his radar on which, being an inflatable with a low profile and radar reflection, we would hardly show up on his screen. The steady woofing gradually faded into the fog in the direction of Harwich and all was still again.

Darkness fell and we decided that if we could not get to Sealand by morning we would fire off a flare. I had never called a lifeboat in my life and thought the inability to sort out my own problems would be a failure. However the idea of being able to paddle across the fast flowing tide in a boat that responded like a log in a river and to actually get to the fort would be one in a million chance even if we could see the damned thing.

142

Suddenly we could hear the ominous 'thump-thump-thump' of a massive engine growing nearer and nearer in the dense fog. It sounded to me like one of the huge British Rail train ferries. The Essex or Suffolk ferry, probably under the command of our friend 'Ginger' who had visited us and shown support on an almost daily basis over the years. *How profound would that have been if he had run us down in the dark and not even known about it?* The fog had now cleared slightly and the ferry appeared out of the gloom. It was heading straight for us!

We could see the port and starboard lights clearly, the fore and aft mast light lined up one above the other as he loomed larger and larger. We tried to make the torch work but it had died during the night either through flat batteries or the ubiquitous damp that gets into everything in a small boat. She passed towering out of the sea about a hundred yards away, totally oblivious to our presence.

We breathed a sigh of relief.

With the fog starting to clear we looked about to see if we could spot Sealand. *Nothing!*

We could see the Sunk lightship flashing out to sea and various buoys. I was sure we couldn't be that far away although the perspective was so different to the view I was used to from the high deck of the fort. The tide had turned and was now flooding. We had for some time been drifting to where I thought it should be. Suddenly a blaze of lights appeared nearby, my father had started the generator up to go to the kitchen and make some tea. It was just yards away, Willy shouted with cupped hands to his mouth as loudly as he could and I whistled to try to attract my father's attention. We paddled like there was no tomorrow across the tide to try and get behind the tower where there is a swirling back eddy from the fast flow of water. My mind tormented in the knowledge that if we missed it, we would not be able to make headway into the fast flowing tide. We would be whisked away into the depths of the dark freezing cold night. Without even an anchor to stop us drifting away, so we could at least have tried to paddle across at the next slack tide. God or someone must have been looking down on us, or more likely felt sorry for us, that night because several things happened.

Firstly, after all the miles we had travelled over the last two days most of which was in the dark or dense fog the boat was unbelievably in the right place just yards away from Sealand.

Secondly, my father fired up the generator along with all the floodlights under the platform a few minutes before.

Thirdly, he was in the kitchen with his head in the chest freezer wondering what delight to issue himself for dinner that night when he thought he heard a shout outside. He didn't have the best of hearing in the world to put it mildly, so for him to hear us was nothing short of a miracle! He rushed outside, heard us shouting and spotted us near collapsed with exhaustion paddling the bastard log across the fast flowing tide from the south towards him. For us, it wasn't happening. We were paddling as hard as we could, but it was clear the tide was going to whisk us away at the last minute out into the cold, dark abyss of the North Sea and snatching salvation from our grasp. The sweat was pouring off us and our arms felt like they would leave their sockets. We started shouting at each other in frustration when one of us missed a beat; this was desperate stuff and if we didn't get to the fort after all this effort all would be lost. We would be taken off by the fast flowing tide into the dark night and have to decide whether to fire our flares off or not.

We had been given a chance in a million and we had to make it work.

Suddenly there was a heavy thud as a rope came flying down from above and landed perfectly placed across the middle of the boat. Willy hurled himself at it like a rugby player scoring a try and took a turn around the lifting strop in the middle of the boat, tying it off. I guess all those years of insisting there was always a heaving line on deck coiled carefully and ready for action had paid off.

Gasping for breath we dragged the waterlogged boat in on the rope as another smaller rope came flying out of the bright lights above. It was attached at the other end to the lifting hook that my father was lowering down as fast as he could. Pulling now on this rope with our last reserves of strength, I reached out and grabbed the cold steel of the heavy hook and shoved it with a satisfying clunk into the large shackle in the middle of the boats lifting strop. Above our heads, the electric hoist hummed into life. The boat started being dragged sideways across the fast running tide. Tipping over on its side at a forty-five degree angle with us clinging on for dear life, until right underneath the winch and whisked out of the water. Swinging from side to side like a pendulum, water pouring out of the self-drainer. Willy and I collapsed in a heap in the bottom of the boat. Soaked in sweat and utterly exhausted staring up at the blazing lights shining down on us with my dad's concerned but delighted face beaming through from behind them as the boat neared the top.

Dad heaved on the rope swinging the boat in over the side, dumping it unceremoniously on the steel deck with us still lying in the bottom of it. Unable to move as water still trickled out of the self-drainer. Half blocked by pieces of bread and various other food from our stores that we had been clambering about all over for the last difficult and no doubt character forming couple of days.

The next day, after a good night's sleep we examined the damage. Clearly the big outboard engine had to go back to the workshop. We hung the small outboard on one of the gun box doors on deck and on the second pull on the starting cord, it roared into life. I wasn't at all surprised.

We managed to arrange one of the small lobster boats to tow the RIB ashore to get the repairs done. We then decided to part exchange the big engine for a different one that didn't have a *'critical rev range'*.

After being adrift in the boat for two days, a large red salt-water boil came up on my leg. It was where the rough oilskin trousers had been rubbing against my calf. I thought nothing of it at first and waited for it to go away. It didn't and my leg blew up like a large red and blue balloon. It was getting serious, so we got on the radio and asked my mother to go and speak to the doctor about how to treat it. By the time she came back with the information, I had to lay on the bed with my leg in the air in a vain attempt to alleviate the dreadful pain. It was twice as big as the other leg and needless to say we had no painkillers. The doctor advised us to put a bread poultice on it, soaked in boiling water. "A bread poultice?" both Willy and I thought my mother was kidding; we had never heard of such a thing. I was in too much pain to get to the radio.

I told him to tell my mother I didn't want a bloody sandwich, I really was ill and could she come up with something a bit more practical! No, she insisted in an amused voice; a bread poultice was an old fashioned cure and would draw the poison to the surface. With that Willy put his doctor's hat on and marched off to the kitchen coming back with a kettle of boiling water and some manky old bread. He carefully poured the water in a bowl, dunked the bread in it and without further ado slapped it on my huge red, inflamed calf. I nearly shot through the roof with excruciating pain.

"Christ! This isn't going to work! You're going to have to cut it open and get the poison out" I told him through clenched teeth.

Willy was now warming to the task and disappeared out of the door in search of a sharp knife. He returned looking very pleased with himself, clutching our fish-gutting knife, which he proceeded to plunge into a saucepan of boiling water, just like they did in the best cowboy films. Delighted with his new position as fort surgeon, he came towards me knife in hand like Jack the bloody Ripper on a fun day out. The trouble was we were laughing so much at this bizarre situation and my leg was throbbing with such excruciating burning pain. Go on, lance the bloody thing, stick it in. Willy finally pulled himself together from his fits of laughter. Reaching across he gave me a leather belt to bite on, took a deep breath and dug the sharp blade deep into the huge pus filled throbbing boil. Blood began pouring out as he puggled around inside the quite large hole he had made in my leg. Working away with a look of sheer concentration on his face, he triumphantly came out with a revolting green sack of poison, about an inch long. He was delighted with his newfound skills and said he would get some disinfectant to put on the wound. Running out of the room to fetch it, he returned with a rusty gallon can of disinfectant he had found in the toilet, behind the pan that everyone had been pissing on for the last few years. Before I could say anything he tipped a good glug into the open wound, bits of rust and grot dropping off the top of the can as he did so. How my leg didn't fall off after all that I don't know, but the pain went away almost instantly and the swelling went down in a couple of hours.

Three weeks later on a fine spring morning, my father turned up in Tiger. After our customary chat and a cup of tea, we launched it for Willy and I to go ashore. The bloody thing wouldn't start. We ended up making our way back with the small emergency outboard until many hours later getting a tow from a friendly fisherman for the last few miles of our journey.

Out on Sealand we were still maintaining the 24-hour watches and monitoring every movement of ships and aircraft. One day we were visited by a large American Air Force helicopter, which flew around us in a circle a few times. I can only assume by its actions it had been sent out by its political masters to obtain intelligence on the new fledgling state in the North Sea. Quite funny, the winch man in the open doorway held up a steel plate and peered over the top of it like the wartime cartoon '*Chad*', a guy with a big nose who was always starring over a wall.
They should have asked their pals at the US Air Force base. They would have put them straight. Since the early seventies low flying USAF Phantoms had visited us. You wouldn't hear them coming at near the speed of sound, but they would pass over with a sonic boom. There was one pilot that had a chequered helmet and an eagle on the side of his cockpit. He would fly over so low with his landing lights on and wheels down that he left a wash in the sea. He would wave from the cockpit, do barrel rolls and give us our own incredible air display. He too got a nickname, '*The Maniac*'. We used to collect rainwater off the helipad when it rained hard and pipe it into our fresh water tanks and whenever 'The Maniac' had been about it always tasted of paraffin or aviation fuel. We couldn't complain; he was a great supporter! Sometimes he would appear with five or six other Phantoms, always leading the way, there would be a big circle of fighter aircraft diving down and roaring up into the sky. Many years later I was emailed by a retired senior US Air force officer who said

that he had invited some English friends to stay, that were living on the other side of the States. They showed him the front page of the Los Angeles Times and asked *"You were based in East Anglia in the seventies, did you ever come across these people?"*

He picked up the paper and saw a picture of Sealand on the front page. *"My god,"* he said, *"how strange!"*

He recounted how in March 1968, he had been flying back from a NATO exercise in Holland. Flying low across the North Sea and had seen us, a small dot in the distance. Deciding to investigate, he turned the jet fighter around and had another look. Fascinated by the aircraft and glad of the company, all be it at a distance, we waved to him. He was enthralled and always visited us when he could, to offer his support. We never met him but he became a great friend and another supporter from afar. When he emailed me, I invited him out for a visit if ever he was ever in the UK or Europe again.

Over the years, we witnessed many interesting aircraft. When the first A10 tank busters nicknamed 'Warthogs' came into service with the US Air force, they would come and visit us. They were very slow, which was the idea, so they could hit tanks on the ground with their Gatling Guns' murderous fire.

In early 1980, we witnessed for the first time American Sea King helicopters refuelling in the air from a Hercules C130 tanker. This involved the Hercules trailing a long hose with a funnel-shaped end on it, the helicopter approaching from behind and inserting a probe protruding out of the front of it into the funnel. There didn't seem a lot of room for error below the whirring rotor blades. What we didn't realise as we watched was that this was new technology and that they were practicing for the failed US rescue mission of the Iranian hostages in Teheran; 'Operation Desert Claw' later to be the story behind the film 'Argo'.

Sealand has always had more than its fair share of air activity. For years, the United States Air force would fly overhead during the night and drop magnesium parachute flares. At first we thought we were under attack but the, almost daily at times, practice became routine. They were launching them from C130 Hercules aircraft flying low over the sea, usually with various helicopters clattering about in attendance. Occasionally the flares landed in the sea very close by, but usually they kept a respectful distance. I assume the purpose was search and rescue practice.

One bright sunny day while alone on Sealand a 'Westland Wasp' anti-submarine helicopter appeared from the direction of the UK. It's high-pitched and very loud screaming engine warning me of its approach as it roared in towards me, nose down and going like a bat out of hell across the calm sea. The small speck in the distance, gaining in size and volume as it grew nearer and nearer. Adrenaline pumping through my veins, the hackles on the back of my neck raised, I ran inside, down the long hallway into the radio room and across to the rifle rack grabbing up the nine-millimetre P38 pistol that my father had carried through the war. Strapping the fast draw combat holster firmly to my waist I ran back down the hall and outside. The entire place was starting to shudder under the deafening noise and vibration of the now very close machine that was swooping around above. I climbed up onto the helipad as the helicopter screamed around in a sweeping turn just feet above my head. The pilot was alone in the door-less machine wearing dark glasses and buckskin flying gloves. Written clearly across the nose of the machine was 'HMS Galatea'.

The pilot stared menacingly at me. I crossed my arms and turned slowly on my heels as he circled, keeping him carefully in front of me. He didn't wave or make any gesture. He dropped the machine to below the helipad. The rotors were spinning under the overhanging structure I was stood on; rust and debris flew about the place stinging my eyes like a sand storm, the deck plates vibrating below my feet. I walked forward carefully and looked down on the rotors chopping through the air below me. "Christ you wouldn't want to fall in that lot" I gasped stepping back.

He pulled away before lunging back in again. This bloke might have been a miserable bastard and I am sure he was there with ill intent, but he certainly knew his onions when it came to throwing a helicopter about. We were just feet apart and he just stared; his eyes piercing through me from behind his dark glasses. This whole scenario must have lasted some ten minutes. Then without even the slightest gesture, goodbye or kiss my arse, with a flick of his wrist on the stick he was gone. Speeding out into the North Sea at low altitude, disappearing over the horizon. To this day I don't know if the guy was doing some kind of reconnaissance or if he had just had a row with his wife and was having a bad helicopter day before taking it out on me, but whichever it was he certainly had an attitude problem. Maybe he was just a miserable bastard and didn't realise that despite my caution; it was always a pleasure and a break from solitude to have visitors. I followed him with the binoculars until the tiny speck disappeared over the horizon. I was on my guard more than usual for the next few days, but nothing materialised from the incident and I never saw the ship. These particular helicopters were the long arm of the navy, reaching out at high speed to attack submarines and ships (In 1982, during the Falklands war, two of them engaged the Argentinean submarine 'Santa Fe' on the surface at South Georgia. Along with another helicopter they hit the sub with AS12 anti-ship missiles and strafed it with machine gun fire forcing it to surrender. It was the first military action of the returning task force dispatched from the UK by Margret Thatcher). In 1976, I saw on the news that she had seen action off Iceland in the so called *'Cod wars'* which ironically was fought over Iceland's arbitrary extension of its territorial waters and fishing limits. Britain claimed historic rights for its fishing fleet to work there. The Icelandic coast guard would tow a wire cutting device across the British fishing boats trawl warps to cut their nets away, thus causing thousands of pounds worth of damage and loss of earnings. To counter this, the Royal Navy were called in to escort the fishing fleet. The warships would at times ram the coast guard cutters in an attempt to push them out of the way. Unfortunately, the frigates often came of worse due to the icebreaker design of the

Coastguards bows. Galatea was herself rammed by the Icelandic gunboat 'Baldur'.

Over the years there were some very special people that made sure we were ok. It almost seemed they gave themselves a duty of care. There was a small ship called the *'Ipswich Progress'* that would pass almost daily on its way to Holland. They would go out of their way to pass nearby, sound their horn and wave. The Trinity House Pilot boat the *'Proceeder'* passed several times a day, taking the North Sea pilots stores and fuel out to the Sunk Pilot cutter, some miles away stationed off the Sunk Head sands. For many years 'Proceeder' and 'Pathfinder' worked in harmony delivering pilots by small motorboats that they launched in their lee, sometimes in the most atrocious weather conditions. They braved this as ships over a certain tonnage are required by law to carry a pilot when entering the Thames. They must have been very hardy seamen because over all the years I very rarely saw the 'Pathfinder' or her replacement 'Penlee' go off station and run into Harwich for weather. I imagine it must have been quite a hard life rolling around in the worst conditions the North Sea could throw at them, 24/7, three hundred and sixty-five days a year. These days they are replaced by small fast and very powerful launches running from Harwich direct to the ships. The pilots themselves still have, in most cases, to climb a precarious rope ladder up the side of the ship in all weathers to get aboard as they have done for generations.
There were some ships that would chat to us on the marine radio on a regular basis like the *'Hoo Ness'* ships from as far away as the Shetland islands, when the conditions were right. Many of them had regular runs across the North Sea or up and down the UK delivering cargos of coal or sand ballast. There was even one ship the *'May Mitchell'* a small coaster that always seemed to be delivering ammunition and explosives to small MOD wharfs around the country.

The one particular skipper who we watched through his career we nicknamed 'Ginger' for obvious reasons. Although over the years we saw his hair and beard colour change to silver, as his ships got bigger and better.

We first came across him when he was the skipper of the 'Suffolk Ferry', a British Rail ship that made regular crossings from Harwich to the Hook of Holland. Each day he edged closer and closer on his way past and would try to throw a letter across from his bridge wing, weighted with a nut and bolt. After several weeks of trying he got one across and we found out his name 'Captain Wylde'. Resplendent in his black uniform and gold braid, he would take off his white skipper's hat and wave it to us on many an occasion.

Over the years he would throw newspapers, exploding cans of beer and even a turkey came flying through the air one Christmas. The turkey didn't quite make it, but it was frozen and not of the feathered variety unfortunately or it might have had more chance! When he moved on to command the very long ship 'Seafreight Liner II' he skilfully manoeuvred it in close enough to reach across and shake my hand from the wing of the bridge without even scratching the paint.

When Willy got married on Sealand, Ginger was in command of the huge 'St Edmund' Harwich to Hook of Holland ferry. Ginger made an excuse to delay sailing and was there to meet the bride at midday as promised with passengers on deck cheering and sirens blasting a salute. The massive ship, dwarfing the fortress with the bride having just arrived by helicopter; she stood on the helipad waving to the passengers and crew in her long white wedding dress. An aircraft flew over, chartered by a journalist, capturing the moment on film. It made for an amazing picture that I have on my wall to this day.

Uninvited Guests

It was August 1978 and I had just turned 26. My father and mother had travelled to Salzburg in Austria to meet our associate Alexander Achenbach; who had been appointed Minister of Foreign Affairs. The meeting was to include several other interested parties, with the intention of signing a multi-million pound contract to reclaim a leisure island from the North Sea. I was told later that tens of millions of Deutschmarks had been raised and lodged with a notary or lawyer in Germany to complete the scheme. He had been gone a few days, explaining as he departed, that if it all turned out the way it had been explained to him by Achenbach, it would be an amazing project. It was to be the start of a new era for us and for Sealand. Always preferring to drive when possible, they left by road in their Ford Granada taking the Dover-Calais ferry.

As usual, there was no contact from them; isolated as I was on Sealand. Days went by, which then turned into a week, when on a sunny August morning at about 11am a large pale blue helicopter arrived. Written down the side in large letters was KLM. The machine went into the hover next to Sealand. I was alone on the fortress and had been going about my normal routine of checking and fuelling the generators that gave power to the place. I heard the roar and thunder of rotor blades above the soft rumbling of the generator's engine. I ran up the stairs, into the armoury, took out the nine millimetre Walther P38 automatic pistol and dashed out on deck.

What I was confronted with was an extremely large helicopter with it's side door open and a film crew filming from above.

The winch man standing in the open doorway was indicating with clear hand gestures that they wanted to land on the helipad, this was obstructed by a strategically placed thirty-five foot mast, placed there to prevent just such an action by uninvited guests.

I waved them away with a sweeping hand gesture several times, but they wouldn't take no for an answer. The pilot brought the huge machine with its buffeting downdraft over the top of the helipad and into the hover above my head. A heavy wooden cover from one of our water tanks just below the level of the helipad lifted off with the downdraft and tumbled end over end through the air into the calm sea far below. Above me, they began to winch down a rather large man who I recognised as one of our business associates. His name was *Winfred Brings,* rotund with a red face and beard. I had met him before and he had been introduced to me as a German tax consultant.

By now I had tucked the pistol into the back of my belt under my jacket, as the cameraman continued to film from above.

Brings who was not the most athletic of people, landed next to the mast in an ungainly fashion. Disentangling himself with difficulty from the harness, he came across and shook my very wary hand. Down behind him came another man, whom I later found out was some kind of professional competition cyclist; a well built suntanned fellow called Oldenburg. I never did understand really how he fitted in.
My first feeling of unease came as Oldenburg approached me from behind and Brings seemed very reluctant to release my hand. His clammy hand shaking mine furiously and hanging on like grim death. His other hand came around and gripped my elbow as he pumped away at my hand furiously. I was starting to feel very uncomfortable about the whole situation and dragged the red-faced Brings around still attached to my right hand so that Oldenburg was now in front of me. The down draught from the rotors was massive, like a giant hand pressing down on us. The noise was of cacophonic proportions and the helideck under my feet was shaking with the vibration of it all. I looked up at the helicopter framed in the bright August sunshine, as people were still disgorging from its belly

one at a time; like fish dangling on a line being lowered to the deck. *My heart was thumping in my chest; it was one of the most threatening and uncomfortable moments of my life.*
Here I was in the middle of nowhere. No backup, no one to call on for help and no one to tell what was happening. I could feel the situation slipping every second faster and faster out of my control; like a runaway train, I couldn't figure out how to put the brakes on. Short of drawing the automatic pistol out of my belt and creating an international incident that would probably end up with buckets of blood all over my newly painted helideck. All captured on prime time television, by the German TV cameras filming from above.

I tried desperately to convince myself these people were ok, as they were business associates of my father, but it just wasn't working in my head. I gave Brings a nudge and broke his podgy grip between finger and thumb and headed swiftly for the ladder to the main deck, with him shuffling along in hot pursuit behind me.

In the entrance of the building, with the noisy helicopter still making it very hard to hear what he was saying, Brings ceremoniously handed me a telex message that he claimed my father had sent for me to read. It stated that he had concluded a successful business deal with the group and that I should let them stay. I was very much aware that it was the easiest thing in the world to fake a telex message and make it look like it had come from whomever you wanted. Also, the fact that he was not keen to release it from his podgy paw for closer scrutiny didn't help my belief in its authenticity. *Why would he not just hand it over if it were meant for me?* The hackles were rising on the back of my neck and I was growing increasingly uneasy. I hardly knew this man; I had met him just once before, although I know my father had been in his company many times.

By now we had moved further into the building to get away from the mighty noise of the helicopter so that we could hear each other talk.

While I was far from happy with the situation; I reluctantly returned the pistol to the armoury, as it certainly didn't seem the appropriate time to start a war in front of TV cameras with people I had met before and my father obviously trusted. All the while my father on the verge of a multi million pound deal that we had worked so hard over the years and suffered so many hardships to bring to fruition.

During our shouted conversation, the TV crew had descended from the thundering machine and started to enter the building. I was telling Brings to take his people back to the helicopter, go back to from wherever they came and return with my father to confirm everything was in order; at which point I would hand over control to him. I was adamant that they could not stay and should return to Holland where they said they had come from with their extremely large and loud helicopter.

Eventually he seemed to capitulate and said they would leave. He then started whining that he had been very shaken up by the helicopter flight and the trauma of being lowered down from the helicopter; he desperately needed a drink to calm his nerves.

I looked at him incredulously and said *"you don't stuff about with helicopters and winch wires having had a drink."*
It would be madness, and I wasn't going to give it to him.
But no, he insisted he really needed it!
"Give me just one drink, and I will go back to Holland and make arrangements to come back tomorrow with your father" he insisted in a begging voice.

I wasn't at all happy with that one, but if that was the only thing between him staying and getting rid of the oily bastard I grudgingly decided to oblige.

I went down the hall, pushing through the TV crew who were milling around with all their kit, climbed down the stairs to the storeroom on the first floor of the South tower and reluctantly returned to the living room with a bottle of Scotch. As I poured out the drink for the red-faced and now very agitated Brings, he side stepped out of the door and slammed it shut behind him!

Amongst much shouting and cursing, a camera tripod with the help of the film crew was jammed in the door handle. I twisted and yanked on the door handle with all my strength, but to no avail.

This moment was the start of a vast learning curve in my life; culminating in a flight over the North Sea in the dark, armed to the teeth, facing unknown dangers and with the backing of some great guys. To this day I can't sit with my back to a door or room full of people.

So there I was *stuffed*… Not just a bit stuffed but totally absolutely bloody *STUFFED!*

Locked in a steel room with two tiny portholes made of bulletproof glass about 10 inches wide on the west side and two half-inch thick steel and riveted doors on the east side that were meant to open out into the hallway.

The noise of the helicopter was still thundering above. I could see its dark shadow on the shimmering sea out of the small porthole when suddenly the large noisy shadow was gone and the sound of roaring thundering engines got quieter and quieter into the distance.

All went eerily silent.

I didn't know if any or all of them had stayed.
Was I locked in a room in the middle of the North Sea with nobody knowing I was there?
I listened and listened but could hear nothing. No movements outside of the room. You could have heard a pin drop it was so quiet. I was starting to think that for some reason they had panicked and left me there. I

wouldn't have put it past them; they were certainly not very nice people and to pardon a pun they were like fish out of water.

It was quite a daunting thought. I couldn't see any way out of the situation if they had done whatever it was they had set out to do and just buggered off. Leaving me in this dark and isolated steel tomb.

I desperately tried the door handle again but even though it turned, the door was solidly fixed in place and had no movement at all.

I don't recall being claustrophobic before, but right now a well-found sense of panic was starting to gnaw and twist at my insides. Locked in a room is one thing; but a steel room with no way out in the middle of the North Sea, compounded by the fact that no one knew I was there is the stuff of horror movies and nightmares! Maybe I would wake up soon and find it was just all a bad dream? I had to make a conscious effort to get a grip on myself.

I listened again and thought I could hear whispering, but wasn't sure. Pressing my ear to the door, I was sure it really must be whispering but still couldn't be certain. There certainly couldn't be the ten or twelve people that had been there earlier or I am sure I would have heard something. I was locked in the lounge and the two doors that it had led onto the main corridor that ran from one end of the building to the other. There were two doors because originally it had been two rooms that we had knocked into one, removing the handles from one riveted steel door, effectively sealing it up from the hallway.

I started to pull down the hardboard ceiling lining and supporting batons that were original from the war, to see if I could climb between the top of the steel wall and the steel ceiling plates. There was a gap but it was only inches wide. As I tried to put my hand through, I was to find I was not alone. My new visitors, who I was concerned might have left, started to smash at my arms with a steel bar from outside in the hall, catching my hand with one of the violent blows. I yanked it in, nursing the bruising.

Well, at least I knew they were still there now and hadn't left me to my fate, although the steel bar confirmed they weren't exactly friendly! The violence and disregard for my well-being or safety they were showing towards me right now when I was only making a token effort to escape showed the extent they were prepared to go to in their mission for control of Sealand.

Then the inaudible whispering began. They were whispering instructions to each other as they went about their work.

I could hear them feverishly dragging what sounded like heavy metal objects or something similar from outside the building. Along the hall and bashing whatever it was into place with hammers on the other side of the steel door.
I couldn't really work out what they were doing. It was very frustrating, not to mention infuriating for me.
I looked about the room and found a small mirror. When I heard them shuffle off back outside again, I pushed the small mirror through the gap between wall and ceiling and was able to see why they had been so industrious. They had built a false wall over the doors into my room. Fashioned from steel sheets and held in place with timbers braced across the hallway, these were what I had heard them bashing into place with sledgehammers. I could hear them returning to their labours, so quickly pulled the mirror back in, not risking another battering by Germanys finest.

I sat on the floor with my back to the wall, listening intently I tried to analyse exactly what was going on outside and just what I was up against. There was panic in their whispering voices. Although it didn't take me long to work out there was only the two of them. They started calling out to Hans, Fritz, Joseph and Uncle Tom Cobbly; all in high pitched almost hysterical voices.
I had to chuckle. I was in a desperate possible life and death situation with armed men who had basically kidnapped and imprisoned me. I was

totally incapacitated, being locked in a half-inch thick steel room; yet there unhinged voices told me I still had the psychological high ground.

It really didn't take long for me to surmise that there was just no way out. My next attempt at escape was to try to dismantle the hinges off the door. They had massive rivets through the steel work, but they also had inch steel bolts in the hinge. I worked away with no tools apart from my mother's metal nail file, a large pair of scissors and a clasp knife I had in my pocket. To my surprise I managed to remove the locking split pin from one and clean up the rusty wartime threads on the bolt enough to unscrew the nut and remove one of them. But the others proved impossible.

I sat down in an armchair, took a deep breath and considered my desperate and frustratingly hopeless situation. I have always been a fighter but this situation was totally out of my control, with no possibility of influencing it myself at all. On the plus side, my efforts had kept me busy and did nothing to reduce the hysterical noises from my seemingly demented captors. This cheered me up a little!

So I busied myself. I manufactured a Molotov cocktail with the whisky by stuffing a piece of rag in the bottle and placed it carefully on the table with some matches in case an opportunity came along for its use. As night fell I got some florist wire that I found in a drawer and used it to fuse the main lighting circuit for the platform, leaving my new friends and myself in the dark. I then switched on the TV that gave me enough light to keep beavering away at my various projects.

Without warning, there was an almighty *crash* as one of them was pounding on the outside of the bulletproof porthole with a sledgehammer. After several blows, it caved in, showering me with piles of thick laminated glass and allowing in the cool night air.

A hysterical German voice shouted out *"Mizter Bates srow out ze riffle, srow out zer riffle now or vee will be forced to shoot you"*
What a polite fellow? I thought *but what bloody rifle you soppy bastard.*

Ah well, the fact they thought I was armed did seem to keep them on the lavatory rather a lot, so I didn't bother to answer.

I hunkered down in the corner near the porthole, determined to stab any pistol bearing hand that might come through it with my clasp knife.

It was now quite late, they had managed to find the circuit supplying the TV and ripped out the wires; plunging the room into deep darkness. I tried using some of the whisky with a wick hanging over the side of an open tin to improvise a lamp but the flame produced by the spirit was too blue and it kept petering out.

I was cold, had nothing to drink or eat all day and was getting tired so decided to get some sleep. I scanned the dark room for something to keep me warm and very patriotically took down a huge Sealand flag that covered a whole wall of the room. How profound I thought.

There was an old fashioned set of headphones on a long lead lying on the stereo, I attached them to the metal door handle and rolled myself up in the flag on the floor amongst the broken glass. I attached the other end of the wire to my wrist.

As I snatched fitful moments of sleep, every movement of my hand made the headphones clatter on the steel door and produced more hysterical noises and rodent-like scampering about from outside.

The morning brought a fine calm day and the heat from the sun started to warm the building. Although I was on the shaded side of the fortress, the small amount of transmitted heat was very welcome.

I was pleased with my efforts to keep my new friends on edge, but I had run out of constructive things to do. It was time to employ a new tactic!

I asked to use the toilet! No answer!
I asked for water! No answer!
I asked for food.... just hoarse hysterical whisperings.

Ha ha! While desperate to reverse the situation and feeling somewhat misguidedly guilty for letting my parents down, I was absolutely delighted with the effect I was having on my vicious captors.

The morning passed uneventfully and as the sun started to creep around the building Brings appeared very gingerly outside of the port hole, the first I had seen of him for a day and a half. He started to talk to me and explained that his friend and employer, Alexander Achenbach had talked him into attacking Sealand and that he really didn't want to be there.

He sat down on the rail some 6 foot away from me, with his red face and silly sailors hat, munching on a piece of raw bacon wrapped in bread. As I engaged him in conversation, I looked around me for a piece of wood to launch through the porthole at him and send the fat bastard tumbling over the side. It then occurred to me that if I did manage to clear Sealand of these scumbags, it wouldn't help if I were still left locked in a room that could become my coffin miles out in the North Sea. No one knowing about the drama that was unfolding just off the UK coast.

He chatted away mostly about his difficult life and how people had cheated on him, how his wife had left him and how Achenbach had something on him that could put him in jail for many years. He was definitely feeling very, very sorry for himself and ended the conversation with *"Young man, never trust anybody!"*

Good advice from a terrorist!

I recalled Brings, Achenbach and a bespectacled guy with thinning hair called Tebroke, visiting by helicopter with some journalists a few weeks before. It was the first and only time that Achenbach ever visited Sealand.

At one point, I opened the lounge door to find the lone Brings kneeling down, rapping the carpeted steel floor with his knuckles. It became clear to me now that he was making sure there would be no way out of the room if I were to be locked in there. They had obviously been planning this for some time.

I had been a hostage in this steel room for some 30 hours with no food or water. A leaking biscuit tin I had found became my badly improvised toilet. I knew my only chance of escape would be to talk my way out.

Now that me and my new pal Brings were 'mates' and I had allowed him to share his worldly advice with me, it didn't prove too difficult.

The one stipulation that they made was that I put my hands through the porthole while they tied them up. Brings with all his twenty odd stone of lard held onto the rope on the outside. While his pal Oldenburg came in and searched me, and the room for weapons.

Unable to find 'ze riffle' that they were so worried about, but satisfied with the results of the search, Brings stopped swinging on the rope and we all trooped outside.
With my hands firmly tied together. I scanned the familiar surroundings for something to use as a weapon. I looked over towards the old 3.7 anti-aircraft gun for the metal bar that we use as a lever on the winch. It was gone!
I looked for the big fire axe that we kept under the winch to cut the wire in an emergency but that had also disappeared.
All that was visible was a huge red crane hook that must have weighed over 100lbs. It would have been far too heavy and unwieldy for bashing Germans with when your hands are tied!
They had done a meticulous job of clearing up and hiding anything that could possibly be used as a weapon.

Typically Germanic, they were very polite and referred to me as Mizter Bates the entire time. I had visions of being very politely asked to step in front of a firing squad please Mizter Bates!

After being outside for some 20 odd minutes, I asked them to untie my hands. Their reaction to this was to scamper to one side of the deck and start a good old whispering session.
After a while it was clear that this wasn't going to happen, so I told them if they didn't untie me I would do it myself. I started to pick at the tight-knotted ropes with my teeth, the whispering became more frantic and agitated, the hysteria was coming back into their voices and I knew what was about to unfold next.
I turned away from them so that I could just see them from the corner of my eye and within seconds they were charging across the deck at me.
I turned to deliver a perfectly timed kick to my new pals bollocks and grabbing the lapel of his slimy synthetic jacket I head butted him with a very satisfying thud on the bridge of his nose. As blood ran down his face, it brought an abrupt end to what had been our blossoming friendship.
In any case, it was his advice not to trust anyone, and if nothing else, I always like to listen to other people's views on life!

I was clinging onto his coat like a man possessed. I knew with my hands tied together I would be lucky to get another grip if I let go. A split second later I had his friend on my back, trying as hard as he could to strangle me, crashing to the riveted steel deck under the weight of him and the not so small Brings. Heavy boots were kicking at me, thudding into my rib cage and back; the wind knocked out of me I tried to roll away and then it stopped.

The ropes were cutting into my wrists, and I was fighting for breath from the exertions I had just been through, as they set about tying my feet together, my knees together and even my elbows. Not happy with that they then tied my hands to my knees.

They dragged and carried me to the side, lifted me onto the rail whilst trussed up like a Christmas turkey some sixty foot above the calm North Sea.

"Let's chuck this bastard over the side" one said to the other.

I have been asked many times if, as they lifted me up to the rail, my life flashed before my eyes. I am sorry to report that all I felt was blind rage and I just wanted to kill the bastards. So much for the bloody Stockholm syndrome, I mean yes I did want to fuck them, but not in the biblical sense! After the little confab in German it was decided that it would be more prudent to keep me alive. But I could tell they weren't very happy and I definitely wasn't going to be on their Christmas card list ever again.

They roughly dragged and carried me down the length of the hall into the radio room and threw me on the bed in the corner. It was now my turn to lose it slightly and I cracked up with subdued laughter. Meanwhile, Oldenburg nursed a bad arm and Brings was examining his glowing bloody somewhat bent nose.

As blood trickled out of his trouser leg, the ever-polite Brings questioned *"Mizter Bates why do you laugh?"*

"Just, you have me prisoner and have been jumping all over me with my hands bound. Yet you guys look ready for an ambulance and I feel fine"
"Mizter Bates I will never understand you" Brings replied in a flat tone.
"No, I don't suppose you ever will."

As the blood attempted to flow back to my hands, I was overcome with agonies. My wrists swollen and tied were giving excruciating pain; my hands felt ready to fall off. *It hurt like hell!* My elbows and knees had been grazed, bruised and banged about in the fracas adding to the pain.

They left me in the room for a few minutes while they went out into the hall for another intense whispering session.
Returning, they came smartly across the room grabbing me roughly and

dragged me off the bed onto the hard floor. I had taken the concealed clasp knife out of my pocket and had been awkwardly sawing away at the ropes binding my wrists. The heavy knife tumbled out of my lap onto the floor with a dull thud. Its discovery bringing with it exasperated sighs from my captors and another kick in the ribs amid much cursing. Dragging me none too gently out of the room, down the hall and back into the living room with much muttering and swearing. They then searched the living room scrupulously yet again as I watched.

"Where is zer riffle Mizter Bates?" demanded the heavy breathing Brings. *Here we go again* I thought. *"What bloody rifle you soppy bastard?"*

He then produced from his pocket a 20-gauge shotgun shell that formed part of my cartridge collection. I had never owned a 20-gauge shotgun in my life.

"Ah, that rifle. I couldn't tell you, I haven't seen it for ages" I replied in a sarcastic voice.

As they departed I asked them to untie the ropes as they were stopping the blood flow to my hands. It was still extremely painful and I feared I might lose the use of them for good if the pain continued and the blood flow was cut off. Wasn't that what they did to sheep's tails? Tie a cord around them until they fell off on their own?

They just ignored me, left the room and locked the door.

Bunch of bastards! It was now after dark, chilly and pitch black. My hands were screaming out in agony and to cap it all I was busting for a pee. I hopped over to the far corner of the room like Skippy the bloody bush kangaroo. Managed to open my flies and do the deed in the corner without soaking myself, which let's face it would have capped an all round pretty crappy day.

To my utter amazement in the dark hours that followed, amongst tears of pain and frustration, I managed to untie all of the knots with my teeth and feverishly massaged some life back into my aching wrists. Thank God for my years spent around fishing boats and experience of working loose seemingly impossible knots. I suppose I shouldn't have been but I was surprised that they didn't come back to untie me or at least check on me to see if I was ok.

I battled in my mind to maintain a positive attitude. In the classic lament of the Roman soldier: *Nil illigitimi carborundum (Don't let the bastards grind you down).*

In the meantime, on his way back from Salzburg, my father stopped off to stay with a friend 'Guy Hawtin' who was a senior journalist with the Financial Times in Germany. Hawtin warned my father that there had been a coup on Sealand.

It later turned out he also phoned the British Consulate General in Frankfurt and offered his services as an undercover informant for the British security services. Giving them what information he had about my father, his associates, plans and aspirations.

What is that adage? Never trust a journalist? How many times have I been told that? by (of all people) my parents.

All the information he gave them was passed on immediately to London.

The cold night came and went as I dozed a few minutes at a time on the hard floor. At about six thirty in the morning I could hear the sounds of a powerful engine nearby. I craned my head out of the shattered porthole and could just make out the blue painted bow of a trawler. Suddenly it appeared from around the corner of the building, the '*Leendert*', a rather fine steel Dutch beam trawler registered in Scheveningen.

Brings, and Oldenburg were running about the deck trying to get organized to lift the re-enforcements up onto the fortress. They swung the lifting derrick out excitedly and started to lower the bosons chair, hanging from the hook, down to the trawler as it motored into position sixty feet below. The electric winch hummed as the wire paid out from the drum. As I watched, I was not surprised to see the wire lift off the barrel, start to birds nest and knot. Oldenburg was now staring over the side at the trawler excitedly as he pressed the down button, oblivious as to what was happening behind him. It always was a very temperamental system and took a lot of practice to get it right; losing concentration for a moment always ended in disaster. Clearly they hadn't practiced. They struggled to get the wire back onto the barrel, but I knew it was a lost cause. Game over! I stuck my head out off the porthole and offered to help but was ignored.

After about an hour, they gave up on the winch idea and reverted to trying to launch the rope ladder over the side. I had gleeful visions of this also ending in catastrophe if they forgot to shackle it on first.

After a short time, some new faces started to arrive on Sealand. The first one was a German lawyer named Gernot Putz. Slim build with dark curly hair and glasses, Putz was a Sealand citizen. He had a small revolver in his hand and held it up to the window in a threatening gesture.
"I see you have a little gun" I said taking the piss out of him.
"Yes and I shall not hesitate to use it if I have to" he replied in a very serious and threatening voice.
"No, I don't suppose you would you little shit".
Funny, I thought, this fortress had been built at vast expense by the admiralty to defend the UK from the German threat during the Second World War and nearly forty years down the road armed Germans are stomping around on it like they had just invaded Poland!

The door swung open and in came three new faces. These were more business like hard cases. Few words were spoken as I was lead outside into the sunshine. The bright sun hurt my eyes, I was unwashed and three days unshaven.

A warm breeze gently blew across the sea from the distant shore. That familiar smell that could almost make your mouth water and had many times in the past made me feel home sick, bringing back childhood memories of sunny days in the country. I took a deep breath of air, taking a moment to savour the smell of freshly harvested fields.

Standing and sitting around the place were at least seven people. One of the new faces, a big man in a blue jacket, started to row heatedly with Brings about the fact that he had told them I was securely tied up and no threat, yet when they opened the door I was untied.

That done, the new guy in command 'Helmut Eck' asked if I wanted to stay, go to England or go to Holland with the trawler.
"I will stay here" I said.
Brings spluttered *"If he stays here you must lock him in ze room he is far too dangerous to allow out!"*

Well, I didn't fancy my dad coming back from Austria and getting himself killed trying to rescue me so I reluctantly said I would go to England. This brought on more heated discussion. The skipper said he would not enter UK territorial waters, as he did not want to be arrested for kidnap or piracy by the British. So it was decided to sail to Holland. The skipper, Hans Snoek, was still not happy so Gernot Putz, the very helpful lawyer with the 'small pistol', said he would write a document stating I went of my own free will. He knocked up the worthless scribbling on a piece of paper. Taking the pen Putz thrust toward me, I signed: 'M. Mouse' and we were in business.

Brings started to climb awkwardly down the rope ladder and got stuck half way. As I have mentioned before, if you have never climbed a rope ladder you will not know that it is an absolute work of art.
"Would you like me to climb down and give you a hand?" I offered condescendingly.
Once again, the ungrateful bastard declined my heartfelt offer of help. Eventually, they managed to coax him down and off the ladder, onto the aft deck of the trawler.

Eck asked me if I had all my possessions. I asked him for the two hundred pounds we kept in a drawer in the radio room. He went to look for it, but it was gone. He questioned Brings who confessed to taking it along with the P38 pistol in a bag he had sent down to the boat. The money was returned to me, and the pistol sent back up to the fort.

While Brings had been desperately hanging on the ladder, the crewman on the trawler had been sitting in the sun peeling potatoes with a long, curved and wicked looking gutting knife of the sort used by fishermen. I suppose when he jumped up to rescue the opulent Brings from the ladder it must have gone over the side.

I was next down the ladder and on the deck.
"Where is the knife?" enquired the mate.
"I don't bloody know!" I replied.
"Mizter Bates hand over ze knife!" continued Brings, a hint of hysteria creeping back into his voice. There goes good old Brings being too polite again.
"Rifles. Knives. What is it with you Brings?" I snapped.

So there we all were on a totally unexpected and unplanned mystery tour to Holland! The happy crew consisted of me, Brings, Oldenburg, the ships mate, the skipper Hans Snoeck and one other guy Hans Lavoo.
Hans Lavoo was a young Dutchman with a large mop of very curly blond hair, who said his girlfriend was a journalist and that he had come to cover the story for her, as she couldn't make it. He turned out to be a lot more involved than he claimed to be.

I have spent a lot of years around fishermen and immediately struck up a good rapport with the skipper Hans, a tall balding fellow in his forties. Hans it seemed was not entirely happy with the situation he found himself in. He was also, he said, unaware that the people he had transported were carrying guns. We discussed his trawler and methods of fishing. He proudly showed me his new electronics and gave me a tour of the ship including the engine room. He was genuinely a nice fellow and no different to any other fishermen I have encountered in different parts of the world.

The weather was fine, and we sailed through the afternoon and late into the night, docking at Scheveningen Harbour, Holland about midnight.

I was somewhat surprised there were no Customs or Immigration to meet us when we put the ropes ashore in the large fish dock amongst all the other trawlers of varying size. I jumped ashore as soon as the boat touched the quay; glad to be free from my captors in a jurisdiction with police and courts to look after me. I was without a passport, not knowing what to expect next but happy to be back on dry land.
Looking along the deserted quay I could see the diminutive figure of yet another of the co-conspirators, Adrian Oomen climbing out of a car. Easily recognisable from a previous encounter by his slicked over thinning hair and Hitler moustache. I had been introduced to him as a Dutch international lawyer. Talking to Brings, he reached deep into his pocket and produced a bundle of cash. Counting out the notes under the dull glow of the street lamps, he paid the skipper for his dark work.

That done he slunk away back into the darkness without approaching me. I wasn't surprised. Gutless little shit I thought. He would never knowingly put himself into any danger. The next time I was to see him was at the International Court of The Hague, where to this day war crimes and evil acts of genocide are prosecuted.

The skipper took me back to his home and helped me book a flight back to the UK. I slept on his sofa and he dropped me to the airport the following morning. After much arguing with the immigration authorities in Holland and the UK about my lack of passport. I was allowed on the plane in Holland and off the British Air Ferries plane at Southend airport in the UK. As I recall, I used my driver's licence for identification and insisted rightly at the time that a passport was not necessary if you can prove your identity. I don't suppose that would work so well these days.

I didn't even have a key on me to get into the family home in Southend, so I made my way to my Grandmother's house to have a bath, a shave and humanize myself again.

I didn't tell my Grandmother too much of what had happened as I didn't want to upset the old lady. I still had not spoken to my parents as they were in the car somewhere in Europe and unreachable.
I was in a bit of a dilemma. *What do I do now? I began scheming.*
I telephoned a fisherman friend in West Mersea. I asked him if I was to build a steel box with a drop down hinged ramp at the top of his mast, would he take me back out to Sealand and crash it onto the platform as we stormed out the front? He was not keen and the more I thought about the idea, it was absurdly dangerous even on a flat calm day which can be few and far between in the North Sea. So I shelved that one.

My parents arrived back later in the day and they were very upset. My mother asked me in tears how I could have thrown away their life's work and my father very aggressively asked me what I had done since arriving back in the UK to resolve the situation.
I have to say I felt like shit and believed I had let them down very badly.

I guess their reaction was the shock and trauma of coming home to such a situation. They didn't even know the circumstances at this stage.

My father was a wonderful man and I loved him to death but he came from a Victorian era, the sole survivor of a family of 5 children. He was brought up to believe you never make excuses and certainly don't say sorry or apologise. To his generation, one Englishman was worth ten others, *there is no such word as can't* and *the graveyard is full of good intentions*. In the winter his father would run a bath in the evening and break the ice with his foot in the morning before throwing him in.

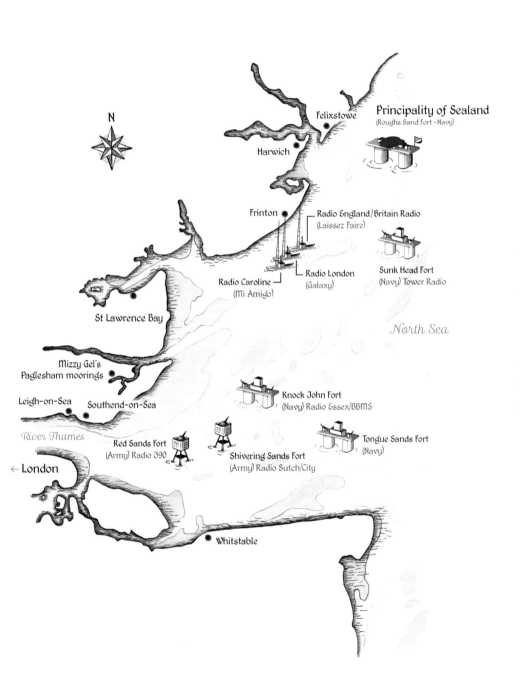

N

Principality of Sealand
(Roughs Sand Fort - Navy)

Felixstowe

Harwich

Frinton

Radio England/Britain Radio
(Laissez Faire)

Sunk Head Fort
(Navy) Tower Radio

Radio London
(Galaxy)

Radio Caroline
(Mi Amigo)

St Lawrence Bay

North Sea

Mizzy Gel's
Paglesham moorings

Knock John Fort
(Navy) Radio Essex/BBMS

Leigh-on-Sea   Southend-on-Sea

River Thames

Tongue Sands Fort
(Navy)

Red Sands Fort
(Army) Radio 390

Shivering Sands Fort
(Army) Radio Sutch/City

← London

Whitstable

Above: Sealand (Roughs Tower) being sunk in place 1942
Below: Home from boarding school. Me and Dad

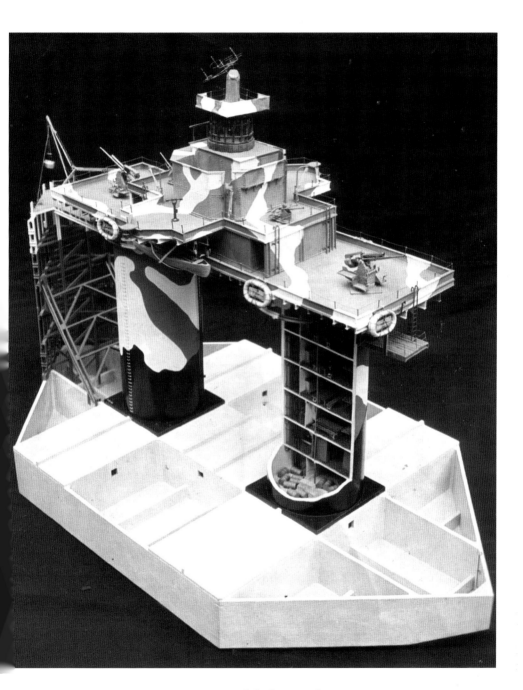

Cut away model of a Navy fort

1

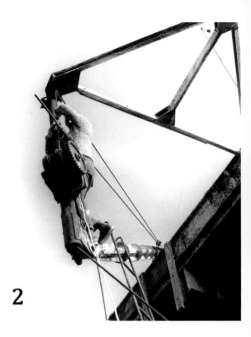

2

3

1. Dad 60ft up climbing onto the Knock John
2. Not going to be stopped...
3. And a bit higher...
4. Not far now...
5. Dad gets to the top!

5

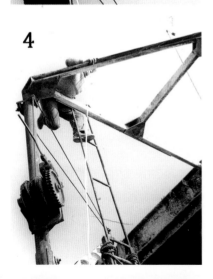

4

Above: Radio Essex DJs   Below Right: Mum and Roger Scott
Below Left: Mum handing out the Radio Essex fan mail

Mum and Dad Radio Essex (Knock John fort)
1965 on Mo Deals boat 'Kestral'

Above: Radio Essex (Knock John); Penny, Mum and me, Christmas 1965
Below: Mum, Me, Bellasco and Dad, Sealand 1967

That's how you climb a rope ladder!

Above: HMS Bembridge
Below: Independence day. Michael, Roy, Joan, Penny, Dave Ford, Jim
Emmons, Dave Belasco, Marjorie Belasco raising the flag for the first time

Above: Sun Newspaper Cartoon
Below: Penny and Dad loading stores onto tug 'Sauria' at Felixstowe dock

Above: THV Vestal
Below: Dad, Mum, Penny, Fruitcake & I

Above: HMS Dittisham
Below: Lunch!

Above: Me & British Rails Suffolk Ferry
Below: The old Mizzy Gel & Walter standing on the bosuns chair

Above: Roland and Walter, 1968
Below: Generator Room

Dad with Mum in the dreaded 'Crate'

Above: Who says we dont wear crowns?!
Mother and me. Christmas 1969 (note the shoulder holster)
Below: HMS Egeria

Above: Me and Dad with Tiger 1972
Below: Mum and Tiger 1972

Above: Mum modelling in the '70s
Below: Our friendly USAF Phantom jet fighter

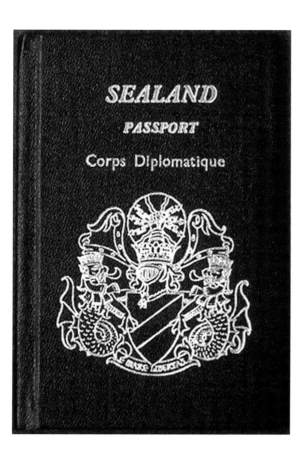

Above Left: Sealand Passport
Above Right: $25 Sealand Dollar Coin
Right: First Edition Stamps
Below: 1977 Edition Stamps

Nº 00240

We did our own health and safety! Me & Dad

Above: *Right to left:* Tebroke, Oomens, Achenbach on his first and only visit
Below left: Winfred Brings clowning about while I'm locked up August '78
Below right: German lawyer Putz with Mum and Dad

Left: Barry Harcus and
Dutch trawler 'Leendert'
which took me to Holland

Middle: The Sun Newspaper:
Do you have any prisoners?
Evert Boss, Dad, Willy,
me & Helmut Eck

Below: Me, Putz, Barry and Willy waiting
for the German ambassadors helicopter

Above: 1978 Me ready for anything
Below: Putz enjoying a last cup of tea before being freed

Above: The assault team. Me, Dad, Captain John Crewdson, Willy & Barry
Below: Mum and Dad in Tiger

Above: Willy and Karen's Wedding Day
Below: Arrival of Dad and Karen the bride

Above: Ginger offering a spectacular sail past for the wedding
Below: Robbie Dawson and Bahadur guarding the wedding

Above: Dad and Bahadur
Below: In my twentys

Above: Wasp helicopter from HMS Galatea,
close enough to see the whites of the pilot's eyes!
Below: Principality of Sealand's Coat of Arms

Above: Havenco founders; Jo & Sean Hastings, Sameer,
Avi, Roy, Ryan Lackey (Uncle Fester) and me
Below: Wired Magazine July 2000 - "Sealand Waves The Rules"

Above: Some of the Havenco Servers
Below: Sealand

Sealand Fire 2006

photographs courtesy of 'The Register'

Above left: James and Liam deciding who is going
to climb up after the Sealand fire, 25th June 2006
Above right: James climbing the hook ladder after the Sealand fire
Below left: My heart was in my mouth as I watched James
Below right: Triumphant James phones his grandfather in Spain

Above: James and Liam inspect the charred remains
of Havenco's generator shed after the fire
Below: Record breaking mountaineer Kenton Cool
raising the Sealand flag at the summit of Mount Everest

Above: James, Ben Fogle (becoming a Lord of Sealand) and Charlotte
Below Left: Mike Barrington, Ben Fogle and James
Below Right: Liam earning an International cap for our football team

At the time, we still had the small fast RIB (rigid inflatable boat) with a 55-horse power engine on the back giving it a speed of some thirty plus knots. It was only 4 metres long so didn't have a great deal of space to operate from. We came up with the idea of making a scaling ladder out of lightweight plastic piping and climbing up in the dark. I set out to look at and price up materials.

That evening a German guy called Kamera telephoned to say that he had been involved with Achenbach's group but didn't like the way it was going. He thought we should know that they intended to re-enforce their position on Sealand with ten Belgian ex-paratroopers armed with Uzi submachine guns in the following couple of days. These mercenaries would be flying out by helicopter.

I was given the job of speaking to him. I remembered Kamera from many years before, when he came to my father with wild ideas that never came to fruition. However, I was grateful for the information.

Kamera explained in his best English that Achenbach's group had only met me, and my parents in London or Germany. My dad had been dressed in a Saville Row suit and expensive shoes. However Kamera had seen the other side of my family and recognized our resolve and determination with Sealand. He had also stayed on Sealand for a short while with Willy and myself and realised we were not the kind of people to just walk away from a situation like this.

I told him that the weather was too bad for us to get near Sealand. Worst scenario if we could not get it back, I would swim some explosives in under cover of darkness and blow the bloody thing up.
He wished me good luck and put down the phone.

Crikey, now what are we going to do?
Well, there is only one way we are going to get anywhere near it in this weather, and that is with a helicopter. *Who's going to ring John up?*

My father called our pal John Crewdson who at the time owned several helicopters at Southend airport. To our delight, he was as offended as we were about what had happened and pledged his unconditional support.

So how are we going to do it?
Well, we could involve the press. Get the BBC and a few national papers out and circle the place with four or five helicopters. Then go in with one in the hope that this would faze the enemy.

Or we just go in, bang crash at dawn and use the element of surprise.

Well, the press idea had merit, but we decided that once we involved the press, word would leak out and the British Government would stop us. Besides, the old fashioned ways are always the best! At dawn, peoples alertness are always at the lowest ebb; they will be half asleep and apart from the horrendous noise that helicopters make, we would have the element of surprise on the, hopefully, sleeping men.

We decided that we would go in at dawn the next day.

I had explained my problem to a few of the local 'hard cases' hoping to enlist their help, but they all decided it was too rich for them. Strange but I have found in my life that at moments of adversity it is the most unlikely people that come out of the woodwork and are prepared to stand shoulder to shoulder with you, *do or die.*

The first person we tried to contact was Willy, a really good friend who was more like family and had spent many of his formative years on Sealand with me as a young man.

We had lost touch with him for a year or so and tried to track him down.

Eventually, we were told he was at the hospital having blood tests. He had been suffering from lethargy and had no energy for anything. He was concerned he was suffering from some diabolical illness and had eventually decided to go to the doctor, who then sent him to the hospital to see a specialist.

We sent my mother to the hospital to see if she could find him. By luck, she located him straight away. He dumped the tests and came straight back with her to help. Obviously he must have just been short of an adrenaline buzz because the lethargy thing just disappeared!

Barry Harcus and Robbie Dawson, good friends who had worked for us over the years and they too were keen to help. The whole thing revolved around the fact that somebody had taken over our home and used violence against me. There was no question of money; it was sheer disgust at what had happened. Later, we could relate very well with the farmers and even the British governments thinking in the Falklands when the Argies marched in and took away their properties nationality and identity by force.

We had the people we now needed a plan.

"There is a sixty odd foot mast at each end of Sealand and a shorter 35ft one in the middle on the helipad. So we are going to have to take the doors off the helicopter and slide down ropes. Does this present a problem John?"
"No, I can put the machine into the hover between the two sixty foot masts. But you can only use one rope each side of the helicopter and try to slide down in unison so that when the weight comes of the machine doesn't become to unbalanced and slew into a mast."

Ok, do we abseil or slide down the ropes?
I decided I didn't want to be attached to a helicopter by a harness that would need unclipping; with the likelihood the bad guys might be firing bullets at the machine or me. *"Let's slide"* I decided.

Ok, do we use gloves or a piece of rag or something to stop the rope burns?
Memories of the accident years ago flooded back of the guy wrapping a
rope around his hand and the ensuing injuries when the flesh was burnt
off his fingers to the bone. Not a pleasant sight, so I was acutely aware of
the dangers involved.
We went to the local ships chandlers, bought a couple of lengths of rope
and decided we better have a practice. We owned a factory in Southend
that was originally a stable. Outside of it there was a gibbet sticking out
where years ago they would pull up hay and haul it in through an upstairs
door. It was nothing like what we would be doing the next day, but could
at least get a feel for it.

Leather gloves didn't work they got too hot and other types we tried were
no good So it came down to using cotton rags wrapped around the hands.
(Not ideal over the North Sea, but not being the military and without their
budget, it was the best we could do!)

We had never seen a film or even never heard of anyone sliding down a
rope out of a helicopter. The term fast roping hadn't been invented. As far
as we knew, we were breaking new ground.

Now came the problem of weapons. My dear maternal grandmother lived
in a cottage in the country. My father, a man of considerable forethought,
had disassembled two automatic pistols that he had from the war and
stored them in my grandmother's loft along with some ammunition. My
father's thinking was that come the revolution, someone was going to
have to save the country. Not realising in this forethought that the country
that needed saving wouldn't be mother England, but Sealand.
The dear old lady never knew they were there.
My mother went off in the car to retrieve them, but we had to go back and
get some missing parts she couldn't find.

It was now evening time and Willy disappeared off to collect some rifled
slugs and large grape shotgun cartridges he just happened to have at

home under his bed. Rifled slugs or 'Sabots' are a solid chunk of lead fired from a shotgun. A shotgun has a smooth bore, unlike a rifle that has rifling or a thread in the barrel to make the bullet spin to give it greater accuracy and penetration, so some very clever ammunition maker came on the idea to put the thread on the bullet instead. The American police use them to smash the engine blocks on fleeing cars and they're also used to stop large prey such as a bear. The large grape is self-explanatory and consists of several large lead balls, again used to stop large animals or people. Perfect for this mission!

I also popped to see my girlfriend Linda. I told her I was going away for a few days and to keep an eye on the newspapers. I didn't explain where I was going, although she knew there was a problem.

I arrived back at my parent's house where Willy had also returned. I went to the cupboard, took out my best shotgun and set about cutting the barrels and butt off with a hacksaw until it was no more than eighteen inches long. I tied a piece of parachute cord through the trigger guard so that it hung snugly around my neck but was long enough to use. Robbie and Barry turned up later and after checking all our gear we decided to get a little sleep. We all crashed on the floor in my parent's front room.

Robbie woke me up in the early hours and unsurprisingly said he wasn't able to sleep. My father came in and we quickly prepared to leave for the airfield.

We all piled into my father's Ford Granada and headed for the airport. We took the back roads hoping we wouldn't get stopped by the police for some silly reason and bring our whole plan to a crashing undignified demise.

They Came From The Sky

It is 3am on a chilly summer's night and a vehicle pulls up in the shadows of the Zero6 nightclub on the fringes of Southend airport, about 35 miles from London. Five ghostly figures dressed in an assortment of camouflage fatigues, armed with semi-automatic weapons emerge in the dark and make for the barbed wire perimeter fence of the airfield.

In the shadow of a nearby hangar can be seen the familiar shape of an Alouette helicopter.
"Where's the bloody pilot?" I quietly whisper as we near the still and silent machine.

The words have hardly left my lips when John appears from the dark shadows of the hanger.
"Come on come on get the doors off!" he commands in an urgent voice.

We lift the aluminium and Perspex doors off the hinges and lay them against the hangar wall. *"Where do you want them John?"*

"Just stuff em inside the hangar door, so they don't go into the rotors when we take off and let's get the bloody hell out of here!"

In the dark, we hastily tie ropes onto the metal seat frames. Aware that our lives depend on the knots that we are tying by feel alone, that in less than an hour we would be sliding down these ropes over 100 foot above the North Sea, facing armed terrorists and on a mission that we had not had time to practice. In those days rappelling from a helicopter was unheard of. The pilot reiterated his concern that if we didn't hit the ground simultaneously on either side of the small helicopter, it would lurch to one side and he would lose control with catastrophic results.

We climb into the machine as John snapped on his safety harness and hit a few switches above his head. The rotors begin to crank round, faster and faster.

The helicopter turbine roars and whistles as it fires into life. More switches are snapped down. With the bright strobe flashing, and reflecting an eerie light off the nearby hangars, the machine rattles and vibrates as the old single engine Alouette came up to power ready for take-off.

The smell of hot TVO aviation fuel fills our nostrils. We follow his example and snapped together the various buckles to hold us safely in our seats for the 20-minute flight over the dark and raging North Sea to our final and probably violent destination.

We look at each other wide-eyed with excitement, the adrenaline coursing through our veins like a warm drug. Checking the loaded sawn-off shotgun on its lanyard is secure under my camouflage jacket, I ensure the breach is slightly cracked open for safety and then pull it into my chest to ensure it doesn't impair my movements on the coming flight.

The headphones crackled into life, *"Everybody comfortable?"* said John looking over his shoulder in his best British Airways voice.
Four heads nodded in the gloom.
"Here we go then," *"Southend Tower, Southend Tower, this is helicopter GOLF ALFA WHISKEY ALFA PAPA, request permission to take off. Destination Sealand with a camera crew to take dawn shots."*

"Say again GOLF ALFA WHISKEY ALFA PAPA?" probed the control tower.

"Dawn shots Southend tower, we are taking dawn shots of Sealand!"

"GOLF ALFA WHISKEY ALFA PAPA permission granted, wind 25 knots from the Southwest, cleared for take-off, have a good flight" came the response.

"Thank you Southend, good watch."

As the pilots practiced hands nursed the controls of an old friend and coaxed the machine high into the air, four silent figures breathed a heavy sigh of relief.

We were off the ground without suffering the ignominious end of being dragged away in handcuffs by some unsympathetic British 'Bobby' before our mission had even begun. I'm not exactly sure how we would have explained to the courts what we were doing skulking around Southend airport at such an ungodly hour, armed to the teeth. On the whole, British Bobbys tend to lack a sense of humour and understanding about such matters. I can't help but think if we had been stopped by one we would have had to bundle the poor fellow up and take him with us then sort the consequences out later.

Twenty long minutes later, in a very fresh South-westerly breeze, we find ourselves rapidly approaching Sealand from the North East having flown along the UK coast past Harwich, Felixstowe and then Bawdsey. Turning out to sea and into the wind, lining up for our approach. We had decided we would fly into the wind to keep the noise down. The decision had been made before we set off that the only one to communicate with the pilot should be my father who sat in the front next to him.

We were concerned that our old friend John Crewdson, who had flown spectacularly in a host of James Bond films, might have a problem with this particular mission.

Our little team consisted of me, my father, Willy, Barry Harcus and Robbie Dawson (Robbie, a great lad, was left at the airport in tears of anger and frustration when the pilot said there was not enough room for him).

With 3 miles to go, John chatting through the headset asked my father if we were armed. We had agreed that we would tell him that we were armed with pickaxe handles but not firearms.

I could hear over the headset John's amazement that we were not. *"Well, I fucking am!"* he declared, pulling back his jacket revealing a short barrelled Smith and Wesson 357 magnum in a shoulder holster nestling snugly under his armpit! Suddenly I didn't feel so bad about the sawn-off shotgun hanging around my neck on a piece of string under my coat, the wicked looking serrated diver's knife on my leg or the various automatic pistols and knives carried by my friends.

With that, John pushed the stick forwards and the helicopter swooped down towards the wild grey swirling sea with wave crests curling and foaming in every direction. So here we were as dawn was breaking, thundering across the North Sea not more than a metre above the angry waves, in a great clattering of rotor blades with Sealand drawing ever nearer. To the east, the tip of the sun is just starting to edge slowly over the horizon.

With the helicopter tilted forwards at a jaunty angle so that the rotors gave the pilot maximum speed across the sea, I unbuckle my safety harness, grab hold of the back of John's seat in front of me and carefully clamber out the door and down onto the slippery aluminium skids a couple of feet below. My foot slips sideways on the damp downward angled metal sending a shock wave of adrenalin coursing through my system! *Christ I had nearly fallen before we even got there!*
Clutching a coil of rope in one hand, John's words before take off resonate through my mind. *"Whatever you do don't drop the coil of rope until we are in the hover or it will foul the tail rotor, and we will crash."*

Now outside of the helicopter with the wind tearing at my clothing, trying to rip my grasp free and hurl me unceremoniously in the sea below; I have a moment of contemplation and mumble under my breath *"What the*

*fuck are you doing here Bates? Dangling out of a helicopter in a gale of wind
without even a life jacket on! Get this wrong and you have had it!"* followed
by *"Don't even think about it Bates! Head down and get in amongst the
bastards! Who the fuck do they really think they are?"*
These guys had lied to me, cheated me, hurt me, tied me up, imprisoned
me and worst of all made me feel I had let my family down to an
unimaginable extent.
They were now about to see another side of me!

My father once told me that as a young Major in the infantry, they made
night attacks on enemy positions with bayonets fixed. You could always
tell which of the men had seen the enemy and was near contact. They
would start mumbling *"Bastards, bastards, bastards"* again and again in a
hoarse whisper. I guess that was their way of psyching themselves up for
action. It was working for me; I was pumped up with adrenaline to
bursting point and ready to explode in amongst my enemies!

I was glad I had thought to try and keep my hands warm on the windy
flight out by sitting on them. It might have been summertime, but it's
surprisingly cold in the early hours of the morning in a hundred knots of
wind chill factor. Besides which, they were still giving me pain. I clearly
had a considerable amount of nerve damage and lack of sensation in them
after being tied up during my forced incarceration by the same people I
would soon be getting to grips with. I turned my head away from the
punishing blast of air from the speeding aircraft and took several deep
breaths as I clung on to the vibrating airframe for dear life.

Looking forwards again, the distant fort had grown bigger as we
approached it at over one hundred miles an hour. Adrenalin coursing
through my veins like never before.

I can see on the deck of the fortress something unusual and out of place. I
strain against the rushing wind to focus my watering eyes and identify a
yellow shape on the deck. As we get nearer I just make out a man in a

bright yellow oilskin coat, *my dad's coat!* He was asleep in a chair.
I later learnt that this was Gernot Putz, the German lawyer. He was meant to be keeping watch but the cold and his nerves had made him drink a considerable amount of 'Geneva' and he had fallen asleep in the chair. He was to tell me later that the first thing he saw as he woke up in the chair was the helicopter appear from under the platform. Men were standing outside on the skids with coils of rope in their hands and in his own words: *"It frightened the shit out of me!"*

Skidding through the air sideways with a sweeping turn, John brought the helicopter in between the two masts perfectly and with a little rocking motion came into the hover.
I dropped my coil of rope as we had done in practice the day before. To my horror it's caught by the strong wind and is trailing over the side of the helideck sixty foot below and dangling over the raging sea. It was also too short.
I climbed back into the machine, put my arm over Johns shoulder and indicated forward, forward, down, down. He obeyed without hesitation. I ripped open my camouflage jacket to release the shotgun underneath, climbed back onto the skid and launched myself straight down the rope.

Hurtling downwards I can see two armed men running out of the building below me, one had a rifle in his hand and the other a holstered pistol. I look up and see my father sliding down the other rope on the opposite side of the machine. The plan was that the first man down would collapse the mast by pulling the base away, allowing the helicopter to land.
The two others, Barry and Willy, were to stay in the machine and when it landed untie the ropes from the airframe so that John could fly away back to base before anyone had a chance to see his helicopter at the scene. Like most great plans, it didn't quite go as arranged!
The mast was behind me and the bad guys were running out of the building in front of me. Under massive downdraught and cacophony of engine noise from above, I headed for the bad guys!
I ducked and glanced over my shoulder. My dad was nearly down and to

my surprise there was Willy brave as a lion, not wanting to be left out of the action, clambering hand over hand along the airframe outside of the hovering helicopter. Determined to reach my father's rope attached at the front several feet away from where he had been sitting. Grabbing it, Willy came hurtling down the rope onto the helipad behind me.

WE WERE BACK!! And we were very pissed off!

Do You Speak English?

I snapped the breech shut and flicked the safety catch off my shotgun in a single, well-practiced movement. Running to the edge of the helipad, I could see the enemy still piling out of the building below me. They were armed but nobody pointed a weapon in my direction. *"Rouse rouse handa ho handa ho"* I shouted above the roar of the helicopter. I had them covered from the roof as my father disappeared down the hatch in the helideck roof onto the ladder in the corner of the building and appeared on the deck below me.

Braced forwards in the combat crouch with his pistol pushed out in front of him; ready to drop the first man to raise a weapon at him.

They were clearly in shock, unsure what to do and I didn't want to take my eyes off them for one second to follow Dad down the ladder. Without even thinking about it, I stepped forwards and launched myself from the helipad out horizontally 4 foot, over an open topped water tank and dropped ten foot onto the deck below, right into the middle of the bad guys and next to my old man.

As I landed with a crash and rolled on the hard steel deck the butt of the sawn off hit the ground. It went off with an almighty *BOOM!* Splattering a large white painted fuel tank in the corner of the deck with grapeshot in very spectacular fashion. In a fraction of a second, their hands shot up in the air indicating unconditional surrender.

We had won the day and I had narrowly avoided committing patricide!

By now, the helicopter had landed, the ropes had been removed and John had departed for home with a big grin on his face; elated with the triumphant news.

Jill, John's wife, phoned my mother who had been awake all night on tenterhooks with Robbie Dawson pacing the floor. Her mind was churning with visions of not just losing her husband but her only son as well. She almost passed out with relief when Jill excitedly told her we were all safe.

We disarmed our prisoners and ordered them to sit on their hands on the ground. I am sure they thought we were going to shoot them then and there as we had to knock them to the floor. We fetched a five-gallon drum and sat Barry on it armed with an automatic pistol and orders to shoot anyone that moved. He took to the job with relish and stared down the barrel unblinkingly.

I went inside to clear the building and ensure there weren't any others hiding. The generators were stopped as they had run them out of fuel and didn't know how to refuel them. Everywhere was a mess. They had even been bathing in the drinking water tanks and had lit a fire on deck made from smashed up furniture to put the electric kettle on in an attempt to boil water. At a later date, when the Falklands war took place it reminded me of the senseless destruction and hysteria the Argentinean conscripts left at South Georgia.

The place was wrecked. These were not the actions of people settling in, more like those of people in a semi-hysterical state.

We got the generator running and went back out on deck to examine our prisoners. It seems my father had taken the lawyer and Sealander Gernot Putz to one side to question him about his friends that had given me such a hard time and tied my hands up so tight.

Putz had blood running down his face from above his hairline. I couldn't quite work out what had happened to him and asked him if he was ok. He nodded his head vigorously, wincing as he did so.
I looked at him again, *"Are you sure?"* I asked looking into his somewhat dazed eyes.
"Yes, yes," he said with his thick German accent, *"I am fine".*
I turned to Willy and Barry *"What's happened to him? Did he fall over or*

something? He looks like he's been run over by a truck?"

"Don't know" they mumbled in unison shuffling their feet and looking sheepishly away.

"Don't know?" I inquired quizzically *"What do you mean? You were here weren't you?"*

Willy could help himself no longer and started to snigger. *"He's had a spot of bother with your dad"* he said with laughter in his voice.

"What kind of bother?" I asked.

"Well, your dad asked him where Brings and the other guy that had held you prisoner were to be found, and well... er... he wasn't particularly forthcoming with answers. So your dad being upset about what they had done to you and your hands and stuff, was cracking him over the head with his pistol butt every time he got the wrong answer."

Unfortunately for Putz, the pistol involved was a 9mm Berretta with a rather savage metal spur on the magazine that protruded from the butt. He also seemed to have acquired a rather colourful black eye somewhere in the proceedings.

Satisfied there were no others hidden about the place. We marched them all down to the bottom of the tower, where we locked them up in the magazine, a fairly airless, gloomy concrete and steel room below water level that we had converted into a jail.

About an hour later a blue and white passenger carrying boat turned up with the '*Daily Mirror*' on board. They shouted up. *"Do you speak English?"*

"Of course we do" I replied.

"Oh", was the somewhat confused response, *"We thought there had been a coup d'état?"*

The boat drifted away as the skipper had trouble keeping it near enough for us to talk in the worsening weather conditions.

"I will talk to you on the VHF radio" I shouted and with that went inside to call them on the radio.

We made contact and started to chat. After a very short while, with the old VHF radio buzzing and crackling, it became clear that I could hear them but they couldn't hear me. My transmitter had packed up.

The journalist started taunting me with *"Come on Mr Bates we know it's all a publicity stunt. You have to talk to us. The truth will all come out in the end".*

The boat went off with the two intrepid news hounds delighted that they had successfully solved the publicity stunt riddle of Sealand and didn't end up making their paper look foolish. They didn't publish.

As we fiddled with the radio and flicked through the channels, we came across two fishing boats talking. One of them was Vic Goods 'Allison Teresa' from Harwich. The other boat was saying that he had heard that we had been thrown off Sealand. Vic said he thought something strange was going on as he had seen a funny looking helicopter with no doors over the place at dawn. He had gotten his binoculars out for a look. He said it had only been above for a minute or two, didn't land and seemed to be flown by some kind of stunt pilot judging by its gung-ho aerobatics antics.

Ten minutes later a tug turned up with The Sun newspaper. Two journalists and assorted crew stared up at us from the large open aft deck as the skipper skilfully swung the ship around and backed in under the fortress. Now you can say what you like about the good old *'current bun'*, but they do like an adventure story and if you can throw in a bit of piracy and a few nasty Germans so much the better!

This time the larger ship was able to maintain its position close underneath. The same questions came out: *"Do you speak English?"*

"Of course we bloody do."

"Oh, we thought there had been a coup d'état?" a puzzled voice shouted back.

"Yes and at dawn this morning we coup d'état, the coup d'état!" Came my triumphant response.

"Bloody marvellous! Absolutely bloody marvellous! Germans as well aren't

they? Well done lads do you have any prisoners?"
"Yes of course we do" I said.
"Wonderful! Can we have a photo?"
" I suppose so" I replied and sent the lads off to get them.
The result was a brilliant photo in the Sun of our prisoners in a row with
their hands on their heads, black eyes, fat lips and all!

All day long the press arrived in droves, accompanied by my very proud
mother. ITV, BBC and a host of newspapers from around the world
wanted to know our story. John did well for his company flying them
backwards and forwards.
Everybody was very happy! Everybody, that is, apart from our three
prisoners. Taking them downstairs one by one, we locked them in the
wartime ammunition store, the 'magazine', at the bottom of the north
tower. They consisted of *'Helmut Eck'* who we were told was the karate
champion of Germany who made his living as a bone breaker in the
Hamburg red light district, *'Evert Boss'* a Dutch guy and of course *'Gernot*
Putz' the German lawyer with the dents in his head and nasty headache.
Putz who had written out the so-called legal document when they had
kidnapped me, Putz, who had waved a pistol in my face and threatened to
shoot me when he had first arrived! (Hmm, as a father myself I can
understand my dad being ever so slightly pissed off with him!)

Willy wanted to take the Karate king down to the cells. *"Do you want me to*
come with you?" I asked, *"In case he gets frisky?"*
"No, don't worry about that," he said. *"Why would I need help with one*
kraut? Get down those stairs you bastard!" he said looking up at the
somewhat giant German towering above him and nudging him towards
the first of seven dark companionways. Eck obliged in a surly arrogant
fashion, giving him a threatening filthy look. *"Go on, bloody get on with it!"*
said Willy giving him a poke in the ribs with his automatic pistol. *"Get*
down those fucking stairs!" He pushed and shoved the large German down
the seven sets of stairs down to the cells, as I watched and tried to listen
from above concerned he might have trouble with the fellow, but knowing

it was something he needed to do on his own. A few minutes later Willy arrived out of the dark stairwell back on deck. He was looking very pleased with himself for achieving the mission on his own. *"Bloody karate crap,"* he mumbled *"fucking Germans, I showed him!"* he declared with a very satisfied look on his face.

He marvelled at the little 'Walther model nine' airmen's escape pistol in his hand.
"You know this is a beautifully made little pistol but its only .25, quite a small calibre. I wonder what the penetration is?" he ruminated quizzically.

"Let's put a piece of wood up at the end of the platform and see how deep the rounds penetrate it." I proposed.
We placed a four-inch bulk of timber against the rail, Willy stood ten yards back and fired. *BANG!*
"You missed the bloody thing" I chuckled.
"No, I couldn't have!" he gasped looking all hurt.
"Well, you did. Look no hole!"
"The barrel must be bent" he declared.
"Ha ha! Make it safe and have another go!"
As I looked down at the gun, I burst out laughing.
"What", said the increasingly irate Willy, who had been shooting all his life and considered himself a bit of a dead eye Dick. *"What?"*
"Look!" I laughed; poking out the end of the barrel was a nickel-jacketed bullet. It was all shiny and you could see the rifling marks where it had spun around as it was meant to while travelling down the barrel. The ammunition must have been as old as the gun that my dad's boyhood friend Pat Coleman, a fighter pilot during the war, must have taken off a German airman. The propellant had only just managed to make the bullet jam at the end of the barrel with the point sticking out like some cartoon gun. *"Hmmmm"* said Willy, looking somewhat bemused.

We just fell about laughing.

It was during this period after recapturing Sealand, while the press were flying in and out on a daily basis for interviews, that something funny happened. I was standing on the top of the fort in the middle of the helipad. I had been told there was an incoming chopper, I was up there, ready to guide him in to land, using hand signals and the airband radio John had provided us with.

John had a nutty American ex-'Nam' pilot working for him, Tom. Tom had been crop dusting farmers fields all over Essex and Suffolk using the little Bell Sioux helicopter. They were the machines used in the Vietnam War (and famously in the US TV series MASH) for evacuating casualties from the battlefield. I was told this bloke was a bit 'off the wall'; a bit messed up from Vietnam. He had been known to fly through trees at the end of crop spraying runs, damaging the rotor blades, his mechanic had told me they were constantly having to repair them.

So this little machine is screaming towards me, with its deafening high-pitched piston engine getting louder and louder by the second. A Small dot that was getting bigger and bigger as he tears towards me. He's low, he's head down and just above the water, but the helicopter is looking odd. It has two large blow up floats bolted on the skids. I'm thinking any minute now he's going to lift up, sweep round and land where I'm standing. It's not happening. He's still hurtling towards me, and I'm now almost looking down at him. He is so near I can see his face, and the shear concentration etched on it, as he leans forward in his seat, staring intently.

I read his mind *he is only going to put the fucking thing between the towers*!

He thinks he can do it!

I'm about to run and dive off the helipad onto the deck below. Seconds before he commits to the point of no return, I see his crazed face through the Perspex bubble.

He knows he's got it wrong.

He yanks hard on the stick, frantically pulling it back into his chest, but the large, air grabbing floats act like drogues, making the aircraft unresponsive.

Slowly it lifts, swoops up, and misses me by feet. All I can see is the large floats, and belly of the helicopter merely feet in front of me. The machine is now climbing above me, clawing it's way straight up into the sky, standing on its tail, decreasing in velocity until it loses nearly all forward momentum and stalls. I stare helplessly into the space above me to see the tail rotor spinning like an oversized chainsaw, no more than fifty feet above my head.

I'm thinking *'Crap this lot is coming down on me, tail first!"*

Filled with the terror of its impending impact, I dived to get out of the way, when out of the corner of my eye I see the machine fall away to the left, and the pilot amazingly regain control. He sweeps round in an aggressive arch, comes in at speed and lands, bouncing heavily on the helideck in front of me. Wild-eyed and covered in sweat, he powered down the engine. The nutty air ace gazed at me through the Perspex bubble, his eyes wide with adrenaline. We both know he fucked up, and that we'd both had a very lucky escape.

It was decided that we didn't need to keep the prisoners; they just presented a security problem and a drain on our resources. We released the Dutch guy Evert Boss, and the German Helmut Eck.

We convened a court and Putz being a Sealander was charged with treason. Held in a sombre fashion in our living room, there were members of the press present, our UK lawyer's son Trevor Conway and several other independent witnesses. Putz elected to represent himself and the charges were read. Putz pleaded guilty on all counts as charged. He was found guilty and he was fined as I recall some 75k DM (about £18,000).

I insisted that for the release of the prisoners the same Dutch trawler the 'Leendert' must be used.

In the meantime, as all of this was going on, the Dutch and German navy appeared over the horizon in considerable force. We had a row of Dutch warships anchored a few hundred yards to the east and a row of German warships anchored a few hundred yards to the west; in line astern, one behind the other. There must have been five or six from each navy, each ship bigger than the fortress itself. Looking back we were not fazed at all by their presence and just mounted one extra guard during the hours of darkness.

I recall flying down one of the lines of anchored warships with John in his helicopter as he mumbled about what he would give for some 'Sidewinder Missiles' right now for his helicopter. I thought I had better add them to our next stores list!

Ominously close they never approached us or tried to communicate with us. I assume sent to intimidate us or possibly launch an attack if instructed but as quietly as they had arrived, after a couple of days they left in the same fashion.

Putz in the meantime had started spilling the beans on the entire nefarious goings on of Achenbach. Divulging amongst other things, that 'Hans Lavoo', the Dutch lad who had tried to befriend me on the trawler that took me under duress to Holland, was in fact the brother of a guy 'Dick Lavoo' that was very wrapped up with Achenbach and instrumental in the coup. Dick was going to put together a commercial radio station to broadcast from Sealand to Europe and the Dutchman that we had captured Evert Boss was his employee.

The Leendert duly arrived as arranged to take our uninvited guests Evert Boss and Helmut Eck away. The weather was fine and calm with afternoon sunshine glistening off the peaceful sea. The skipper and mate waved to me as the boat circled the fortress. They hung around for no apparent reason down tide and to the north at the opposite end to the lifting hoist we would need to unload it. As Putz and I watched it from above. I was starting to smell a rat. Things just didn't feel right. Putz was getting very agitated and furtive. Looking a bit more 'potty', if that was even possible, than usual. He kept manoeuvring himself nearer and nearer the side. It became clear to me that he must have been given a message by someone, probably a journalist, to dive over the side when the boat arrived and they would pick him up.

It wasn't that simple. The guy couldn't swim, it was a very long way down being low tide and to help him with his decision-making I told him I would shoot him if he did so. Obviously I wouldn't have shot him and I could tell he was pretty sure I wouldn't. In fact by this point I had become quite fond of the silly bastard. It was easy to forget how he had waved a gun in my face at our first meeting, like some hardened wartime Gestapo officer, saying he would shoot me if he had to. I could imagine him quoting the words of many a German officer at the Nuremberg war crimes trial *"I only obeyed the orders"*.

I was trying to make him see the futility of jumping. I could see he was well up for it though in his somewhat distraught mental state. I had visions of going in after him to stop the soppy bastard from drowning himself and was preparing myself to do just that. I am sure he could see this as his last and only chance of escape from his indeterminate period of imprisonment. His wife certainly didn't seem too interested in sorting out his release and had only very grudgingly sent a box of letters and paper he had requested several times to our lawyers. Sometimes I would look at him and he would be a total, forgive the pun, 'fish out of water' and needed looking after almost like a child. Other times I would look into his eyes and see a snidey, over-clever bastard who thought that because he was a lawyer he had to be cleverer than all those around him. He could not believe that we could read him like a book. He came from a very sheltered world; only greed and the thought of making a fortune could have got him into the trouble he was now in.

I took him inside and sat him down with Barry and Robbie before he launched himself over the side into space and probable oblivion. But before that happened I noticed Hans Lavoo on the trawler once more. *"Hans old son, how are you?"* I shouted down to him warmly.
"I am fine thank you Michael" he said like a long lost friend returned home.
"Do come up and have a cup of coffee and a look around Hans"
"I would love to" said the conniving little bastard, who no doubt hoped to encourage Putz to dive over the side. With that he jumped in the bosons chair and Willy hit the up button on the electric winch, whisking him off the deck and into the air from the gently rolling Leendert. As he came level with Sealand's deck, the hoisting derrick was swung in one smooth

motion. I reached out, got hold of his cherub-like blonde tresses and dragged him over the gunwale.

"Got you, you bastard!" I roared. I still had a lot of anger in me and was delighted with myself getting hold of this two faced lying bastard!

We frog marched him down the hall to the radio room and sat him in a chair.

"So Hans, you are not the innocent bystander whose journalist girlfriend just happened to ask you to take part in what turned out to be a kidnapping" I probed.

"Yes I am" he declared.

"But Putz has told us that you and your brother were involved in the coup and that Evert Boss is your employee" I said growing more and more impatient with his lies.

"It's not true! I know nothing of this" he squealed *"and I don't know anyone called Boss"*

Hmm, I thought, *what now?* We can't really start pulling his fingernails out and it would be bad form to start wiring up his testicles to the mains electric. Having said that, we had just fixed the generator and it would probably be a good way of load testing it!

Then a moment of blinding inspiration hit me! I turned to Willy and Barry and gave them a conspiratorial wink.

"Take the lying bastard outside and shoot him!" I boomed.

I heard the words come out of my mouth like something out of a crappy old B movie. Delighted with their new mission, they dragged him off the chair kicking and struggling through the door and out of sight down the hall. His arms and legs were flying everywhere, but Willy and Barry were having none of it, he was going like it or not. It was so difficult keeping it all together until they got him out the door. I had to look away from him so he wouldn't see my face contorted with suppressed laughter; he probably took that as me washing my hands of it. I collapsed against the wall heaving with fits of hysterical laughter. Sliding down it to the floor, I was on my knees trying to keep my hand over my mouth in case he should hear me and spoil the ruse. I just couldn't stop; my eyes were

195

streaming and I was racked by spasms of hysterical laughter.

I was trying to pull myself back together, when suddenly a thought hit me. *Shit! Did Willy really see my wink? Maybe he hadn't clocked it and they were really going to do the poor bugger in!* I looked around the corner. Much to my horror Willy and Barry had taken to the task with a huge amount of enthusiasm and were dragging him far too quickly kicking and screaming down the 50ft hall towards the door onto the south deck. In his eyes (and I think possibly in Willy and Barry's eyes) to certain doom. Three-quarters of the way down the hall he capitulated.

"I will tell you everything. Don't shoot me, I will tell you all I know!" he wailed.

They brought him back ashen faced. He readily agreed to sit down and write all the facts of his and his brother's involvement in a statement arranged by our new German legal advisor Gernot Putz. Willy and Barry looked somewhat disappointed and I breathed a heavy sigh of relief.

So Eck and Boss went, and Putz and Hans stayed.

We negotiated Hans's release a couple of weeks later using a Dutch journalist as an intermediary and the Dutch newspaper De Telegraaf paid for a helicopter to take him away.

As part of the agreement, his brother 'Dick' met my father in our UK lawyer's office. Where he signed papers saying he would have no more involvement with acts of aggression against us, or anything more to do with Sealand.

That left Putz, now released from his cell and allowed to wander around as one of us. We now had to suffer his lousy coffee making skills, bad washing up and dubious legal advice.

The German Government in the meantime contacted the British Government to complain that one of their nationals was being held against his will on Sealand and, as the nearest neighbour, what were they going to do about it. The British Government was quoted in the Press, as saying there is nothing they could or would do.

Meanwhile diplomatic phone lines were burning hot.

In a communication marked *'CONFIDENTIAL'* from 'Mr Furness' of the Western European department entitled 'Troubles on Sealand' which was copied to the UK Government legal advisors and the MOD, Furness quotes a phone call:

"Mr. Schaapveld, Minister at the Dutch Embassy telephoned me today about a telex message that the Dutch Government had received from a lawyer representing Mr. Achenbach, who recently staged a "Coup" against Major Roy Bates, to seize power at "Sealand" (Roughs Tower Fort) in the North Sea, but was later ousted by a "Counter Coup" organised by Major Bates.

According to Mr. Schaapveld, the telex was from the Dutch lawyer (Mr A Oomen of The Hague), states that a Dutchman, Hans Lavoo and a German Gernot Putz, are being kept under armed guard on "Sealand", after being man handled there, and Achenbach requests urgent intervention by the Dutch Government for their liberation. Whilst "Authorising" the Dutch Government to set foot on "Sealand" in order to achieve this. Mr Oomen requests an early reply from the Dutch Government.

Mr Schaapveld was familiar with the background to the case and the inhibitions the British police felt they were under, following the court ruling some years ago that Roughs Tower Fort was outside British territorial waters and therefore outside the jurisdiction of the court. I had to admit that I did not see any easy way, against this background, in which we could offer any satisfactory comments on the approach the Dutch Government had received, despite the evident embarrassment to HMG caused by the antics of Mr Bates and his associates/rivals on "Sealand".

Mr Schaapveld said that he had three comments to make on a personal basis.

1) If Britain advanced her territorial waters from 3 to 12 miles, would not this automatically solve the problem? (I commented that no doubt it would but that the issues involved were somewhat wider than the embarrassment caused by Major Bates and the Roughs Tower Fort);

2) Could not the recent events be treated as an act of piracy on the high seas, and thus open the way to intervention by any state?

3) Was it feasible to think of a Dutch patrol vessel "passing by" the Fort and somehow happening to take appropriate action (I said this would be unlikely to reduce the embarrassment caused to the British government by the present situation).

I undertook to look into the whole question of "Sealand" again and give Mr Schaapveld some sort of reply as soon as I could. Could you, therefore, please discuss the approach from the Dutch Embassy with the Whitehall departments concerned, and let me know what reply I can give to Mr Schaapveld? Is there any chance of a British patrol vessel "passing by "the Fort and somehow knocking it into the sea? (Mr Schaapveld added the comment that he had himself only yesterday passed close by on the Hook of Holland /Harwich ferry)."

A note on this letter dated 24th August says:

"while the above was being typed, Mr Schaapveld telephoned to say that the Dutch press this morning reported that Mr Lavoo had been released had been released from his captivity at Roughs Tower Fort, and that therefore the immediate issue was over as far as the Dutch Government was concerned, although they clearly might find themselves further involved in the affairs of Sealand as its lively history progressed.

Mr Schaapveld said he did not know whether the German (about whom you have received representation from the FRG here) had also been released.

Assuming that he has, then we can consider the problems of Sealand in somewhat slower time, but no doubt the same sort of problem might be thrown up at any moment until the British Government feels itself able to take some effective action over its property in the North Sea."

A further note a few days later from the Western European Department and marked restricted states:

"Dr. Niemoller telephoned again today to tell me that one of the sons of Conway and Conway Lawyers of Westcliff-on-Sea had visited Sealand yesterday and was able to meet Herr Putz. Apparently the general conditions of Herr Putz confinement are unsatisfactory; Consequently, Herr Putz nerves are beginning to suffer.

Dr. Niemoeller said he understood the predicament of HMG; he was now considering the use of a helicopter to land a German Embassy official on Sealand to attend to Herr Putz immediate welfare. I could not foresee any objection but undertook to confer with the MOD and Home Office."

In the mean time, Sealand was receiving a constant stream of journalists from around the world rumours, and speculation about European government reaction to the situation abounded.

Richard Clarke from the Western European Department wrote to Furness the MOD and the Home Office:

"Dr. Christophe Niemoeller, Counsellor and legal and Counsellor Affaires at the German Embassy, telephoned again today to pursue the case of Herr Putz, who is still being held prisoner on Sealand as a result of the recent attempted "Coup". (As you are already aware, Dr. Niemoeller and Herr Lincke (Counsellor) discussed this case with me at the end of last week).

According to Dr. Niemoeller, the foreign ministry has been informed by a Dutch journalist that Mr Bates was now pressing Herr Putz wife for a ransom of 57,000 DM, that being the precise value of some precious stones that are known to be in her possession.

Once again I reiterate HMG's policy towards Sealand. I outline the stance that has been adopted by the MOD, the Home Office and the Essex Constabulary in the light of recent events, but, in response to another hint as to the possible German intervention, admitted that something would have to be done to release Herr Putz, though by whom and at what date, I would not wish to speculate."

A hand written note by one of the recipients of this letter stated.

"You may like to be aware of this latest episode in the ludicrous history of 'Sealand' in which a British Court ruled in 1968 was outside UK jurisdiction. At least we have the Dutch Embassy out of our hair and the FRG Embassy are???? About pressing the interests of the German Putz who has fallen foul of his British fellow adventurers."

Meanwhile, the German Embassy in London contacted our UK lawyer Lionel Conway and he put them in touch with my mother who was in the UK at the time.
The conversation started *"Bonn demands the release of Herr Gernot Putz."* My mother's firm reply was *"Bonn can demand whatever they want but Putz has been charged with treason after joining an armed attack on Sealand. He has been fined and is under house arrest until the matter is resolved. However, if you wish to speak to my husband then you are welcome to send a representative of the German government if they would care to charter a helicopter."*
"We will not pay for a helicopter unless you guarantee his release" was the response.
"I can't do that," said my mother, *"and that is my final offer."*
The next day Dr Niemoeller met my mother at London Southend airport

where John and his trusty helicopter sat on the tarmac ready at his disposal.

Niemoeller was a very mature, tall, sallow complexioned and cadaverous looking diplomat whose diplomatic credentials declared him the chief legal advisor to the German embassy in London. Niemoeller waved his diplomatic passport at the Customs and Immigration and demanded unhindered right of passage. Police and special branch respectfully in attendance.

"Diplomatic Immunity" honked the old boy as he strode through the immigration control.

"Whoa, just a minute," said my mother, *"if you want to visit Sealand you have to undergo a security search."*

"But I am a senior diplomat of the Federal Republic of Germany and I have a diplomatic passport. You cannot do this to me. It is against the Vienna convention!"

"No search; no go." was my mother's stern response.

With steam coming out of his ancient diplomatic ears, he acquiesced to the search. This presented my mother with another problem as she was on her own with no one to frisk him.

"Young man," said my mother turning to the nearest uniformed policeman, *"Would you be kind enough to search him for me?"*

With absolute glee, the young fresh-faced blue uniformed British 'Bobby' went about a meticulous search of Germanys finest.

The trauma didn't end there for the old boy. When the helicopter eventually landed on the Sealand helipad, he was taken from the machine still waving his diplomatic passport around like a magic wand and leant up against it, FBI style; legs kicked apart with the weight on his hands and searched again.

"Why do you search me when you are all armed?" he winged, now sounding a little worried.

"Well, perhaps if you controlled your nationals in a proper fashion we wouldn't need to be armed" was the swift response.

The ubiquitous diplomatic passport was removed from his bony grasp, and he then became the proud owner of a Sealand immigration stamp. He should be very pleased with the collector's value. It is still to this day the only diplomatic passport with a Sealand visa in it.

So there he was in a foreign land and with no friends, apart from the security thing he was treated with the utmost of respect. I took him to the living room and offered him coffee. Putz was despatched to make it for him.

"Where is your father?" he demanded somewhat more sheepishly now.

"He will be here in a while" I responded.

"I need to speak with Her Putz."

"After you have spoken with my father" was the answer.

My father made him wait like a schoolboy for half an hour and then came in the room.

"Do you and your government recognize Sealand?" was my father's first question.

"No" exclaimed the cadaver somewhat arrogantly.

"Then we don't recognize your diplomatic immunity. So if you don't behave yourself as our guest you will be thrown in the cells. Do we understand each other?"

"About Her Putz?"

"You can't have him," responded my father, *"he stays here until his fine is paid."*

"Can I speak with him?" he pleaded.

"Yes you may." With that, my father left the room and Niemoeller was given half an hour with Putz. We then ushered him to the helicopter and wished him Bon Voyage. The helicopter left; mission unaccomplished.

After the Niemoeller visit, there followed a rather funny introduction from the 'Western European Department' sent to the 'British Embassy' in Bonn entitled 'Sealand':

"I enclose a copy of a somewhat petulant note on Sealand, which we have received from the FRG Embassy here and on which we are consulting legal advisors with a view to our eventual reply.

The FRG Embassy has sent us the attached note "Assuming that the British Government will take all suitable steps to free Putz quickly and safely from his false imprisonment." Putz is a citizen of the FRG, and the German Consul has recently been to see him, in a well-publicised helicopter flight. Until receiving this note the FRG seemed content to accept our explanation that as a result of the ruling by the Chelmsford Crown Court in 1968, Roughs Tower is considered by the Home Office to be outside of British jurisdiction. I also understand that the FRG Embassy is incorrect in assuming the imprisonment of Putz to be an act of piracy committed on the high seas since such an act can only be committed from a vessel and not from a fixed site.

So far as we can judge, Putz has been involved with the so-called Prince of Sealand, Roy Bates, and his 'imprisonment' is not necessarily entirely involuntary.

The FRG Embassy may feel that they have lost face as a result of this affair, whose funny side they may not appreciate- hence the attached note, couched in strident language. I do not think we need hasten to send a reply but should be grateful if you could let me know which points in the note relating to international law we should cover in our reply."

It seems from the above that some diplomats do have a sense of humour and that the world famous German lack of it won through with the pompous note below.

"Botschaft Der Bundesrepublik Deutschland

The Embassy of the Federal Republic of Germany presents its compliments to the Foreign and Commonwealth Office and has the honour to draw its attention to the following matter:

The German national Gernot Ernst Putz is being held prisoner by members of the so-called "Principality of Sealand" on the former anti-aircraft fort

"Roughs Tower" 7 miles off Harwich. The Embassy understands that the former fort is the property of the Crown. This was confirmed by a letter of the British Embassy in Bonn of the 26th of April 1977. The representatives of the so-called "Principality of Sealand are British citizens.

There is no state by the name of "Principality of Sealand" recognized by international law. Therefore the imprisonment of Putz is in away an act of piracy, committed on the high seas but still in front of British territory by British citizens.

The Government of the Federal Republic of Germany assumes therefore that the British Government will take all suitable steps to free Putz quickly and safely from his false imprisonment. It would appreciate early information on the steps taken and their results.

The Embassy of the Federal Republic of Germany avails itself of this opportunity to renew to the Foreign and Commonwealth Office the assurance of its highest consideration."

By this time dear old Putz started to crack up a little, he had written to his wife and she had failed to answer his letters. The marriage, as I understood it from the long in depth chats we had, was somewhat shaky. This due to his infidelities with a client who was a female jockey, whom had procured his services to act against her husband who had a predilection for making his wife perform with the family pet. That as best we could ascertain through the language barrier, much arm waving (and fits of laughter) was an Irish wolfhound. It was at this stage in my life that I really wondered if there were any normal people in the world!

Putz was allowed to wander around, as free as we were in the confines of a fortress at sea and now had his own room in the main building on deck level. We were keeping twenty-four hours a day watches, three hours on and three hours off. It is very exhausting, even though I had lived that life in the past, because you never really get into a deep sleep and relax. One night, just after retaking Sealand, Willy came into my room in the dark about 2am to wake me up for my watch. This was always the best watch because although there is always more chance of being attacked at dawn, the sun coming up in the east is so wondrous as it appears over the dark horizon, all the tiredness goes away with daylight and the strain is off after spending hours peering into the darkness and listening for unknown enemies.

This morning was not to be like that.

Willy came to my door, which I always left open when asleep clutching a mug of cocoa, a plate of biscuits, a torch under one arm and a shotgun under the other. I am not one to dwell or whinge about needing therapy or counselling, but I was certainly having a bad dream that night and in my mind I could see Brings coming in the door. I had a 9mm Walther P38 pistol under my pillow. Still in my sleep, I sat bolt upright in bed, slipped it out from under the pillow and pointed it dead between the eyes of the red faced sweating aggressor Brings who I could see standing in the doorway. I really must still have been fast asleep, tired from the watches and a little head stuffed from my recent experiences.

A little tiny spark in my brain said: *No, fire a warning shot!* I raised the barrel above Brings head.

Again a little tiny spark said: *Don't mess about nail the bastard before he gets you!* The barrel came down to the shadowy figure behind the torch in the doorway.

Fortunately, the other spark came back. I raised the barrel, still convinced it was Brings framed in the steel doorway and fired a round into the ceiling above his head. *BOOM!* The pistol sounded like a cannon going off in the confined space of the steel room, the bullet ricocheting about the walls. Willy hit the floor covered in cocoa and biscuits. A clattering of metal as the shotgun landed on the steel floor of the hallway. I woke up with a start and realised what I had done.

Later my mother asked me what the next thing I did was. I dropped the magazine out of the P38, cleared the action and made it safe. Replaced the fired round, snapped the magazine back into the pistol, pulled the slide back to put another live round up the spout, put the safety on and placed it back under the pillow before enquiring *"You alright Willy?"*

Willy dug the bullet out of the wall studding where it ended up and wore it around his neck for years as the one that nearly got him. I still have a copy of the 'Brendan Voyage' a story of Irish monks and boats made of leather telling how they probably discovered the Americas before the Vikings or Columbus. It has a bullet score across the spine from that night.

I guess it just goes to show what stress can do to your head!

I had trained and trained for years with weapons and very rarely miss with a pistol. My father taught me, who himself was taught by a fellow called Grant Taylor, an expert in instinctive shooting. Grant Taylor had instructed the original 'G men' who went on to be Americas FBI. Most situations concerning drawing a pistol and letting a round off in defence, happen within a distance of five yards and like shotgun shooting, both eyes are open. With training your lead eye (in most people the right eye) takes control of the aim. Taylor was a nutter who during the war was taken ashore in Northern France by British commandos. He was escorted to a chateau where a group of pilots from the First World War, who were now senior officers in the Luftwaffe, were having their annual reunion bash. British Intelligence had got to hear of it and decided knocking out a group of such senior officers in one place was a chance too good to be missed.

The commandos got him right up to the building, kicked the door in and put him inside. His choice of weapons surprisingly was two pistols, a left and a right. He charged in pistols blazing. The most sober and alert were dispatched first as he worked his way through them until he cleared the room. His theory was that while a submachine gun would have been good. A pistol with its short barrel can easily cover the whole room with just a flick of the wrist (That's what makes short weapons so dangerous and liable to cause accidents).

Grant also taught the SAS instinctive shooting, a method of hitting targets without aiming through the sights. Basically if you point at something with your finger and then look down it, you will be surprised to see that you are mostly pretty much spot on target. It involves drawing the pistol whether it is from shoulder holster or belt, and getting two rounds off into the centre of the target as quickly as possible, the 'double tap'. All the while dropping into the combat crouch, leaning and bending forwards to present a smaller target and putting yourself in the position that if you are hit you fall forwards and can carry on firing. The idea being not so much to kill your opponent, as to stop them and knock them down as quickly as possible. Putting them out of the game, so they are no longer a threat to you or others. Despite what you see in the films, it's not feasible to draw a pistol and guarantee you are going to hit your target in the leg or arm just to 'wing them' as they say in the cowboy films before they do you some damage. Hence going for centre target and getting off two rounds.

My father had at the end of the war, taught the services use of weapons in clearing streets and houses, a very dangerous job involving firing through doors, walls and even ceilings above your head. He also went on to teach the Essex police small arms, when the previously unarmed local constabularies were told they needed armed response units, he advised what weapons to buy and technique.

Even as a boy, my father would take me to the police pistol range and I would shoot with the police both on the indoor .22 range and the full bore outdoor army range that he had permission to use.

I would like to think I am very safety conscious with small arms and have always trained others the same.

We had been under threat of attack for years with no one to call on for help and very often I was alone on Sealand for weeks on end. I carried a pistol in a holster on my belt or had it on the table next to me in the evenings next to my cup of tea. At night it was under my pillow. This was not over a short period of time, but for years and years from the age of fifteen. It was like a mechanic on call would have his tool bag nearby or a doctor his medical kit. Just a tool! Ready to grab up and use if, and when required.

It seems I was not the only one to feel the strain; Willy came back from visiting his father in Somerset with several gallons of very strong scrumpy cider, which we shared with Putz. He started running around the place with a piece of rope around his neck shouting *"You hang me now!"*
He really did start to lose the plot. One day he saw somebody making a big pot of stew and declared with a sly demented sideways look: *"I know what you do! You put me and the stew in the box you lift the stores off the boat with. You put it on ze 'Vinder' (the electric winch) and you lower me over the side and leave me to die!"*
The wonders of imagination I thought. *"Look Putz old chap do you really think we would waste a perfectly good pot of stew on such a project? Even if we had that in mind"* I said, but he wouldn't have it.
We took the flag down one day because the wind was getting up and we didn't want to see it getting blown out. We were running out of flags and being hand made by a sail maker, they were expensive. Suddenly, over the roar of the wind, we heard a loud hoarse voice *"You do it? You do it now?"*
"Do bloody what now? Stop being so loud Gernot!" I shouted back at him.
The raucous honk started again, *"You shoot me and you don't want it to be under ze flag, so you take it down!"* he screamed in a hysterical voice.
"Please Gernot old chap, you are giving me a bloody headache. Go and have a sit down in your room and chill a little or something. We keep telling you that we wish you no harm. You survived the first few minutes of our counter attack and now like in the 14-18 war is the time to relax and be exchanging photos of your kids!" I replied soothingly.
The demented whelk eyes stared at me out of an unwashed, unshaven face as he turned and shuffled off a broken man wrestling his inner demons.
"Have a shower and a shave and sort your bloody self out!" I shouted after him.

He definitely couldn't work us out. We bought him piles of cigarettes, cooked for him, fed him and the worst he had to do was wash up now and again or make some bad coffee.

Not only did we not lock him in a room, we gave him a key so that he could lock us out. Bizarre really!

One dark night I could hear him shuffling about in his room and scratching at the walls. I tried the door and it was locked.
"You alright in their Gernot?" I asked concerned for his wellbeing.
The hoarse panicky voice came back *"I know what you do, you pour petrol under the door and set fire to me."*
"Ay?" I replied somewhat confused.
"You burn me to death in my room and make it look an accident!" he squealed.
"So come out then you twit and stop being so daft."
"Never! I never come out!" was the reply.
There were some holes in the steel wall of his room where wartime pipes or cables had been removed. He had blocked the bigger ones with a suitcase and stretched across the small room his fingers and feet shoved in the other holes like some children's cartoon character. He wouldn't move at first to our disquiet and we got quite concerned about him. But then we saw the funny side of it!
He stood like this all night mumbling incoherently to himself on the other side of the door. The door rattled open in the morning, he staggered out, a broken and shattered man after his self-inflicted nightlong ordeal.
Mumbling in a rasping voice *"I give up, do what you want."*
"Cup of tea old chap?" was the stern response from his nemesis.

Over this period, I went ashore to Felixstowe ferry to meet our lawyer to sign some papers. While I was there some of the local fishermen tried to get me to confess that it was all a publicity stunt and wouldn't have it any other way.

While our guest Putz was staying with us, a journalist told us that Achenbach had held a meeting the day before with some mercenary type, who had attended in a fancy uniform covered in gold lanyards and scrambled eggs. He had conspired about using some kind of nerve gas on us and he was coming out that day to do a reconnaissance.
Gas? Bloody gas? What an unpleasant bastard! The message had come via our lawyer. We asked how the fellow would be coming out; Boat? Plane? Helicopter? We were told that nobody knew, but he would turn up today so watch out. Ten minutes later a small white twin-engine aeroplane was spotted coming towards us at speed from over the horizon in the direction of Belgium.

The plane circled above us, then banked and descended until it was quite low and level with the platform.
"So what nationality is the registration of that plane chaps?" I asked the lads as we watched it circling menacingly lower and lower.
"I think its Belgian" announced Barry with a very convincing air of authority on the subject. We had erected chain link fencing around the place to explode any incoming shoulder launched missiles, but hadn't reckoned on being gassed!

"Gas us would you?" I mumbled under my breath. *"Barry, give me the shotgun and a couple of those rifled slugs."*
I opened the action, removed two cartridges and slammed the heavy shells into the breech and snapped it shut. *BOOM! BOOM!*

The aircraft seemed to falter, wobble and then race off towards England. It landed at London Southend airport in Essex amid complaints of what had happened and the pilot pointing to a hole in the fuselage. I don't know if there was or not, but it was very close; I did give it plenty of lead and it was certainly a bit bigger than a duck!

A Special Branch detective based at London Southend airport told me later that they were expecting the plane. Our lawyer had alerted them and warned them that there was a threat of gas being used against us. They had ignored the pilot's remonstrations that we had blown a hole in his aircraft and had gone over the plane in fine detail with an explosives and gas sniffing device. He also explained to me that if they had jettisoned gas canisters over the North Sea, it was very unlikely that the sniffer device would have picked up any traces by the time it reached the UK.

At this point, Putz started to follow me around like a lost puppy and would ask me to wake him up when it was my watch. I remember saying to him that he could go on watch with some of the others at a more civilised hour if he need to spend time with someone but he wasn't keen. He would insist I wake him in the middle of the night to keep me company. One very dark night, we were sitting quietly on the deck and as usual he was smoking furiously.

"Why do you light your cigarette bent down under the rail and hold it in the cup of your hand?" he asked curiously.

"Because if there was a sniper out there, he will aim for the light" I responded. He was horrified and cut right down on his smoking after that while on watch with me.

"Well, they're your mates" I said sarcastically!

He went on to tell me that he had always wanted a black Porsche and to have some children. He explained that he could afford the car and wanted the kids, but had always been too cautious to have them so early in his life. But after his experiences with us, he now realised how precious life was and how he should really get on with it while it was there. He swore that if he were ever released, he would have the car and the children. *I often wonder if he ever did!*

One dark, windy evening about nine o'clock at night, Robbie came hurtling into the kitchen with horror on his face. *"It's Putz! I think he's lost it! He is sitting on the outside of the rail and threatening to jump!"*

We ran outside on deck into the darkness and there he was sitting on the outside of the gunwale with the look of sheer terror on his face. His bloodshot eyes were bulging out on stalks and he was foaming at the mouth. Sixty feet below him the raging seas were rolling through the towers and for the time of year there was a very chilly easterly breeze. *"I jump! I jump!"* he was screaming at the top of his demented voice.

I thought he can't be drunk because there wasn't any booze about. Maybe it was just the effect we had on people?

My father turned decisively to me and said, *"Get a torch. If he jumps, I will go in after him with it and keep him afloat until you can launch the boat."* He really had lost the plot; he was a hairs breadth from falling over the side, never mind jumping!
"Sorry Dad, but there is no way I am going to let you jump over the side into the freezing North Sea some 60 foot below in the dark. If you survive the drop, by the time we launched the boat you would be hundreds of yards away in the dark on a strong ebb tide. Secondly if the crappy old rubber torch doesn't work or breaks in the fall we would never find you in the dark. But most importantly, we didn't invite the bastard here in the first place and when he did turn up he didn't exactly have a bunch of flowers in his hand did he?"

Putz watched from the rail, his eyes bulging from their sockets like organ stops. He was wearing my long ski jacket that I had lent him to keep out the cold. It was made of a shiny material and not conducive to keeping a grip on the cold metal RSJ girder on which he sat. He kept shuffling his bum further towards the edge.
I said to my dad *"Ok, if you want to go ahead with that plan I'm younger and fitter. I will jump in with him and you can pick me up in the boat."*
The old man wasn't very keen on that idea so I said *"What's the difference you or me? If you can do it, I can do it?"* I insisted.
He looked at me with annoyance at first, but after some arguing acquiesced to my way of thinking.

I don't suppose that Putz realised just how near to losing him we were. To cap it all, I knew he couldn't swim as he had told me before in conversation.

There is nothing more difficult than spotting a man in the water in the dark. That's, of course, if he can swim and if he doesn't break his neck in the fall. Even in daylight the drill on boats is that if a man falls over the side at least one crewmember should watch him and not take their eyes off him for a second as the boat turns to pick him up.

There was just no way around it. Even though he was only a couple of yards away from me, there was no way we could have rushed the idiot and have got a grip on him before he fell.

Every time we looked at him, his quivering buttocks slid nearer the edge. I could see that his hands gripped the outside of the RSJ girder with white knuckles. He had no possibility of saving himself if he slipped further and quite how he didn't fall off, I really don't know to this day.

I would say apart from this adventure into the macho world of guns, boats and daring do, it was the first time he had been in a more dangerous situation than driving a car down the road. He was certainly not used to looking after himself and surviving. He probably never had the need in his comfortable lawyer's office.

If he was bluffing, and I am sure he wasn't, he hadn't got a clue as to the danger he was putting himself into sitting where he was and behaving like that.

"Gernot," I said, *"just to be clear about what's going on here! It is dark and rough, and you can't swim. Even if you could swim, we wouldn't find you in the dark with the tide and weather as it is. If you jump you will without doubt die! And if you die, the fish and the crabs will eat you, pull out your eyes and devour your genitals. Worse than that, you will be my nearest fucking neighbour for Christ knows how long, until the bones wash away. To be honest, I could really do without that! Do what you want we can't help you, you useless bastard, just fucking get on with it. I am fed up with trying to talk you out of it!"* I hissed.

We turned to walk in. *"Oh and by the way take my fucking jacket of before you jump."*

We went inside to the kitchen and sat drinking tea whilst we waited in silence, only talking in hushed tones. Looking at each other across the table and not saying a lot.

To be honest, he was quite a weak man who had been overcome by greed and got involved with something that he was not programmed to deal with and had shot his bolt.

There was nothing else we could do; he had flipped his lid. I hate to say it, but we had almost got a bit of a soft spot for him by this point, and felt responsible for his welfare. We had certainly denied him nothing; he had shared food and drink with us. He lived with us including cold early hour armed night patrols and talking about his life and its tribulations. Twenty minutes later a very cold and sheepish Putz came in.

"Cup of tea old boy?" chirped Barry.

Dad and I looked at each other and breathed a silent sigh of relief.

It wasn't long after this that we decided we had to get rid of him. Not in the mafia and concrete overcoat sense of the phrase, but because if he didn't go soon, all of us will be lined up on the rail ready to jump while he watched on with a demented grin.

The funny thing is he came as an invader but we gave him two hundred quid travelling money and I gave him yet another one of my jackets to help him on his way.

To say Putz was shocked and surprised at the sudden change of events for him would be an understatement. He wasn't sure whether to be happy or cry. As I recall, he did a bit of both.

We had made the decision on the spur of the moment. We launched the boat with Willy and Putz in it and gave them ten minutes head start before radioing the Coast Guard: *"Thames Coast Guard, Thames Coast Guard, this is Sealand, do you receive please?"*

214

"This is Thames. Go ahead Sealand"
*"We are landing our uninvited guest of several weeks Gernot Putz on
Harwich town quay in ten minutes time. Please be good enough to inform
the Customs and Immigration for us"* I replied.
"No problem at all sir and best wishes from all here" was the reply.

Willy dropped Putz off and raced away at thirty knots. Putz was left with
his two hundred pounds and instructions on how to get to the ferry
terminal that would take him back to Holland.

I was told later that Special Branch took him off the ship to interrogate
him and he had to take another ship six hours later.

Our Lawyer, Lionel Conway, later wrote to MI6 and suggested that if HMG
would like any information about the incident they should contact him
and he would be happy to explain in detail. Needless to say they did not
reply.

The German Embassy wrote to the Deputy Under-secretary of State
Department of State for Foreign and Commonwealth Affaires:

*"I refer to our telephone conversation on Friday concerning the German
national Gernot Putz who is presently held prisoner by the "Bates" family of
Westcliff on Sea on "Sealand". You might be interested to see a copy of the
so-called (Sealand) judgment of the 30th August 1978 showing beyond any
doubt that Putz is under false imprisonment. This has been admitted
repeatedly by Mrs. Bates and was equally established by a member of the
Embassy who saw Putz last Monday.*

*UK Legal Counsel for government commented that the only point of
international law in the German Embassy's note is the rather despairing
suggestion that the activities of Mr. Bates are equivalent to piracy. For
obvious reasons, I should prefer not to enter on to these grounds in further
correspondence with the Embassy.*

I believe from the newspapers that Mr. Putz has now been released from his captivity, and Dr Niemoeller confirmed to me on the telephone yesterday that this was so. Accordingly I wonder whether we can now regard the chapter as closed and, at least evade giving a substantive reply to the German Embassy's note."

They did however write to the German embassy:

"The Foreign and Commonwealth Office presents its compliments to the Embassy of the Federal Republic of Germany and with reference to the Embassies note of the 12th September 1978 and have the honour to state that to the best of its knowledge Herr Gernot Putz is no longer suffering the restraints referred to in the Embassy's note.

The Foreign and Commonwealth Office avails itself of this opportunity to assure the Embassy of the Federal Republic of Germany the assurance of its highest consideration."

The bizarre thing about all the legal wrangling and reference to international law in the Sealand saga is that all the way through Britain's legal advisors have always told their masters, the Government, what they (the Government) wanted to hear. After all, the lawyers are not paid to tell them unpalatable but obvious facts. There were countless legal opinions written in the sixties and seventies for HMG by their legal departments.

How could they possibly claim ownership of the territory? The Crown built it illegally in international waters at a time of war. Because it was during the war in Europe nobody bothered to complain or take them to task on the subject. After a brief period of time at the cessation of hostilities, they were abandoned in international waters on the high seas. Becoming *'Terra Nullius'* or nobodies land according to *'Jus Gentium'*, the Roman laws that allowed nations to live in peace with each other and on which international law is still based today.

This produced another illegal act; 'Any structure built by a country in international waters must be removed by that country when it has no more use for it and abandons it'.

My family has owned the Sealand fortress nearly fifty years. A lifetime or more and about five times longer that the UK occupied it. Sealand also commissioned international lawyers to give legal opinion as to its status. Not surprisingly they upheld our viewpoint

I suppose all bullshit aside; the proof of the pudding is in the eating. If the British government thought they owned the Fortress, why did they try or even feel the need to buy it from us? Why did they try to take it from us by force and then subterfuge? Why did they try to starve us out? Why did the police officer have to ask permission to visit us to question me about the Trinity House incident? Why did they revert to gunboat diplomacy? Why did they not act when asked by the German and Dutch governments to invade?

So it was left to us to sort out our own international incident and send Putz on his way.

Needless to say, we are not holding our breath waiting for him to send the fine payment, let alone the two hundred pounds we gave him or even my jacket!

I did bump into him again a couple of years later. I was crossing the border from Holland into Germany using my Sealand passport as usual, when an overzealous German border guard stopped me. I was effectively arrested because he didn't recognise the passport. I was held in a tiny booth on the border crossing. I was most indignant and asked to speak to my German lawyer Herr Putz.

Putz, bless him, came along and sorted it all out for me. By the time Putz turned up; the border guard and I were getting on like a house on fire. He had a new out Beretta M9 pistol with a double column magazine that I had heard of but never seen before. We had taken it to pieces on the table to find out how it worked. *What a nice chap!* After being released, Putz took me back to his office in Hilden for coffee. I forgot to enquire about the jockey, the wife, the Porsche or the intended children.

Wearing a suit and driving a nice car, he certainly didn't look the demented nutter from a few years before that I had last seen grinning up at me from the boat as it sped away. In fact, he seemed genuinely pleased to see me. But then I suppose if you will excuse the pun yet again he was a fish out of water during his time on Sealand.

After all this we wrote to the Dutch bar council at the International Court of the Hague, complaining of the actions of 'Adrienne Oomens' the Dutch international lawyer who paid the fisherman that took me to Holland. He had also telephoned my mother when we had all the troubles with them, threatening her and our family with violence. My mother and I went to the International Court of The Hague, to which we had given transcripts of the taped menacing telephone conversations and other evidence against him. We arrived on the Harwich Hook of Holland ferry late afternoon. We were ushered through Customs and Immigration by officials who came on the ship as soon as she berthed, escorting us with our Sealand Diplomatic passports from there to our hotel. We were in court the next day.
A strange place to be; where despots and tyrants had stood trial for mass murder, genocide and war crimes.

The hearing lasted a day and Oomens, an arrogant but physically diminutive little man with thinning hair and an almost Hitler-like moustache, had to explain himself to the bar and a council of his peers.

The result was he was suspended from practicing for a period of time as a punishment for his actions. I can't help but think in this modern age with the constant terrorist threats we live under, that if it had happened now, the penalty would have been that much greater. To this day 'KLM', the Dutch national airline, have not been brought to account and have never acknowledged any responsibility for bringing out armed men from a Dutch airport to perpetrate a kidnapping.

On the fifth of December 1978 'Lord Kennet' asked a question in the House of Lords. Whether a British national is occupying a wartime gun platform called Sealand, seven miles off Harwich?; Whether he is holding or has at anytime been holding a German national prisoner there?; Whether they will make a statement on the facts of the matter and on their legal and political implication?

The answer, which came from the Right Honourable 'Lord Goronwy-Roberts,' Minister of State, Foreign and Commonwealth Affairs.

"My Lords,

A British national, Mr. Roy Bates, is living on a wartime gun platform called Roughs tower, 7 miles off Harwich. The gun platform remains the property of the British Crown, but it lies outside of British territorial waters. In October we were informed by the Embassy of the Federal Republic of Germany that a German national was believed to be held prisoner there. To the best of our knowledge the German national in question left Roughs Tower some time ago. The British Government built the tower for wartime use and ceased to use it at the end of the war. The Government has not used the tower since but continues to keep it under surveillance. If pressed the minister was to say that extension of UK territorial limits was under study at the moment but no decision has yet been taken.

We are keeping the situation under review. If we discovered that Roughs Tower was being used for purposes detrimental to the security of the United Kingdom, we should have to consider taking appropriate action.

As I have said. Roughs Tower is beyond our territorial jurisdiction. There are no present plans to exercise the proprietarily rights of the Crown over the tower."

The background notes go on to explain that official communications between Her Majesty's Government and the Governments of the Netherlands and the Federal Republic of Germany pointed out that the events on Roughs Tower were not taking place on British territory and were not subject to British jurisdiction. Reiterating the 1968 Chelmsford Court decision.

While all this was going on the German terrorists made a complaint to the UK authorities that we had unlicensed radio transceivers in the UK for communication to Sealand.

During the seventies there were no mobile telephones and so we had been using medium frequency radiotelephones on the ship-to-ship frequencies. The first ones we had built from scratch by a friend of ours called Tom but they often went wrong, putting us without contact while they came ashore for repair. So we started using either ship-to-ship radios or sometimes converted tank transmitters that could be put on the maritime frequencies. We had one at our office in Southend and another at our home nearby.

These sets required a dipole long wire antenna on the roof and a high antenna out on Sealand where the sets were prone to lightning strike damage.

During electrical storms, static would build up on the fortress. On one occasion I could hear a clicking noise getting louder and louder and speeding up until it was a loud buzz. It was coming from the 3.7 inch wartime anti-aircraft gun barrel that alarmingly seemed to be acting as a static collector under the black threatening sky of an impending storm. Nobody wanted to go near the thing for fear of getting a massive belt off it!

It was certainly a very eerie effect. We tried to earth out the fort to the sea with a copper strip because we assumed that the concrete towers insulated the platform itself from it. We were not quite sure what that meant for us if there was a lightning strike.

The delicate diodes on the transceivers were always going wrong. The radio would be on during waking hours or until the static noises become unbearable in the evenings. It was great after so many years of solitude to be able to speak to each other and keep in touch with events in the UK. We had to make out we were both ships, Sealand was 'Lady Jane' and shore side was 'Nomad'. It was an open secret around the east coast and we had many friends on fishing boats and ships that would call up during the day for a welcome chat. We also had a simple code when discussing important things so that people listening in on these open ship-to-ship channels could not understand what the conversation was really about.

There was never any problem with having the radio equipment on Sealand but we kept a low profile as the UK laws were very strict on the subject and prosecution and confiscation with large fines was the norm for any illegal broadcasts from there.

The Dutch international lawyer Oomens, who I had seen pay the skipper of the fishing boat when I was kidnapped, informed the UK authorities about the radios. A ten-strong police unit raided our house and office with warrants under the Wireless Telegraphy Act, the same act that had closed down the pirate stations. They also had warrants under the firearms act.

When I had cut down the barrels of my side-by-side shotgun to use in the retaking of Sealand, I had thrown the barrels into the bottom of the office filing cabinet and never given them another thought. Fortunately, not a week before the police raid, I had remembered that they were there. I fished them out from under the files, put them in a bag and gave them to a local fisherman friend 'Lenny Rook' to dump at sea next time he went to work.

The police turned the office upside down, pulling all the draws out of the filling cabinet. They confiscated the radio equipment from the office and the one at our home. My father was charged and had to go to court a few weeks later.

After the police and telecoms people (who in those days were the Post Office) had given their evidence, my father was found guilty, given a fine and it was ordered that the radio equipment be destroyed. It didn't really matter to us as we had already replaced it. There were many reasons why we could not lose radio contact, especially in emergencies such as illness or coming under threat.

A more important development to come from the case was that we had the opportunity to tell the court that in international law it was illegal to cut off the communication of small isolated communities. It was against their human rights. The judge instructed the Post Office to give us a postal address, which ended up being: Sealand Postbag, IP11 9SZ. We still use this to this day.

The judge also instructed them to give us telephone communications, which they said they would do in court, but after the case a 'Mr. Baker' from the Home Office radio regulatory department wrote to our solicitor Lionel Conway. He explained that it would not be possible to arrange a radio link as Sealand was not in the UK and it was not a ship either so under the Wireless Telegraphy Act 1949 there was nothing they could do. A year later the same gentleman seems to have changed his tune in a letter to a 'Mr. Masters' at the Post Office, 'Mr. Baker' explains:

"Roy Bates has been attempting to obtain an international call sign, presumably with the intention of establishing a commercial radio station on Roughs Tower, which would not be subject to any form of control. Following correspondence with the Foreign and Commonwealth office, it has been decided that the presence of an ungoverned radio station just outside UK territorial waters is a situation to be avoided and I am now writing to say we will reverse our previous decision and are now prepared to approve the provision of a radio link under the Post Office Omnibus Licence (clause 1h).

The Foreign and Commonwealth Office have asked us to say that any reference on public documents or publications or the Post Office telephone directory should refer to Mr. Bates, "Roughs Tower" and no reference should be made to the Principality of Sealand.

I would be obliged if you would let me know if you will now be able to provide a telephone service on the lines envisaged in Mr. Simpsons letter of 16th October 1979."

Strange how attitudes change, however by the time they had written backwards and forwards to us and worked out how it could be done it was going to be hugely expensive. They priced it well beyond our financial capabilities at the time. So we carried on with our radios and eventually moved over to amateur 2 metre sets, which were much more compact and easy to use, although the antennas where quite large and not easy to hide. They were however very directional so in theory would have been hard to detect unless you were in between the two stations.

It's A Dog's Life

Throughout the seventies my parents travelled extensively while I looked after the fort sometimes on my own, our friend Mike Todd would call me on the radio every few days from his ships radio to make sure I was ok. In 1971 my parents were invited to appear on a TV program in Japan where the audience had to guess who they were. They came home the slow way visiting the Philippines, Thailand and India. One of their trips took in the USA by Concorde and a private jet down the east coast of America to Freeport in the Bahamas. My father had a meeting there with the owners of the Xanadu Beach Resort Hotel and marina complex that had been owned by Howard Hughes. It was there that the infamous billionaire recluse had lived locked away from the outside world in the penthouse suite for four years.

In 1979 my father was invited to Riyadh in Saudi Arabia to discuss placing a hugely powerful radio station on Sealand to broadcast the word of Islam to the UK and Europe.

There were trips to Barcelona and unofficial meetings with what turned out to be representatives of the Spanish government who thought there might be an angle with Sealand to reclaim Gibraltar sovereignty for Spain.

There was always something and whenever they went away they said *"One day son it will be you doing all the interesting travelling and meetings!"*

We had just been through very traumatic and exciting times. Things on Sealand were starting to get back to normality. We had repaired most of the damage done by the attackers and we were looking to the future.

We did however feel under constant threat; we had been told by a reliable source that a 'contract' had been put out on me and my father's lives and it was to take place in the UK. Our lawyer informed the local police, giving them details and requested permits to carry a concealed side arm for self-defence. This was refused by the Chief Constable of Essex.

We talked about how to combat this threat and improve security. We made a hanging gun rack under the radio room table to house our sawn off shotgun, ready to be snatched out in an emergency. We also secreted a small automatic pistol in the air vent in the lavatory. We discussed the idea of electronics and radar alarms, infrared heat sensing equipment and a multitude of even more bizarre ideas.

One such idea being to cross the North Sea in our fast RIB, land on a beach in Belgium in the dark and make our way to Aachen on the border with Germany were Alexander Achenbach, the man behind the coup lived. We were told he was still plotting our demise and assassinating him there in a pre-emptive strike seemed a reasonable idea under the circumstances.

We worked out how much fuel we would need to get across the North Sea, the logistics of getting to his house and getting back to the pickup point on the beach. After all, if it was ok for the Israeli Mossad to do such things in the interest of state security, then why not for us we reasoned. A little extreme perhaps, but none the less it was discussed at length and in great detail. Eventually without even knowing it, he got a reprieve.

We decided on a slightly more down to earth approach; we decided the less risky, less controversial and most cost effective way forward was a guard dog. A German Shepherd dog would have better hearing and senses than us, and if nothing else give warning of any intruders. Also a plus point, there would be someone sensible to talk to while alone on Sealand that wouldn't give too much backchat. Talking to yourself while on your own for weeks on end is not really the way forward, it is the thin end of the wedge and was to be avoided. Yep, a dog seemed a great idea.

We searched through the telephone directory and called all the local kennels around Southend until we came up with one that had a large male German Shepherd.

"Come on Willy," I said pleased to have found a four-legged candidate for the job, *"you're the expert on dogs. You're the country boy. Come and advise me on this hound."*
We set off in the car for the kennels, set back from the A127 Southend London Arterial Road behind a pub called the Dick Turpin.

In a barn behind the kennels, we were introduced to a tall, dark haired man who said he would go and fetch the dog. The door opened and in bounded this magnificent tall, underfed German Shepherd. It ran around a tractor parked in the middle of the barn. Peed up one of its wheels while scanning the space around it and assessing the situation, before charging up to Willy and smartly bit him on the backside. The man was mortified and Willy was rubbing his sore bottom mumbling something about *"shooting the bastard thing."*
"He doesn't normally bite people," said the man worriedly (No doubt seeing his cash sale going out the window) *"He is a good natured dog, honestly."*
He was still making excuses to me as I said I would have him. He was so busy trying to talk over the top of me that he missed what I was saying. Money changed hands and on a bitterly cold January day I became the proud owner of my very first dog.

I don't know why we never had one before. My father had been brought up with a dog in the house when he was young and so was my mother but we had only ever had cats.
We took him for a short walk and then drove him home in the car. We had a conference about what we would call him, as he didn't seem to have a name. My father decided he wanted to call him *'Bahadur'*, Ghurkha for brave. Taking him for a walk on the seafront, he was delighted with his newfound freedom and kept nipping at my fingers in a playful but quite

painful way.

The next day we drove up to Felixstowe Ferry, towing our RIB behind the car on a trailer. We launched the boat as usual on the beach and started loading our stores into it. Bahadur sat on the beach watching the procedure with interest. Suddenly, he charged down the beach and launched himself into the fast flowing tide of the River Deben and was swimming about like an Olympic athlete. There was no stopping him and it took some time to coax him back to shore.

He was freezing. It was bitterly cold and he was due to be taken out on an open boat in the middle of winter. I took the clean sheets that my mother had washed for me out of my kit bag and dried him off the best I could on the beach.

We loaded the now sheepish, subdued and shivering hound into the boat and set off for Sealand.

Arriving under the fort, Bahadur sat quietly in the boat with me holding on to his collar while Willy hooked the lifting strops onto our crane, we were all lifted some sixty-foot into the air and the boat was deposited on deck.

We took the shivering, dejected and soggy fellow inside and introduced him to everybody while he went through another somewhat undignified drying off with a towel this time.

He adapted to life at sea really well, although there were some snags. The first obstacle that had to be surmounted was the fact he didn't take a leak for several days. At first we thought it funny and he would eventually adapt but as much as we watched him, the more he wouldn't do it. He just could not get his furry head around the idea that there were no trees to piss up! He would wander about looking forlornly for something green to relieve himself on. We stood large oxygen cylinders up and led him over to one of them hoping he would think it a tree to get his bladder going, but he was having none of it. We lifted his leg for him against the cylinders. Eventually, first myself, and then Willy had to pee up the bottle while he watched. Before he finally got the message that it was ok to do it and

unleashed what seemed an endless torrent with a huge look of ecstatic relief on his face.
We were in hysterics it was one of the funniest things!

We trained him to attack anyone that pointed a gun in his direction. We built a dog flap so that, on the command, he'd go out of it and patrol the deck; doing a circuit of the building in the dark and then come back in again. We taught him a word that when dropped into conversation would turn him into a snarling monster. We bought piles of books on the subject of security dog training and he was a very willing pupil.

We worried that one day he might get too excited when barking at a passing ship and fall over the side. So we trained him to never put his paws on the RSJ rail that surrounded the outside deck. He made a toy out of a small white plastic fender, which he would carry around in his mouth and drop at your feet. But when he got too excited woofing at boats, he had been known to drop it out of his mouth on to the flat top of the rail. This was a worry as sometimes they would roll over the side while he was distracted and he might have launched himself after it and been lost to the sea. Had he fallen over the side we would not have been able to rescue him unless the RIB was there and the weather fine. Even then the chances were slim.

One horrendously stormy night I woke to find him gone. He never normally left my side and I sensed there was something wrong. I was alone on Sealand and because it was such a wild night I had locked the outside doors and gone to bed. Secure in the knowledge that no one and nothing could get near the place in such stormy weather.

Hitting the generator start button on the wall next to the bed, I jumped out of bed in a panic as the lights all came to life around me.
Where the hell was he? I never slept with the door shut or curtains closed in my room, so I could better hear boat engines or incoming helicopters or worse someone already on deck trying to break in the front door, but

right now the whole place was shaking with the roaring violence of the storm. Snatching up a torch and throwing a coat on, I ran out of the room calling him. I searched all the rooms in the main building. I unlocked the front door, the force of the wind nearly tearing the door handle from my grasp. He might, I thought, have gone out of his dog flap to spend a penny. I trudged around the stormy deck in misery, despairing more and more that he had for some reason or somehow fallen over the side in the storm. Maybe he had heard the seas breaking around the towers and leant over too far, looking to see what it was and had fallen over.

Clinging onto the icy rail as tightly as I could, I leant forwards and peered into the darkness below. All I could see was huge white crested foaming rollers breaking against the towers and surging around them in a maelstrom of violent weather. Rain was blowing across the deck horizontally and stinging my eyes as I searched every nook and cranny where I could think that he might be, the wind all the while trying to blow me off my feet.

I climbed up the steel ladder onto the helideck, stuck my head through the hatch and peered through the horizontally driving rain, desperately calling his name.
Returning back down to the deck, I looked once again over the side into the seething caldron of driven spray, rain and wind lashed waves. There was no way anyone or anything could have survived down there.

He wasn't there. I went back inside devastated.
My best pal had gone, disappeared.

I wouldn't have it. I started searching the rooms again calling him, shouting above the fury of the storm. He never left me for more than a minute; I knew he must be lost forever.
The whole fortress was roaring with a deafening noise; the deck beneath my feet was shaking and vibrating in the wind. Outside forty-five gallon oil drums were crashing and rolling around the deck like runaway trains.

I sat down in the kitchen and put my head in my hands, trying to imagine what he must have gone through and the terror he must have suffered before drowning in the cold rough sea.

Suddenly, over the fierce roar of the storm I thought I heard a bark. I ran outside again and looked down into the crashing waves. I heard another faint weak bark behind me. I ran back into the building and looked down the dark companionway to the first level in the South tower. He can't be down there I thought, he can't get down the steps. He was able to climb up the steep wartime companionways if carried down, which I had done once to familiarise him with it, but he couldn't get down them.

Stepping down the hatch onto the first rung, grasping the coamings around the edge, I reached out for the railings and half ran-half slid down the stairs to the bottom. Through the noise of the storm, I could now hear desperate scratching and whimpering noises coming from the food store. There he was locked in the storeroom in a total panic trying to get out! *I don't know who was the most pleased to see who?* When I opened the door he burst out and jumped up at my chest knocking me to the ground, nibbling and licking my face frenziedly. It would be fair to say we were both very happy and my watery eyes weren't caused by the storm force wind alone. I worked out that during the storm he must have heard noises down the tower. The sound of seas breaking about and had fallen down the ladder in the dark by accident luckily not breaking a leg or tumbling down the barely gated lift shaft in front of the ladder. He must have then wandered into our small storeroom full of tinned food, bags of flour and dried foods, with its wartime half stable door and serving hatch and accidentally managed to push the door shut behind him trying to get out in the dark.

Words can't describe how relieved I was to find him! I slung him over my shoulder like a bag of spuds and carried him up the stairs through the hatch and into the hall. I went back to bed with the bloody great lump of dog curled up at the other end of it like a puppy and not moving a muscle as the storm roared around outside unabated. He was very subdued for a few hours getting over his trauma. The next day with the storm having passed over he was soon back to his usual boisterous self, none the worse for his ordeal.

One of the hardest things to teach him was to look up in the air to spot helicopters. Which to me were the greater threat due to their speed of getting to us from the moment they were heard or seen. He knew they were a threat and could hear them coming long before anyone else but would just stare down at the sea wondering why there was nothing there even as the things flew over the top. He couldn't get his furry, wing nut eared head around the idea that certain things flew. Eventually, when he got the hang of it, he would point to them with his nose up and tail wagging like a gun dog pointing to ducks in the classic pose.

One calm sunny summer's afternoon hearing splashing sounds I ran to the side to see a very large seal some forty-foot below. It was high tide, so there was no noise or movement from the flow of water below and the sea was gin clear. I looked down at it in fascination for five minutes, studying its grey and black colouring and enjoying the unusual chance to be at one with nature. Having studied it for long enough, I leant over the side and said *"Hello Mr Seal and how are you today?"* in a welcoming voice. Its bemused face was a picture! It kept looking around as I spoke, but didn't have the thought process to look up and spot me. It must have been there some fifteen minutes before swimming off looking very confused and none the wiser as to where the voice had come from.

For a couple of years after the German incident, whenever alone on Sealand, I would sleep out in the open on deck in a sleeping bag. This was not a new experience for me as I had slept under the stars when Walter and Roland were out there for years on end. I would lay some wood on top of the gun boxes (wartime ammunition stores on deck) that sat against the building just below the helideck level. This allowed me to see around the horizon for 180 degrees. I have to say I got used to it despite the thin chair cushions I used as a mattress and only slept inside if the weather was really rough and windy or when I woke up soaked through from the rain. Invariably when it started to rain I would stick with it hoping it would stop before it got too heavy. If it was a bit windy or threatening rain I would make a bed up on the deck under the outrigger that stuck out over the side of the building. This solved the rain problem until the wind changed or it rained so hard the deck flooded and I woke up from my slumbers in a pool of water.

I would have a nine-millimetre pistol under my pillow and a pump action shotgun loaded up with grapeshot next to the makeshift bed. Bahadur, our faithful old dog, would lie down next to me on his bed.

I was determined I'd never be caught out by invaders again.

When the skies were clear, it was amazing to be under the heavens with no reflected light from a city or roads and to watch the stars twinkling trillions of miles away. Shooting stars ripping across the night sky every few minutes, some bursting as they hit the earth's atmosphere. The craters on the moon were clearly visible with the naked eye and in fascinating detail through the binoculars. It was amazing to think that some of the lights I could see in the heavens were emitted from stars of long gone distant galaxies. To this day I always sleep with all the windows, curtains and doors open whatever the time of year. This has caused a few problems for me over the years, as it's not everyone's cup of tea. On a clear night on the fort, you could see the distant glow in the sky from Southend, Ramsgate and other far off over the horizon towns. In daylight on a clear summer's day with a heat haze on the horizon, we could see what I can only describe as mirages. Distant light ships far beyond sight and over the horizon would appear looming in the sky in a heat haze. Things that we read about but very few people get to see.

As time went on, Bahadur started getting trouble with his toenails and a couple of them fell off on the deck. We thought it must be because of the steel and concrete. We had always worried he might get the doggy version of scurvy (if there is such a thing) but he would always go to the apple box and steal one whenever he had the urge for something green. We had a freezer devoted to his food and sacks upon sacks of dried dog food for emergencies.

We took advice from the vet and soon realised he had to be taken back to the UK for his health.

We were somewhat concerned that he might end up in quarantine under the UKs strict rabies laws even though we knew he had not been in contact with any other animals of the four-footed kind. Strictly speaking this should have been the case. At every seaport there are pictures of rabid dogs; teeth barred and slavering at the mouth incorporated in anti-dog smuggling posters. Six months locked up in quarantine would have broken his heart.

So a plan was formed to get him ashore and relieve what was probably the doggy version of trench foot.

Willy was to skipper the RIB and to drop me, and the dog off on Felixstowe beach at the mouth of the River Deben. At a certain time of the tide, the beach is sheer and we could get the boat very close, nose on to it without hitting the bottom with the propeller.

Like all good plans it was simple.

I would launch the dog, an excellent swimmer, over the side and he would swim to the beach. While he was doing this I would jump off the front of the RIB onto the beach, thus keeping myself, and my shoes dry. I would call him, he would come obediently to heel and would start walking down the road like any normal dog walker out for a stroll. Meanwhile, Willy would go into the harbour, get the boat on the trailer and meet me a mile up the road with the car.

What could possibly go wrong with that plan? Willy put the nose of the boat into the beach and I jumped ashore, pleased that I hadn't even got my feet wet.

"Here he comes" shouted Willy as he launched Bahadur over the side of the little boat.

I guess you have to ask yourself, *is it possible to forget how to swim?* There was this dog that a few years ago could have out swum Johnny Weissmuller, who had now forgotten how to do it. I mean, he didn't just make a hash of it, he sunk like a bloody stone. A head and a paw came out of the water for a moment then he was gone and not coming up for the traditional three times before drowning.

I charged down the beach into the water and was soon up to my neck feeling around for him. Eventually getting hold of a hand full of soggy fur with one hand and the safety rope attached to the RIB with the other. Looking up at Willy who was falling about with laughter in the boat. I dragged Bahadur up the beach where he had a good shake and sorted himself out; seeming none the worse for the experience. We then squelched of up the road looking to the world like disaster victims.

Needless to say his feet started improving on medication from the vet and like all old sea dogs he developed a taste for Guinness and real ale. Amusingly, he would cock his back leg up and put his foot on the tree for support when he had been on the therapeutic Guinness. He did take a little toning down after his security training and there was nearly an unfortunate incident when an unsuspecting blind man crossed the street in front of me and pointed his white stick at him. Bahadur assumed it was a gun and flew at him like a missile. I managed to make him drop to the pavement before getting to the poor fellow.

I guess he could have done with counselling after his years on Sealand. In the bank one day a little boy flung his arms around his neck. Bahadur loved children but when the father with a look of sheer horror on his face tried to retrieve his child he was growled at over the kids shoulder.

He also couldn't be left alone. I suppose after years on Sealand one to one or with a bunch of people 24/7 he couldn't cope with solitude.

One time when my parents were away, I borrowed their car. A rather plush Ford Granada Ghia that they were very proud of. I was out on a date with my girlfriend and misguidedly thought the best thing to stop him fretting would be to take him with us and leave him outside the restaurant in the car. I thought he would see me through the window and be settled.

Not Bahadur.

I suppose I must have been a bit distracted with my date. When I got back to the car, he was staring out of the window at me with a very sheepish look on his furry face. I opened the door and the headrest off one of the seats fell out onto the road. He had wrecked the car. He had pulled off the sun visors, chewed great lumps out of the walnut dashboard, but worse, he had eaten the seats. The inside of the car was a write off. I was dumb struck.

Strangely enough, Bahadur seemed to suffer no ill effects from the large amounts of foam we assumed he had ingested, although he was a little subdued for a few days after. I took the car in for repair hoping my parents wouldn't notice the damage, but there was no getting away from it as the upholstery came out a shade different in colour and there was nothing they could do with the deep teeth marks in the dash. I was resigned to having to explain to my parents what had happened and received a considerable bollocking when they got back along the lines of dog cruelty. I think they would have preferred it if I had left my girlfriend in the car and taken the dog in the restaurant.

It didn't end there. My pal Robbie, who when not with us on Sealand made a living driving his own taxi, gave me a lift a few weeks after this to collect some engine parts. I said let's take the dog into the office with us as he's not very good with cars. But no, Robbie insisted on leaving him in the car explaining we would only be five minutes. He's not very good with cars I said again. But Robbie who had a massive soft spot for Bahadur was insistent even though he had seen the damage done to my parent's car. We were only five minutes and he did only have time to destroy the driver's seat. Luckily Robbie thought it was the funniest thing in the world. Unsurprisingly that was the last time Bahadur ever got left in a car.

The old soldier eventually contracted hip problems as many German Shepherds do and his poor old back legs would give away. He was really fit and happy in himself but the bloody legs just wouldn't work. He would try to get up and collapse in a heap with a howl. I suppose if he were a human they would have just given him a hip replacement operation. I can't imagine the cold years patrolling the decks of Sealand in all weathers would have helped. We read in a newspaper about a firm in America that made a special harness with wheels. We got one sent over straight away and the old warrior got himself a new lease of life. He could often be seen proudly walking along Southend seafront with my mother and father, pulling himself along with his powerful front legs.

Willy in the meantime had met a new girlfriend called Karen. We were on our way out to Sealand on a calm sunny day, zipping along at some thirty knots, Tigers engine buzzing away at full tilt when he leant across to me and said right out of the blue *"I'm thinking of getting married"* I was shocked, it was the first I had heard of it.
"What do you mean you are thinking of getting married?" I shouted over the engine noise.
"Well I am getting married" he said."
"You're getting married? Have you discussed it with Karen?" I asked.
"Yes" he said with a beaming smile on his face. *"I have asked her and she said yes."*
I was dumbfounded and was trying to think of ways to get him out of what surely must have been an accidental promise of commitment; surely he must have been drunk or something? I had not even met this Karen at this time, but he had told me all about her. He could see the shocked look on my face and explained *"I want to get married to her, I haven't known her long but have fallen in love with her and know I am doing the right thing! Can I get married on Sealand please? It would be a first and I would like you to help me arrange it"* He said in a gleeful voice.
I realised then he was serious and had made his mind up, so agreed to help him in every way I could.

I talked to my father about it and we worked out the best way forwards was to write to the Archbishop of Canterbury, who is the head of the Church of England, and ask for his help. We were aware that the Queen is the spiritual head of the Church of England and this might cause the

236

Archbishop some possibly insurmountable political problems in helping us. We wrote to him mid-January and by the 7th of February 1979 we had an acknowledgment from 'Lambeth Palace'. Willy was on tenterhooks, he really wanted to get on with this marriage thing now he had decided to commit and he wanted the wedding to be in the spring or summer when the weather would be kinder for the outside event he had planned.

By April he was getting despondent and thinking it was just not going to happen, when a letter turned up from the 'Lay Assistant to the Archbishop.' It read:

"Dear Roy of Sealand,

I am writing to confirm what I said to you last Friday on the telephone. You had previously told me of the wish of a young couple who live on Sealand to be married there according to the rights of the Church of England. I have undertaken to let you have some observations on this unusual request.

Having taken advice, the position would seem to be as follows (assuming that neither party has been married before and has a partner still living)

1) Sealand is not part of the United Kingdom and is not part of any UK diocese.
2) A marriage solemnised there according to the rites of the Church of England would, provided there is no impediment to it, be considered a true marriage in the eyes of the Church.
3) But to be valid in the eyes of the State marriages need to be registered. A marriage on Sealand cannot be registered in the UK. A problem could therefore arise if the couple later wished to live in the UK. It seems likely that if such a marriage were challenged in the UK courts, it would be recognised as valid. But this cannot be guaranteed.
4) If a Church of England clergyman takes a marriage service on Sealand, he will not be in any breach of the law of the land.

It would seem from the above that if you wish a Church of England clergyman to take a marriage service on Sealand the way is open to you to issue such an invitation, subject to what is said above."

Willy was delighted; it now meant we could get the show on the road for him.

A few days later a letter arrived at our lawyer's office from the Bishop of Colchester, who had been instructed to make the arrangements, informing us that the service would be conducted by the 'Reverend James Chelton' the Vicar of Harwich.

In early May 1979 the world looked on as Willy and Karen married on a beautiful calm sunny day. The Vicar arrived by fishing boat from Harwich with some of the guests, amongst much ribbing about his leather bag carrying all his Godly paraphernalia. If he was asked once, he must have been asked ten times if he had a hammer and wooden stake in the bag. A tall kindly man in his forties with grey hair, he changed into his robes and emptied his bag of holy water and crosses etc onto a table in the radio room, while armed men looked on pulling his leg. He took it all in good stead, even blessing Bahadur. He was, after all, the Vicar of a seafaring town and was I am sure accustomed to such banter.

The helicopter arrived carrying the bride, radiant in her long white wedding dress, and my father (Her mother was meant to accompany her but was afraid of flying so had to make the journey by boat). It circled the fortress once, before landing gently in a flurry of rotor blades and down draught blowing on the waiting guests below. John, in his pilot's uniform, proudly opened the door to help them out as they stepped from the helicopter. It was quite spectacular!

Meanwhile inside, Willy under my supervision had a stiff drink before making his way to the altar.
"You still have time" I whispered to him conspiratorially. *"We can put the*

ladder down the north end and I can launch the boat and pick you up for a quick getaway. It's not too late."

"No" he said resolutely. *"I have made my mind up I want to get married."*
The Sealand Fortress looked great in its new coat of paint that Willy and I had worked tirelessly to apply for the special day. The guests were all dressed up in their finest as yachts, ships and photographers in planes buzzed about, cheering and sounding their horns. Eventually with the service and reception concluded, the bride and groom climbed into our small RIB with Karen still in her wedding dress. They were lowered down to the calm sea and roared off in a cloud of spray to their honeymoon.

The day had gone perfectly!

The Unforgiving Sea

Nineteenth of December 1982 an hour before midnight with a gale of wind crashing about outside, I was sitting at my desk on Sealand reading and listening to the international distress frequency 2182 kilohertz on the marine shortwave radio. I often did this when the weather was bad in case I was able to hear a weak signal and offer help. Every half hour ships carrying such radios were obliged to listen and not speak for a three minutes silence period and the normally busy channel of ships calling up other ships or shore stations would become totally quiet. The world over you could hear a pin drop. The idea being if a ship was dismasted or had weak batteries, perhaps even a lifeboat transmitter or was just a long way away from the coast stations, the distress signal might be heard by someone hopefully nearby. I could sometimes hear ships as far away as the Mediterranean when the conditions were right. Suddenly the booming two-tone noise of an international auto alarm distress signal came crashing out of the radio speakers, filling the room with noise followed by the words *'Mayday'* spoken three times, then the longitude and latitude position of a nearby ship called the 'European Gateway'. She was sinking some three miles away from me. I ran to the porthole and could see searchlights cutting through the stormy night sky. I knew the European Gateway was a ferry that carried commercial trucks and could have a large amount of people and trucks on it making their way home for Christmas. I switched on the short range VHF radio and could hear the urgent radio chatter on channel 16. The 4,263-ton European Gateway on passage from Felixstowe to Zeebrugge had been struck amidships by the bulbous bow of the incoming 'Speedlink Vanguard,' a slightly smaller ship of 3,414 tons, tearing a two hundred foot gash down the side of her.

The European Gateway immediately rolled over on its side and started to sink in the now southwest storm force ten conditions. Harwich lifeboat was launched and the Speedlink Vanguard with great presence of mind launched a ships boat in the horrendous conditions. Another large ship, the 'Danna Futura' her searchlights illuminating the scene, was positioned by her skipper between the weather and the casualty, giving a lee with its bulk and somewhat aiding the rescue.

Two fast Trinity House pilot boats were the first on the scene, with great bravery and skill under the stormy and freezing conditions, they managed to take 48 survivors off the stricken ship. Harbour tugs, lifeboats and helicopters rushed to help.
Of the seventy crew and passengers; sixty-four were rescued and six were missing. Searches were carried on by sea and air for most of the night but at 5am they stood down and waited for daylight.

It was known amongst the truck drivers that certain of their colleagues would sleep in the comfortable beds in their truck cabs in the bowels of the ship, even though this practise was illegal and not condoned.
When daylight arrived I could see the ship lying on its side half submerged on the edge of the Cork sands. It was an unbelievable sight. We had a very powerful military telescope and I was able to see every detail of the ship in the clear conditions.
A hole was cut into the side of the ship and divers entered her to search for survivors.

Five bodies had been located and one was missing. Questions were asked in the Houses of Parliament on ferry safety and praise was heaped on the rescuers that did such a valiant job that bitterly cold and stormy night.

Over the next few days I watched in fascination through the telescope as the salvage teams fought to remove fuel and other hazardous cargo from the wreck. The company charged with raising the wreck was 'Weissmuller Salvage', coincidentally the same firm that used to tender the radio ships. When the weather fined away enough they sent a crane barge from Holland. I watched through the telescope as they worked away on the hull, the men running around on the side of the ship like little ants and bright welding sparks flashing into the night as they continued their work. After a few weeks, pyramid style metal shapes appeared on the side of the hull, the crane barge was brought into position parallel with the wreck and moored by rows of huge anchors. It was reported on television that all openings on the ship had been sealed and that they were about to roll the ship upright using very slow but powerful winches on the crane barge, the pyramid shapes being used as lever and anchor points for the huge wire hawsers.

The first attempt was a failure and more work was undertaken, with more men running about and the sparkle of welding being carried out both day and night. This time it was more successful and slowly but surely she was winched to an upright position. I could see through the telescope huge volumes of water being pumped out of the hulk back into the sea. As the water level inside the wreck dropped; she lifted with the flood tide.

The ship, which was built in 1975, was repaired and sold off to a company in the Mediterranean where she has had several name changes since the tragedy.

Spangles Muldoon

In 1984 I met my future wife Lorraine, 'Lozi' to her friends and family. Proposing within days and having survived a couple of rocky moments in our engagement, she suggested a wedding in a year or so. I am not the most patient man in the world and when I decide to do something I like to get on with it. Taking advantage of an unfortunate incident with some nightclub doormen who had set about her sister's boyfriend, which resulted with me, not him, covered in blood and yet another broken nose caused by a knuckle duster one of the spiteful bastards pulled out of his jacket pocket. Her father, an ex doorman himself ran to get the car. He explained later he had a pickaxe handle in the boot of his car and would have helped me but decided there were too many of them! Well I suppose at least he took us home with me bleeding all over the back seat of his Jaguar. Lorraine nursed my bruised and battered face, beside herself, shaking as she tried to clean me up and horrified with the state of her fiancé. Grabbing the moment, I suggested we got on with it and married next week. She dragged it out another couple of months but I got my way!

We were married in the spring of 1985 and it wasn't long before she was pregnant with our first child. Her first experience of Sealand was when six months pregnant with James. Not the most athletic of women and without her husband's passion for boats and the sea, she tried her best to get involved. There was a problem with the generators so I took her heavily pregnant out to Sealand with me to see what I could do.
It was her first visit and she has never forgotten it.
I was down the tower in the generator room working on the wiring of one of the machines when both generators put power into each other. Smoke started pouring out of it as it caught fire inside. I stopped the engine and crawled across the floor to the door, trying to keep below the acrid fumes. Outside the door smoke was pouring out of the hatch at the top of the companionway above me and I could see Lorraine's horrified face

starring down at me.

"*Get outside into the fresh air!*" I shouted to her.

"*I'm not going anywhere without you*" she said.

"Just get outside so I can deal with it!"

"*No I'm not going!*" ...Bloody women!

I ran back into the room and found a fire extinguisher and emptied it into the electrics of the now smouldering and silent machine.

Running up the ladder to the deck, dragging Lorraine through the smoke behind me, I could see more smoke pouring out of the other tower.

"*Right you stay outside while I go back in a sort the fire in the other generator room*"

"*No, I'm coming with you*" was the reply.

Aargh! There was no time to argue, I ran down the hatchway into another smoke filled room, stopped the engine and emptied another fire extinguisher into the insides of the smouldering machine.

She was never that keen on Sealand after that!

July 1986 my beautiful wife Lorraine gave birth to our first son James without, it seems, any ill effects from his mothers smoke inhalation. With a birth weight of 10 lbs 2oz, he certainly made his mothers eyes water. We were both very proud of him and would show him off at every opportunity. You would think we had invented having babies. He was an absolute delight to us apart from when he was put to bed he would howl half the night and the more his mother comforted him the worse the crafty little blighter would get. We were getting no sleep, so eventually I insisted that his cot was put in the living room of our one bedroom flat. This worked quite well after he realised he wasn't getting his own way and just got on with the not so unpleasant idea of sleeping.

He then took the opposite tack and whoever woke him up in the mornings would get howled at for what seemed like hours. He would be inconsolable. I remember going away on business for four weeks and coming back really excited to see my son. Lorraine nervously said "*Don't wake him up you know what he's like!*"

"Rubbish" I replied dismissively, "he will be so pleased to see me he will forget to howl."
"No please don't wake him" she pleaded.
"Rubbish" I repeated, "he will be delighted to see his dad."
How wrong can you be? He opened his angelic eyes, took one look at me, his bottom lip started to quiver and he howled and he howled and he bloody well howled for what seemed forever, amid bouts of not being able to breath, the blubbering and whimpering noises combined with the tears must have obscured his vision, I convinced myself, and he couldn't have realised it was me. Oh well, that's fatherhood for you, highs and lows, he is grown up now and isn't quite so bad in the mornings.

Over the five years that followed, Lorraine gave birth to Liam and Charlotte. I would take all the kids out to Sealand with me in their school holidays and we would have great fun teaching them to shoot, fishing and making zip lines and various assault courses for them to go round. I have always made sure they have all been involved over the years with boats, helicopters and Sealand including my beautiful daughter Charlotte who used to love getting involved.

So there I was one morning whilst James was still a baby, wrestling the much-loved little monster into a nappy, when the phone rang and the voice on the other end of the line said with a deep tone "Hello, my name is Chris Carey and I would like to meet with you to discuss some ideas."
It was a name I had heard but I knew nothing about the guy. He explained that I might remember him as the DJ 'Spangles Muldoon' on Radio Caroline and that he had then gone to Ireland where there was a radio free-for-all and launched 'Radio Nova'. Not being able to hear him clearly over all the honking, I arranged to meet him at his house in Camberley Surrey the next day.
Chris was a larger than life fellow and lived in a fabulous house with a swimming pool. On the drive there was a Rolls Royce sporting the number

plate 'The 60s'. The house was strange, it had a tiny chapel in the roof where its former owner prayed to his gods and there was a large mezzanine type balcony one floor up that made up the living room. On the wall was a huge TV screen some six foot or more tall. The picture on it was blurry and crap but in the 80s this was the coolest thing I had ever seen. We talked into the night as he explained to me that he had a satellite radio station that nobody listened to. It could only be received on a television set and who the hell wanted to listen to radio on their TV. He told me that the channel he rented was on the 'Astra satellite', it cost him fortunes and he couldn't get any advertising revenue because of the lack of listeners.

So we hatched a plan. We were to put up a powerful AM medium wave radio station on Sealand and re-broadcast his licensed UK satellite signal. He in turn was going to give press interviews, wringing his hands together, complaining that we had stolen his signal and rebroadcast it across the UK and into Europe thus giving him the listeners he needed to get the advertising in. It got late and he asked me to stay the night so we could talk some more the next day.

The next day we talked and schemed some more, Chris was a man possessed about everything he got involved with; he was in overdrive all the time. I was not surprised that later in life he suffered a stroke, as his blood pressure must have been constantly through the roof. How his lovely long suffering wife and PA 'Sybil', herself a radio presenter, kept up with him I don't know. She was far more steady and sensible or so it seemed to me at the time.

Chris also had a business running where he was cloning satellite TV smart cards and selling them in the 'Exchange and Mart' and other such media prior to the Internet. This was huge business as everyone wanted to get Sky TV and he was offering it on the cheap.

Every time Rupert Murdoch's Sky brought out another smart card, Chris had teams of programmers ready to copy them and unscramble the signal. I have read since that Sky spent £30m replacing cards with more sophisticated ones to try and stop him.

Chris took me to his Eurotech factory on an industrial estate in Camberley where the cards were made. He proudly showed me around the factory and then took me to the studios of his radio station, 'Radio Nova.' It was a rebirth of the station he had owned in Ireland.
We then went down into the warehouse below the studios, where he showed me a large transmitter in a crate, explaining to me that it was a television transmitter that he had bought and one day, if all went well, he would like to see it out on Sealand. He said he had bought it without any specific idea of where he was going to use it. This man was seriously cooking on gas.

I went away with my head-spinning full of ideas. We had to get bigger generators and a crane to lift all the bigger and heavier gear aboard with. We would need vast fuel, food and water storage to be able to withstand a siege if there were to be any political problems.

Chris had given me some money to source equipment with and I found two large stainless steel tanks that a friend of mine had; one for fuel and one for water. I gave him a deposit for them. I also sourced a couple of fuel tanker pumps that we were going to use to fill the tanks from on the supply boat some 60 foot or more below.

I then went in search of a small crane to position on the corner of the deck on Sealand to lift all this plant and machinery aboard. Chris and I had endless arguments about what kind of crane we should get to do the job. He was one of these people who always knew best, even when it was not his field of expertise, and would get angry and bombastic if things weren't going his way. In fact there was no choice, they had to go his way.
This didn't bode very well with me as I was of a similar disposition.

We heard that there were transmitters and generators in Holland that had been impounded by the Dutch authorities from a radio ship the 'Magda Maria' that was going to broadcast the station 'Radio Paradise' off the Dutch coast. She was an old 670-ton German coaster built in 1957 and some 170 foot long, which had been fitted out as a radio ship in Ireland. Just before leaving there was a rush job to fit a 280-foot aerial mast. As she approached the English Channel, in worsening weather conditions, the top half of the mast collapsed and disappeared over the side leaving about 130 foot of mast behind. In August 1981 the Panamanian registered ship anchored off the Dutch coast in international waters. It was swiftly boarded by the Dutch navy and towed into Ijmuiden harbour under protest. It wasn't until May 1986 that the courts ruled that no laws had been broken and gave the ship back to the owners. A hollow victory for them because the ship had been looted, wrecked and had to be towed to the scrap yard. However somewhere along the line they had managed to get the generators and transmitters off her and these were what we were making our way to Holland to look at.

Chris, Sybil and I arrived in the Netherlands and hired a Mercedes. I drove the car to Katwijk, near the lovely coastal town of Noordwijk where we met the owner 'Ben Bode' at a smallholding just outside the town and we got to inspect the kit. This was not new to Chris as he had been involved with these generators and transmitters before in the Radio Paradise project. There were two 10KW AM transmitters made by 'Continental Electronics' an American company and one 30KW Fm transmitter. These and three 100 KW Mitsubishi generators sat in this barn in Holland.

We had them start the generators, inspecting them closely. All seemed good and that evening, in the hotel at Noordwijk, Chris paid £50,000 for the whole package and arranged for Ben to find two 40-foot shipping containers to have them fitted in.

Ben, true to his word, arranged the containers and over saw the fitting of the equipment in them, the generators in one container, and the transmitters in the other. Not an easy task under the circumstances. Chris and I still hadn't worked out how to get them to Sealand. He was of the opinion that a helicopter could lift them and fly them over the North Sea to their new home. I thought we would have to take them out in bits. Dick Palmer, who used to work for my father in his youth on Radio Essex as engineer and Fort Captain, advised Chris that they could be lifted using a scaffolding frame and winches.

I couldn't see that one working. We ended up in the North of Holland looking at a huge ship with a crane on it but that plan, not surprisingly, came to nothing.

We returned back to England and a month or so later Chris returned to Holland to inspect the final fitting of the gear in the containers. Eventually having put many hours in setting it up the way he wanted it with his friend and fellow radio DJ Brian Mackenzie, Chris decided he wanted to test it all before the time and expense of taking it all out to Sealand. Legend has it that nobody in Katwijk got a signal on their television sets for about two hours that night as Chris blasted the airwaves with his test transmissions on dummy load.
First he plunged the area into darkness as he overloaded the electrics, then he fired up the generators to get the transmitters back online. The police were called and the owner of the smallholding where it was stored and tested wanted to throw him out. Fortunately by the time the authorities got their act together he had completed his transmitter and load tests.

A little while after we got back from our adventures in Holland, Chris telephoned me and made arrangements for the delivery of the Antenna mast base, along with some huge heavy long bolts that were to fasten the thing down to the deck. These were serious bolts; each one must have weighed 30 kilos or more. They were to go through the deck and lock into the huge girders running through the generator room below.

The next thing to turn up was two satellite dishes that must have been a meter and a half across, along with the receiver boxes and instructions on how to aim them at the Astra satellite and acquire the signal. Chris had also told me he intended to hand out dishes and receivers for free to the new fledgling local radio stations that were popping up in the more remote parts of the UK. He planned to give them live programming via satellite for them to intersperse with local news and some of their own adverts.

Everything was buzzing along at a great pace until one day he phoned me and said we can't go ahead with it. I was gob smacked to say the least. He had pumped so much money into the project and now he had decided to stop just like that with no explanation at all, apart from mumbling something about his wife having said she would leave him if he carried on with it. He told me he was trying to cancel the antenna and that we could keep the satellite gear and fuel tanks along with anything else he had bought for the project.

So there we were with all sorts of useful bits and pieces including some of the biggest bolts I had ever seen let alone find a use for.

I later learnt that Chris was coming under a huge amount of legal pressure to stop making the smart cards that was obviously giving him a fantastic income. He relocated the factory to southern Ireland where I guess he thought he would be able to continue manufacturing them without legal recourse from Murdoch.
This proved not to be the case, he was arrested in June 1996 on evidence from the 'Federation Against Copyright Theft' and in April 1998, having sacked his legal defence team and representing himself in court, Chris pleaded guilty to conspiracy to defraud BSB Sky. He was jailed for four years.

But the story doesn't end there. While serving his sentence in Ford open prison in Kent, which is a low security establishment, Chris took a break from his job in the stores and walked to the perimeter fence A white Peugeot car pulled up and Chris jumped in as it sped off. He had obviously had enough of being locked up. The police watched all the air and seaports expecting him to run to Spain but there was no sign of him. It seems most of his assets worth some £2.5 million had been liquidated and sent abroad.

Murdoch, it is said, put a £100,000 price on his head. Hell hath no fury like a Murdoch scorned.

A year later detectives working for Murdoch's News Corporation tracked him to New Zealand where he had been living under the alias Chris Broady. He was arrested and charged with entering the country with a false passport.

After being extradited back to the UK, he had fifteen months added to his four-year sentence and a further twelve months for obtaining goods by deception.

He served his sentence and I heard nothing from him until 2008 when the phone rang and this deep resonating voice at the other end of the line said *"Is that Michael? This is Chris, Chris Carey."*

"Well there's a blast from the past what are you doing these days?" I said in a surprised voice.

"This and that" he replied, his voice a little slurry. *"I have an idea he chirped, Sealand needs a local radio station for its subject's right?"*

"Does it Chris?"

"Yes of course it does and if the signal happens to extend a little over its borders and into the UK that would be just one of those things right?" He pressed.

"Chris I am doing other things right now and I am not too sure about such a project but I will certainly think about it."

A week later, in his usual imitable and pushy style he phoned me to say *"I've bought all the kit, an FM transmitter and the antenna. It's all in my garage and ready to go. Dick Palmer will come out and install it. When can*

251

we get on with it?"
"Oh Chris," I groaned *"I am really not sure about taking this direction, let me think about it some more."*

A little while later I heard he had another stroke while in the Canaries setting up another station, complications had set in and he died age 62.

He had told me a story over dinner one evening of how in an earlier stage of his life he had created and run a very successful radio station in Dublin, Radio Nova. They had studios in Dublin linked to the transmitters and antenna up on a mountain above the town. The transmitters were in a shipping container that was in need of a coat of paint. Chris who was still festering over a visit from 'the boys', who demanded protection money from them if he wanted to stay on the air, decided to drive up to the transmitter site and inspect the paint job that the student he had dispatched with paintbrushes had achieved. When he got there at dusk he couldn't believe what he saw. The lad had painted the container in psychedelic multi colours and to his mind looked a bloody mess.

The light was fading fast and prior to driving back down the mountain Chris found the need to take a leak. He wandered over to the huge antenna mast towering into the sky and started to pee up it as he stared up into space aimlessly, still fuming about the paint job. He noticed a bolt missing in the lattice tower above his head, then another and then another. It was a calm and still night and the IRA had decided to give him a little reminder of why he should pay them. He got a team of welders in who worked on it through the night making it secure.

An adventurer willing to push boundaries. The world is a lesser place with his passing.

Sealand TV Channel 5

1987 saw the arrival of a very colourful character, Wallace Kemper. Wallace, a wealthy American from New Orleans, said he was in the banking business and owned a company called "Ewing oil". There was even a Bobby Ewing on the board of directors; all sounding straight out of the hit TV program of the time 'Dallas'.

I don't know how he came in contact with us, but my parents had several meetings with him in London and he had huge ideas. Wallace wanted to build a one thousand foot antenna tower on, or next to Sealand, and broadcast commercial television from 5pm-2am into London and the south east of England using a powerful seven megawatt transmitter. Programming was to be sent to Sealand via satellite for rebroadcast from studios in Ireland, and he had contracted topless page three model Suzanne Mizzi to be the main presenter.

Advertising rate cards were published with the logo 'Channel 5'; for a 10 second advertising slot we were to charge £3.5k, and thirty seconds would be £10k.

Running costs were estimated at £180k a month. Launch date was to be 2nd September 1987, Sealand's twentieth anniversary.

My only involvement in the planning was obtaining a propagation map from a guy that had developed a computer program which showed the footprint of the projected coverage.

Then the plan was changed. We were to bring in the oilrig *Tran Ocean 1,* which was to be fitted out in Germany with the antenna mast transmitters and accommodation. It was to turn up ready to go, and be positioned right next to Sealand with an adjoining catwalk.

Staff were employed, including ex Royal Navy Andy Legg. He and his young family were moved up to Mistley in Suffolk to be near the job. Others were placed on the payroll.

Rumours started to circulate that Wallace was going to be charged with some financial fraud, but before the days of the Internet it wasn't easy to gain information on such things. When confronted, Wallace dismissively reassured us that it was nothing but a misunderstanding, and would "blow over".

A man turned up at my fathers house with £20k cash in a briefcase;

payment sent on account from Wallace for the project.

The German company which owned Trans Ocean 1 hadn't been paid so work came to an abrupt halt.

Wallace became increasingly difficult to contact. My father gave the £20k to the company that owned the rig, as they were threatening to pull out without payment. This held the rig for another month or so.

Then the bombshell dropped. A journalist told us Wallace was in jail for fraud.

When he was released his words to us were *"The British courts imprisoned me for something I didn't do. I'm not staying one more day in this god damn banana republic"*.

With that came the unceremonious end of Sealand TV Channel 5.

Along Came Havenco

Prior to July 1997 when Britain handed Hong Kong back to China, there were reportedly 4,000 fake Sealand passports sold for $1000 each to its concerned residents. We knew nothing of this until one day the phone rang with an American voice introducing himself as being from the Miami Sheriffs office. They were looking for information on a fifty year old man called Torsten Reineck. Reineck the owner of a gay club in Las Vegas claimed to hold a Sealand passport. A few days prior to this there had been the high profile murder of fashion designer Gianni Versace who had been shot outside his Miami house. His murderer, twenty seven year old Andrew Cunnan, went on to kill another four people before eventually being cornered on Reinecks houseboat three miles away from Versace's house.

In early 1999 I started getting email out of the blue from a guy called Sean Hastings. Sean told me he had a really interesting idea; he even had a name for it *'Havenco'*. He described the idea of computer servers connected to the Internet and based on Sealand to run offshore companies from around the world.

It took a bit of explaining to me because at the time I hadn't got a clue what servers, UPS and all the other jargon he was using were. Once we had established that it was nothing to do with tennis or parcel deliveries, it started to make a bit of sense. I was not brought up in a world of computers like my children have been. To me they were obviously very useful if you could only make the bloody things work. My world as a young man was my father getting me to type some letters on an old fashioned mechanical typewriter and presenting them to him to look at and sign. It didn't matter how well I thought I had done or how perfect I thought the spelling was; he would always find fault and make me type the bastard things out again. I suppose it helped me learn typing, but I certainly didn't appreciate it at the time. I used to hate it. Oh and Tipp-Ex, that white stuff you could paint over the mistake with and then re type the word, *"You can't send a letter like that"* the old man would say throwing the letter back on my desk. I bloody hated the whole thing. So when the first hugely expensive electronic type writers came out with some sort of spell checker we all thought it was magic. They too were not the easiest things in the world to use, but they certainly improved my life and saved me hours of unfulfilling work.

Sean explained that he wanted to set up a server farm; racks and racks of servers, which are basically just dozens of computers. Each one owned by a customer, used to store information and process online transactions. There are server farms all over the world but Sean wanted a jurisdiction where the data could not be seized or subpoenaed by any of the world's governments. The idea was to attract customers from such industries as online gaming and secure data storage; even before 9/11 companies were starting to store data off site to remote locations in case of natural disaster or war destroying their vast caches of information.

After much negotiation by email, we eventually came to an agreement and Sean came to meet me at London Southend airport. He had chartered a helicopter to take us to Sealand so he could inspect the site and meet my father who was there at the time. The day had a very inauspicious start to it, I had gone to the airport with my mother and my young son Liam, whose eleventh birthday it was.
My first impression of Sean was him striding through the airport doors, as I put my hand out to introduce myself to the long haired, ankle length leather coat clad, computer entrepreneur he tripped spectacularly, launching himself through the air and landing at my feet. I looked down at him and said *"You must be Sean, you are using the wrong protocol old chap there is no need to prostrate yourself in front of me I'm not the bloody pope you know."*
He laboured to his feet, hand bleeding and rushed into the bathroom to

deal with it. He didn't look very happy.

'Oh god' I thought *'We have a right humourless miserable bastard here, what have I let myself in for?'*

He returned sporting a handkerchief wrapped around his hand, he apologised explaining that he had been travelling all night from the States and that he and his slim dark haired wife Jo were extremely tired and jetlagged.

We went out onto the runway and walked to the waiting helicopter. The pilot gave us life vests to put on, we then climbed into the machine and strapped ourselves in. The starter whined and the jet engine burst into life; with that the pilot nursed the controls and the machine, with a clattering of rotor blades, lurched into the air. We were on our way! Sean had perked up by now and was talking to me through the headsets in the noisy helicopter. Far from being tired now, you could see the excitement on his face, it was I think his first helicopter flight but more importantly he could see his carefully laid plans coming to fruition.

Sean was taking loads of photos with his new digital camera as we descended out of the sky to land on Sealand's heli-deck.

My father was expecting us and was delighted to see my mother in the helicopter. After the introductions, I gave Sean and Jo the guided tour. Some of the lights weren't working down the towers so I took a torch. The poor old place needed some work doing to it and I thought this project was just the thing to kick it back into life and tidy the fortress up. Sean was impressed with what he saw. He could really see how this was going to work. We sat down and had a chat with my father and in what seemed like no time at all, we were back in the helicopter clattering across the North Sea back to London Southend airport.

After lunch in the Anne Boleyn pub near the airport, full of enthusiasm, armed with his photos of Sealand and its infrastructure; Sean and Jo headed off back to the United States.

It seemed I would finally be able to bring my father ashore for good, at the ripe old age of 78 and having already had a couple of minor strokes (unbeknownst to him) it was certainly about time.

A couple of years previously, whilst alone on Sealand, my dad had a recurrence of the malaria he had contracted during the war. He confessed to me that he had become delirious with fever and was convinced Sealand was about to come under attack. He wrapped himself up in a blanket and sat at the end of the long steel hallway cradling a pump action shotgun; waiting to take on his imagined enemies. When the fever cleared he carried on life as normal.

A Sealand company was promptly formed and contracts were signed. A little later an Anguillan company was formed and named Havenco. Sean was CEO (Chief Executive Officer) and he appointed 21 year old 'Ryan Lackey' CTO (Chief Technical Officer). Ryan had worked with Sean on another project in Anguilla some time before, involving online gaming and they had discussed the idea of putting Internet servers in a favourable jurisdiction where there would be very little red tape or local government interference.

There obviously had to be certain ground rules as far as I was concerned. No terrorism, no child pornography and no drugs trade. They wanted no spamming. There was some objection initially that any rules should apply, but I explained to them as much as we were under our own jurisdiction we still shared a responsibility to the international community at large. A week or two later, Ryan turned up at my parent's door in Southend. I opened the door to a very pale, bald, mumbling young man and he was dressed head to foot in black like a Ninja, including black army boots, he even had a black rucksack on his back.

"Hello, I'm Ryan Lackey" he mumbled in a monotone whilst struggling with the eye contact thing.

I ushered him into my mother's front room as she made him some tea. Ryan explained to me how a sever farm worked and how satellite and microwave links would feed our data onto the World Wide Web. He explained that he was an MIT drop out that had been working on and using computers from a very early age. He lived and breathed the things. I think this was probably the first and last time he took time to explain things to me clearly.

In the months to come, he would sulk, mumble and look down his nose at me, as well as walk away when being spoken to. There were many occasions when I was close to punching the petulant bastard. It came to the point that I would make him come back when he did this and stand in front of me like a child until he had answered my questions clearly and concisely in his infuriating monotone voice. He absolutely bloody hated it, who wouldn't? But I wasn't going to have people making decisions that involved me without consultation.

I suppose it was not really his fault, he had been brought up in a world run by micro chips and considered people like me unintelligent, because I wasn't on the same level of technical knowhow as him. I am certainly not used to being treated like that and we rapidly grew to hate each other. He wasn't a very happy man in himself. As I recall he didn't even keep in touch with his parents back home in the USA because he 'didn't get on with them'.

I wasn't alone though; he treated all the crew on Sealand and the boats the same way. He probably didn't know it, but all the Brit staff were under strict instructions to look after him, make sure he was safe, warm and dry and under no circumstance to lay a finger on him. We had some real hard cases amongst our staff and many a time they came to me explaining what a struggle it had been not getting 'Uncle Fester', as they called him, by the throat. It was a very rare thing to hear him do his mumbling laugh.

It's a shame really, because a bunch of people working in isolated places like Sealand can bring out great comradeship and great humour in the most dire of circumstances and he missed it all with his extreme lack of social skills.

I read an article on the Internet recently saying that when he left Havenco, he went to work for a US company in Iraq, which was contracted to rebuild the internet and communications infrastructure. After two months he left and formed his own company. His previous employer was quoted as saying its lucky he left when he did as they were thinking of selling him to the insurgents! That did make me, and some of his former Sealand co-workers laugh!

I don't suppose he will read this unless there is a digitised version he can read on his laptop and a coke machine nearby holding gallons of the sickly stuff. At one point we were getting through more coke than diesel for the generators, trying to keep him supplied. He lived and breathed computers and had his coke loaded fridge in the NOC (Network operations centre) down the windowless tower. He would sometimes hardly leave the NOC for days and slept in there night after night. He would wander about in his slippers and lounging trousers. To be fair to him he was very good at what he did and I am sure sometimes we forgot just how young he really was.

I was invited to America, by Avi Freedman he said he wanted to meet me and explain to me what Havenco would be all about. Avi was the main investor and technical advisor. He had made his fortune by selling his ISP (Internet Service Provider), a company that he had started in 1992 called Netax in Philadelphia and was a very wealthy man.

Crossing the North Atlantic I was amazed to realise I was looking at ice flows out of the aircraft window in the sea far below.

My plane made a gentle landing at Logan international airport in Boston, Massachusetts on a very cold winter's night. As I approached immigration my phone rang, it was Avi telling me he was running a little late but would be there soon.

There was a very heated argument going on between a Hispanic looking chap and the immigration officer in front of me. You could see that no way was this fellow going to be allowed in the country. It wasn't the most friendly of first impressions. When my turn came it went easily, having explained I was there for a business meeting, I was waved through with the ubiquitous *"have a good day!"*

I spent ten minutes waiting in the lobby when the automatic doors swished open and in lumbered this rotund, bearded guy, dressed in shorts, t-shirt and sandals.

"You must be Michael?" he announced cheerfully as he thrust his hand into mine, *"I'm Avi".*

To say I was a little taken aback by his Arctic conditions dress code would be an understatement. The doors swished open again and he led me out into the swirling snow and icy pavement mumbling something about not quite remembering what car park he had left the car in. After a couple of wrong turns and with visions of his toes dropping off in his Jesus boots, we managed to locate it.

He drove me back to his apartment in the Cambridge area of Boston, pointing out all the interesting aspects of the city, including the jail, which was a tall tower block with the exercise yard on the roof.

At the apartment I met his lovely dark haired wife Gail. Childhood sweethearts, they were a charming couple and clearly still very much in love. They would hold hands and stare into each other's eyes for minutes at a time.

They had sorted out a blow up bed for me in one of the spare bedrooms. The place was sparsely furnished and the shipping boxes that the TV and other bits of furniture came in were lying around. There were framed pictures of them with the price label still on the glass covering some of the picture. There was no tea or coffee in the house, no food or any knives and forks. These people were seriously eccentric!

Before I turned in, Avi asked me where I would like to go to dinner the following evening, as he had to leave early for work and might not see me until then.

"Do you like Ethiopian food he asked?"

"Sure" I said, *"I eat anything."*

I turned in shattered from the long journey, only to wake with a start at 6am.

Ethiopian food? The bloke must be taking the piss out of me! I had visions of Bob Geldof and Band Aid, standing on stage telling the world about the famine and dying children. They are all starving to death in Ethiopia; all you ever hear of the place is famine, droughts and the odd kidnapping. He must be having me over.

I got up and walked into the lounge. Avi was already up, sitting on the sofa and working at his laptop.

"About this Ethiopian food thing?" I started.

"No, no it's true" he insisted he had seen an advert for this restaurant and wanted to try it.

I wrapped myself in warm clothes then went down stairs and over the road to a doughnut place for a cup of coffee, while musing how strange these people were. As I stood outside on the sidewalk, nursing a polystyrene cup full of coffee, hunched against the cold and the vibrant city was starting to come to life; the sound of car engines and horns filled the air. I walked over to a second hand car lot and looked at the prices.

I was struggling to get to grips with the fact that this seriously wealthy guy lived in an expensive apartment, in a very expensive part of town but survived on takeaways with cola and dressed himself in shorts, sandals and a T-shirt, while all around him were wearing thick coats and scarves. The whole thing was a culture shock to me!

Gail was very sweet, she showed me around the town, its historic buildings dating back to when it was the colonial capital and the State house from where the US Declaration of Independence was proclaimed in 1766.

At midday Gail said *politely "Michael do you have juice bars in England?"* At the word 'bar' my ears pricked up, I had seen enough culture for one day.

"I don't know but I will try anything once!" I responded cheerfully.

We went into this shabby old shop that had been converted to a bar, with hippy cushions, throws on the furniture and beanbags on the floor. The place was quite busy so it was obviously popular. The choice of drinks was pretty much carrot juice, more carrot juice and anything else that could be mixed with carrot juice apart from alcohol, *yuck!*

True to his word Avi took us to the Ethiopian restaurant for dinner that night and, while sitting on what I can only describe as wicker toadstools, we ate some unidentifiable meat in soggy pancakes. It was an experience, but I don't think I will be rushing back for more.

We were joined by Avi's friend Rob Seastrom; 'RS' to his pals. A larger than life, big tall man who seemed to be as red necked as they come. Avi asked me if I had ever fired a machine gun. RS had arranged for us to go the following day to the Manchester Firing Line Range in New Hampshire where the laws would allow us to fire various weapons.

Avi had wanted to do this for some time but had never got around to doing it. He had never fired a weapon of any sort before and was hugely looking forward to the experience.

The next day we loaded ourselves in Avi's car and headed north for the range, some fifty miles away. The protocol was quite simple, you went up to the counter where the guy ascertained you were over 18 and he then asked you to take your pick of the weapons hanging on the wall. I was handed a 9mm Glock pistol with a box of ammo, some ear defenders and directed to the range. This was great!

It was a proper range with targets that could be winched back to the firing position at the press of a button for analysis. Worlds away from what I was used to. The sound of gunfire and the sweet smell of cordite permeated the air. I delighted in the prospect of sampling a pistol I had only read about; with its ground breaking technology of a mixture of metal and plastics to reduce the weight and make it easier to live with. It is surprising how heavy and annoying it can be when you have to carry the things about day in and day out, even to the lavatory where they have a nasty habit of crashing to the floor at an inopportune moment and especially when you're in a hurry. I know I am not the first person to rest one in his underwear while sitting on the pan. In fact, I remember reading an article about why women didn't make great natural police officers, sighting the fact that their skimpy underwear didn't have enough material in it for such emergencies.

Anyway, it was a fine thing to fire and seemed accurate. I then tried the

.45 calibre version, which had a fair old kick to it and rounds hit the targets with solid man stopping thuds.

Avi meanwhile was having a great time with his Glock. Most of the rounds were going wide of the target but he was having the time of his life, chuckling with delight every time he squeezed the trigger.
His friend Rob then turned up with a Heckler and Koch MP5, the favoured weapon of Special Forces around the world. They both blasted away with it to no huge effect. I tried to explain that to control the thing, one should fire in short bursts of two or three but they were having too much fun ripping up the range. The biggest problem was reloading the thirty round magazines to keep up with them. It was a great day out and we all had a lot of fun.

Over the period I was there I was shown the very best of hospitality wherever I went. I was also taken to see Avi's former ISP building in Philadelphia, the whole system and workings of how it functioned from servers to powering to cooling them and the network operation centre that monitored everything. I found it fascinating.

After my first trip to the States I seemed to get asked to go across more and more to discuss things or pick up equipment and even sometimes large bundles of cash to pay the staff. On one occasion, I was asked to go to Philadelphia, where one of the investors wanted me to pick up some money on behalf of Havenco.

When I arrived at the bank with him there was a problem drawing the money out as they were not used to just handing over large amounts of cash, even though he had it in his account. I hung about in banks with him all day long until it was finally sorted out.

By the time we left the bank it was late afternoon and I was due to fly home that evening. The investor offered to drive me to the airport on his way home to his family.

"There's the cash" he said, thrusting a bulging supermarket shopping bag into my hand. I opened the top and could see bundles of twenty, fifty and hundred dollar bills.

Hmmm, quite a responsibility! Supposing the bag split and they all blew down the road in the chilly winter wind that was buffeting the car! Dropped at the airport, I wished my colleague goodbye and headed smartly into the terminal.

This is no good, I thought, *I can't walk around like this, you can probably see the money through the bag and I'll end up getting mugged and loose $100,000 of someone else's money. Then what?*

I hadn't even signed for it. I went into the luggage shop and bought myself a large bum bag or fanny pack as the yanks call them. Dragging all of my luggage into the disabled toilet, I transferred all the bundles of crisp dollar bills from the shopping bag into the bum bag. They fitted but it was a bit snug. Either way I felt better now they were in a secure bag around my waist.

I strolled out into the concourse and checked my flight time, feeling a whole lot better about the situation, secure in the knowledge that the money was in a safe place and it was just a matter of making my way home without being mugged.

I had a couple of hours to kill before my flight, so I wandered about drinking coffee and reading Americas jaundiced view of the world in their newspapers.

Bored now, I wandered over to a video machine I could see in the corner. It proudly announced on the screen that it belonged to the US Bureau of Tobacco Alcohol and Firearms. Interested to see why they should have what looked like a games machine at the airport I started to push some of the on-screen buttons. Almost immediately there popped up a heading:

Currency Regulations
It is illegal to export more than $10,000 without declaring it and obtaining permission.

The penalty was confiscation, a fine or even imprisonment.

I could feel my face drain of colour as I read this; it was the last thing I had thought of. Being mugged was one thing but having it taken off me by the good guys seemed crazy.

Checking my watch as it was now getting near flight time, I hurriedly phoned the investor.

"Hey I just read the US regulations on currency controls. It's illegal to take more than $10,000 out of the country without declaring it"

"I know" he said in a chilled out voice, *"don't worry about it."*

"Don't worry about it?!" I said in a worried tone. *"They have currency sniffer dogs and everything! And if they find it they will take it away! It's a huge amount of money and it's not mine to lose!"*

"Don't worry about it" he said again *"if you lose it, you lose it and we will have to find some more."*

Wow, what a seriously laid back dude I thought.

By now they were calling my flight over the airport PA system. *Shit,* I thought, *I had better get on with it.*

I marched off to the security gate with my bag over my shoulder and the now worrying bum bag around my waist. I was the only one there apart from the half dozen security people. As I walked towards them I was trying to be as chilled and relaxed as possible, even though my pulse was racing. I threw the bag on the x-ray conveyor, slipped the bum bag off and threw it casually on the belt behind it. No money-sniffing pooches I noted thankfully.

Now I am one of those people who will drive around looking for a parking meter and having found one, I am so pleased with myself, I forget to put the money in it and still get a bloody ticket!

I got through the scanner with no problem, casually grabbed my bag and sauntered off.

"Excuse me sir!" a female voice was calling, *"Sir, excuse me!"* louder and more urgent now.

I looked back and fifty feet behind me was this uniformed lady covered in guns, nightsticks and cans of CS spray, not to mention the obligatory

handcuffs. *Dangling from her hand by the strap was my bum bag containing the 100k!*
"Is this yours sir?"
Shit... I think that was the longest walk of my life.
I strolled over to her joking about my stupidity. *"I would forget my head if it wasn't screwed on"* I quipped reaching out to take it from her grasp.
"You have a nice day sir" she said charmingly.
"I will" I said gratefully.
I have to say I didn't relax until the plane was in the air.

I got back to England and through Customs uneventfully. Arriving home, I threw the thing into an old filling cabinet and locked it. The money was then used to buy generators, other kit for Havenco and pay wages.

I got my friend Mason, a middle aged cockle fisherman from Leigh-on-Sea, to deliver a pile of steel with his fishing boat 'Paula Maree' so we could re-build the lifting gantry to unload the generators and supplies that we would need for our project. Up until now the heaviest thing we had needed to lift were 45-gallon barrels of fuel or our small RIB 'Tiger'. From now on we would need to have the capacity to lift several tonnes at a time.

I went on the trip with them to deliver the steel, accompanied by Ryan and Simson Garfinkle, an American journalist from 'Wired' magazine; every Internet entrepreneur's choice of reading material. Havenco was to make front page in this publication around the world.
We left from Leigh-on-Sea in the dark early hours of a chilly spring morning and after a fairly calm trip we spotted Sealand some four hours later on the horizon. Ryan and Simson started chattering away, asking me questions about the structure and how much accommodation there was etc.

Arriving underneath the fortress, the wind had freshened a little but with the young flood tide making a calm area under the lifting derrick, the unloading of the large steel beams and welding gear went well. The three of us were winched up one at a time on the bosons chair and swung over the side onto the steel deck 60-foot above the sea.

It was interesting to watch Ryan's face as he first glimpsed his new home for the next few weeks. I showed Simson and Ryan around and answered their questions as Simson snapped away busily with his camera. The guided tour done, Simson returned to the boat with me. Ryan stayed to start organising Havenco's infrastructure. The weather moderated to a bright sunny morning on our trip back to the UK.

A few days later I was asked to collect another $100k. I flew to New York and was surprised to find that it was again thick snow. So much snow in fact that the taxis were not working and the only way to get into town was on a bus. I waited in a queue for over an hour, freezing in my thin jacket and shoes, wondering how Avi would cope under such circumstances. Eventually a bus arrived and we all piled on gratefully into the warm interior. The bus driver, a big black fellow asked for the fare. I only had a $20 bill. He asked me to get off the bus because he couldn't or wouldn't change it. I refused having waited so long in sub zero conditions. He was getting quit irate and definitely wasn't very understanding considering the exceptional weather conditions and the fact that I was a foreigner in his country. To be honest he didn't seem the sharpest cookie in the biscuit barrel. As things were just starting to get out of hand, a very kind gentleman leant across and said warmly *"there you go buddy, it's the least we can do for you"* and paid my fare. The driver grudgingly drove off. We hadn't got very far when the bus stopped in some random street nowhere near the railway station I was heading for and everyone started to get off. Thinking this was the end of the line; I asked the driver if we were at the station.

He gave me a deadpan look and mumbled *"Nope"*

"So why have we stopped I asked?"

"Broken down" was the sullen reply.

"Oh, well I can hear the engine still running, so what's the problem? Has the clutch gone?" I enquired.

"Broken down" was the brain dead response.

"Is it the gearbox then?" I continued. *"Broken down."*

Coming from a background of being able to fix an engine with a rusty spanner, sail a broken down boat home or catch a fish with a bent nail and piece of string I was struggling to understand the mans thought process or lack of. I really think he must have been on drugs or something; he certainly didn't have the intelligence to drive a bus on a sunny day, let alone in two foot of snow.

Eventually, with the help of the other passengers, I got to the train station on foot.

After half an hour on the train, bugger me that too broke down. We were ages waiting for another one to turn up and take us on our way. On this occasion, I had to pick up travellers cheques from the 'AAA'. That's not American Alcoholics Anonymous, but some American travel organisation that happened to offer the service free if you were a member. We had already spent all morning trying to get the bank to issue travellers cheques, but they said there would be too many so they couldn't do it. Can you imagine their faces when an Englishman and an American turned up with $100k in cash in a brown paper bag and asked them if we could buy 'some travellers cheques'. It was like being back at school again doing lines. I can't remember how many I had to counter sign in front of the clerk but we had to take what denominations they had and some of them were quite small.

There followed another flight back to the UK with pockets full of travellers' cheques, which was hopefully not as illegal as cash.

On yet another trip, Avi invited me to a party in Philadelphia, now I don't mind a good old party now and then and this sounded fun. It was someone's birthday; one of his mates no doubt from the Internet business. I flew to Boston and met up with Avi and Gail. I stayed with them that night in their apartment after dining with them on the obligatory sushi, it seems Ethiopian food was ok for an experiment but sushi was the staple diet of your average Internet entrepreneur.

The next day we made the three-hour drive to Philadelphia. Avi very proudly pointed out to me the twin towers as a symbol of America's greatness, just visible in the distance as we trundled down the highway past New York at a sedate 50mph. Who would have guessed that within months they would be smashed to the ground with thousands of innocent people dead? A devastating crime against humanity committed by a small group of fanatics that were to change the world. Making countries go to war and make travelling by air a tedious and time consuming experience to be avoided if at all possible.

The other drivers on the road seemed to stick at the low fifty mile an hour limit very carefully. We stopped at a toll booth and the young lad who took Avi's money was awestruck by the car *"Hey man isn't that an M3 BMW only one of whatever in the country."*

"Yep" said Avi proudly *"I bought it off a friend who had ordered it and didn't have the money to pay for it when it turned up."*

"Whooah" said the intrigued lad *"how much was it man?"*

"About a hundred grand" says Avi.

"Whooah, what do you guys do for a living?" asked the boy.

"Internet shit" says Avi as he floors the accelerator and roars away with burning rubber until he reaches 50 mph and backs off the accelerator. Now I like a nice car to drive but to me it was blue with four wheels, but that lad must have spotted an extra bar on the radiator grill or something because to me it just looked like an ordinary car. It did accelerate though and when he floored it we all joked about whiplash until it got to that magic speed of 50, when he backed off the pedal. Later in the day I took over the driving and, much to everyone's disgust, put it through its paces a little. But as I explained to my friend Avi and his wife, when you are a non-drinker there is no urgency to get wherever it is you are going. There were however constant cola and toilet stops for them because there was no reward at the end of the journey!

But the end of the journey was stranger still. We drove to a lovely tranquil suburb of Philadelphia, where there were nice houses set in their own grounds with trees and grassy areas between them. Really picturesque with squirrels running up the trees, the American dream as I would imagine it. Avi found the right house and banged on the door. The owner, a man in his late thirties with shoulder length curly hair, opened it and was delighted to see him and Gail. They explained who I was and we were welcomed warmly into the house.

"There is food on the table and drinks in the fridge" he said, sweeping his arm around theatrically toward the kitchen. *"Help yourself."*

Avi and Gail led the way, there were crisps, Pringles and a birthday cake on the table and water and cola in the fridge.

Hmm... I thought there must be some beer and solids somewhere, but look as I might there was not. I looked around and everyone was clutching a soft drink. There must have been thirty or forty adults around the place and not one of them was drinking alcohol. This was bizarre; a soft drinks party that we had driven hundreds of miles to attend. Even if I tried I don't think I could have found that many non-drinkers in one place other than attending a meeting of Alcoholics Anonymous and even most of them would have been liars. These people were high on life and having a great time.

I kind of convinced myself that because there were a few kids around that it was a teetotal party and when I was told we were going to go down the road to have some fun I thought it would liven up. We all piled into some cars and everyone was very excited, I hadn't worked out quite where we were going but whatever it was we were going to do the evening had to liven up.

We turned off the highway and pulled into an industrial estate and parked next to a wooden building with a veranda, on which stood a couple of rocking chairs looking like the set from a western movie. There was more excited chatter as we all stood in line. After waiting some ten minutes, no doubt a subtle ploy by the owner to raise the excitement to fever pitch, the door was flung open and everyone charged in. Inside were 1960's era pinball machines, of the sort I remember from when I was allowed to go to a café for lunch while at prep school. These machines had been lovingly restored and were going down a treat with the teetotal gang, which had reached about fifty strong by now. I was given some tokens, flicked a few balls, made a few buzzers ring and went outside to sit on a rock and assess the situation. I lit up a cigarette and phoned up Alan Beale who was to become Chief of Security on Sealand. I told him about my day and how strange it had been. As I chatted away, both of us laughing about these bizarre clean living people I had gotten involved with, a brightly coloured sign caught my eye on a building across the street. *'Swedish models'* it proudly proclaimed. This looks a bit more interesting I told him through fits of laughter across five thousand miles of phone line. I walked across for a better look, it stated in smaller print 'Volvo Agents'.

Meanwhile the revellers started coming out of the building jabbering away about the pros and cons of a straight pull on the plunger or a deft flick of the wrist. Everyone mounted up again in the cars and formed a convoy racing off to the next venue. It was a huge restaurant on another industrial estate. Comprising of a long hall with one long table at one end that accommodated the fifty odd people of our group. I was sat in the middle somewhere; food was brought out and consumed with great gusto and much monotonous chatter about Internet stuff. Not a drop of alcohol was to be seen, I poured myself a large glass of water and gave up on the idea. That night, on leaving the restaurant and having been very kindly invited to stay with Avi and Gail, I managed to convince him I would be bad company and if he wouldn't mind dropping me off at the 'Holiday Inn' near his house. Before long I fell in with a group of New York businessmen at the hotel bar, who were having a good old time drinking and smoking while discussing the merits of different boxers and American football. The day had been saved! I should have known, when staying at their apartment in Boston I had asked where the nearest bar was and in response they both gave me blank looks and shook their heads, gesturing confusion with upturned hands.
"Well I know you don't drink but you must have seen a Budweiser sign or something nearby?" They hadn't!

With the initial seed money in place, Havenco started to source generators, satellite equipment and racks of computers to get the service up and running. I heard them talking about employing oilrig supply companies and heavy lift helicopters. One conversation was even (Ryan's idea) to have automatic machine guns on every corner of the fortress to blast anything that came near the place. Needless to say these were to be computer driven, without a human being anywhere nearby.

"Ryan" I said in a restrained voice as I could muster. *"What about the hundreds of yachts with families on board that sail past in the sunshine cheerfully waving every year, are we going to blow them away? Blast them into oblivion by a Robocop machine?"*

"Hmm" he said, *"I guess you are right. So what we need then is six marine grade pump action shotguns and a few shoulder launched missiles!"*

"Oh God" was my bemused response.

I thought perhaps it was time to get involved and offered my services. While I didn't know a lot about computers, I had been around the sea and the practical side of it for years. The way they were looking at it, the first stage $1m seed money would have been blown in a couple of months. They promptly made me Chief Logistics Officer.

I got on the phone to re-employ some people that had worked for Sealand in the past and put Alan Beale in charge of the crew and works. A kind of, 'Fort Captain' although his official title was 'Chief of Security.'

Alan stood six foot and a few inches tall, ex Coldstream Guards and built like a brick shit house (I often wondered where they would have found a horse big enough to carry him around). He was also very good with boats, machinery and even building work. Along with Alan came his saxophone that he could be heard puffing into with great gusto some evenings. On being asked by a journalist if the others enjoyed his music, he commented, *"We don't really socialise after working hours."*

Colin Simpson was asked to come back. Colin was dark and swarthy with a strong Suffolk accent and was an agricultural engineer, working on farms since a boy and could make anything out of nothing (and often did) when he put his mind to it. Not very good in the reading and writing department, he could fix almost anything including radios and eventually computers.

Ryan told me he needed somewhere to live in London when he wasn't on Sealand and said he had found an apartment overlooking the River Thames in Docklands, East London. I took him up to look at it and he decided it was just what he needed. It became Havenco's London crash pad.

The apartment was right on the river with fantastic views of the newly built Millennium Dome opposite and all the busy tugs pulling lighters laden with cargo backwards and forwards. There is a lot of tide running through this part of the river and I would stand on the balcony to watch with fascination the expertise of the skippers and crew who made their work look so easy from many years experience. Being a 'Thames Lighterman', as they used to be known, is a hallowed and venerable profession.

Needless to say that the first thing Ryan did was quickly close the curtains to keep all that nasty daylight out. I think I was the only one that opened them, much to everyone's disgust when I visited them. I remember opening the curtains on arrival one day and Ryan nearly jumping out of his pale skin at this huge ship going past the window.
"Shit I haven't seen one as big as that!" he exclaimed.
"Ryan people pay hundreds of thousands of pounds for a view like this, there are things like that going up and down day and night you won't see them with the curtains shut!" I responded a little condescendingly.

A couple of week's later Wired magazine sent out a photographer by helicopter and took pictures from the air of us all standing on Sealand's helipad. Some of the investors were there for the photo shoot; Avi, Gail,

Sameer Parekh (American Internet entrepreneur and libertarian, who was in the process of making himself very wealthy by selling his company 'C2Net' to 'Red Hat.'), Sean and Jo Hastings, Ryan, my parents and me.

We had had a meeting the day before in the London apartment. Sameer, small framed and dark skinned, lay on the sofa jet lagged and stroking his long black hair in an effeminate fashion, as they talked gobbled-gook Internet stuff about what to do next. Come to think of it there was quite a lot of hair about, both Sean and Sameer had long black locks half way down their backs. Sean favoured the more macho 'Matrix' look with long black leather coats and gloves.
On the speakerphone joining in the conversation was Joichi Ito who was another very wealthy Internet tycoon from Japan; he had fingers in all sorts of pies including banking worldwide.

The media was buzzing with the Havenco project, but the problem was that having gotten all this publicity, when potential customers contacted us we didn't have a service to offer.
Havenco then for reasons only they would know, employed their own PR guy 'Bill Scannel'. Larger than life Bill had a friend that worked at the Independent newspaper, so stories about Havenco started to appear in it on a regular basis. I explained to my colleagues that while all publicity was good publicity, the Independent didn't have the biggest circulation in the world. Let alone the fact that it was far too soon to take publicity. Sealand has never had a shortage of publicity when we could be bothered or find the time to take it and the Sealand/Havenco story was big news. We were getting people placing orders for servers and we didn't have any of the infrastructures to support them.

We bought the diesel hydraulic RNLI lifeboat winch from the end of Southend pier, used to launch their 'Atlantic 21' RIB with a full crew. It was being replaced in a refurbishment and was in pristine condition. It was a massive lump of machinery and having negotiated its purchase for a reasonable contribution to the RNLI charity, I had to work out how to break it down and get it off the end of Southend pier to then ship it out to Sealand in small enough parts to lift with the current crane. Then get it re-assembled and fixed down at the other end. Fortunately I had a boat with a substantial hydraulic crane arm and we were just able at high tide to lift the pre-broken down parts off the pier and onto the boat. My skipper Paul Marchant then ran the machinery down to Sealand, some five hours away, as soon as the weather was good enough.

I don't know who did the PR or marketing for the manufacturers of the winch, but for a machine made specifically for lifting boats full of people in adverse conditions with safety constantly in mind; I think I would have called it anything other than a 'Plummet winch'. It wasn't the most reassuring name to see scrawled down the side of it at a very jaunty angle as you were lifted over the side, dangling some sixty-foot in the air either in a RIB or the bosons chair.

Next on our shopping list was a big ex military 22ft RIB with an inboard diesel engine, followed by dry suits, life jackets and ex RNLI crash helmets to protect the users from not just dangers of getting bashed over the head by swinging crane hooks but also the elements when doing forty knots. Pretty soon we had re-engined the RIB with a brand new Volvo and made all sorts of modifications so it could be lifted onto Sealand with our new crane. It was after all our main physical contact with the outside world. Alan built a special waterproof box that was strapped down in the front that we could carry delicate computer servers and other items in without getting them wet or damaged. We also had special waterproof suitcases to put them in to make double sure they were safe.

I searched about and sourced generators in the UK, paid for out of the magic bum bag fund and arranged delivery to a local boatyard where they were craned on to one of my fishing boats to be delivered to Sealand. We had the first generator broken down into two parts to ensure the new winch could lift it. The second genset we took out in one piece, having weighed it on some hanging scales and working out we could lift it. They were identical machines that I had got from different places. Both 100KW generators driven by Gardner diesel engines, enough power to supply Havenco's first stage.

It all sounds quite simple but they needed to have a building erected around them, complete with cooling and exhaust outlets. They needed to be wired in, which is when we found that because of the precise power requirements of the computers, we had to get electronic governors on the engines. This meant getting a specialist in with all his kit, no simple task when that person has to come from the other side of the UK, or further afield. We would have the fort's crew phone the night before to confirm that the weather forecast looked ok and then hope when the engineer turned up at the pickup point the weather would be good enough to take him out.

This guy came out and did his work on the generators, and then had to come back a week later to make fine adjustments.

We needed a satellite link as backup for the Havenco service. Sean, Jo and I travelled to Holland along with my young son Liam to pick up the kit somewhere near Amsterdam. We then had to get yet another specialised technician out to Sealand to set it all up and point it at the satellite.

Sean then arranged the purchase of forty severs from somewhere in the Midlands.

They came in kit form, as this was the most economical way to buy them. So when they reached Sealand the lads had a production line going to assemble all the circuit boards into the cases. Some of the guys had never touched a computer before, never mind built one!

In the meantime, Ryan and Sean had arranged a costly roof survey on a building seven and a half miles away in the UK, with the intention of putting two huge microwave dishes on them to connect us up to the Internet. The survey to ensure the roof structure was strong enough to support the massive weights involved cost £20,000 and was a huge waste of money; as we ended up using an antenna the size smaller than that of a satellite TV dish.

We then had to arrange 'E1 data lines' to take the data from the dish receiver to the Internet hub Telehouse in London's Docklands.

By now Sean and Jo had based themselves in Amsterdam (I have no idea why) and they imported their much loved and much travelled 'if-it-was-it' dog 'Wasabi'.

With the increasing amount of staff on Sealand trying to put together the infrastructure, fresh water became a problem. For the previous thirty-three years we had managed by collecting enough rainwater, storing it in large tanks on deck. Water is heavier than fuel and the thought of having to start lugging hundreds of gallons of it about again in drums didn't go down very well with me. I suggested a water maker or desalination plant to convert seawater into drinking water, quite an expensive, very clever, and extremely delicate device to use. They are very prone to malfunction.

We had one delivered to our local boat yard and duly shipped it out for installation. The lads on site did a grand job of connecting it up to a seacock on the first level from the bottom of one of the towers. The seacock was originally put in place to flood the magazine in case of fire.

Not long after, I got a concerned phone call from Alan to say that the water feed pipe through the side of the tower had a crack in it and water was slowly leaking in. While it wasn't a huge problem, it could get worse; the 6-inch cast iron pipe might suddenly fracture completely and flood the tower to the outside water level, submerging the lower floors.
I spoke to all sorts of people for advice on what to do and decided to get some special quick setting concrete that would set underwater and plug the hole from the outside. Sealing the pipe off from the open sea. It seemed like an easy job, and I was up for the challenge of doing it myself.

I went to the local dive shop and bought scuba gear complete with a huge set of swim fins that would go over the top of the size 12 boots that were part of my dry suit. I had completed a diving course many years before in

Corfu where the Welsh diving instructor had become a friend. He had taken me down to forty-two meters on my first open sea dive where, to my horror, my demand valve started making very loud strained squeaking noises every time I took a breath. Looking back, it was madness taking a novice down to that depth without qualifications. Unsurprisingly it wasn't an accredited course, so I came away without any certificates. Ready for the job in hand, Alan and I launched the RIB just before low water when the tide would be slack and got it tied up in position over where the inlet in the tower should be. We had one of the lads lower a weight on a piece of rope down the lift shaft inside the tower to the fractured pipe to get the depth of where the inlet should be. He then came outside and lowered it down into the sea so that I would be able to work out roughly within a foot or two where to expect the hole to be. It all sounded very simple and well thought out. Alan and I mixed the concrete plug and sealed it in a plastic bag. I slipped over the side of the RIB with a rope attached so that I could be pulled up in case of problems. I followed the weighted rope down until I got to the end and felt around for the hole. It should be easy to find being some 8 inches wide.

The tide didn't seem to want to stop flowing even though it was dead low water and I had trouble maintaining position in the right place. It would be an exaggeration to say the visibility was nil; it was worse than nil and an underwater torch I had just made it worse.
It was like diving in a thick soup. I couldn't find the 8-inch hole but found one about 2-inches wide. I couldn't work out what that would be; when the realisation struck me. Over sixty years of barnacles and sea life had reduced the size of the hole to such an extent that putting concrete in it would not work. I swam to the surface and described to Alan what I had found. We decided to try plan B, which involved a wooden bung and a club hammer.

Down I went again with the bung and hammer attached to my wrist in case I lost them in the soupy water. I found the hole once more and tried bashing the bung in with a heavy hammer.

It just wasn't happening. We had to re-think about the whole situation.

I was disappointed I had failed and some of the others said from the start that we should have got professional divers in. Eventually, capitulating, I agreed to get a local professional dive team in from Harwich. They came out in their own RIB and dived over the high water. I have to say that as much as I wanted the hole sealed up, I got a perverse sense of satisfaction when these trained professionals also failed in their mission. We eventually got our local commercial marine engineer Steve Cocks to meet the RIB at Harwich and he was brought out with all his kit to try welding it from the inside. It was a very outside chance; as being cast iron it required special welding rods and being constantly wet it was an almost impossible job. To everyone's delight he managed to seal the crack and then patch it. We then sealed the whole area in a box full of concrete constructed around the damaged area.
It shows how the smallest job at sea can run hugely out of proportion!

We had an engineer come to visit who specialised in coating concrete with a material to allow us to use one of the bottom floors as a fuel tank. He assured us this product would form a membrane over the concrete surface, we would then have the room sealed off from above and have breather pipes going up to deck level to allow the fumes and gasses to escape. We would have the perfect fuel tank, capable of holding thousands of gallons and if we were ever put under siege again we could run for a very long time. He went off to work out his quote, while we worked on a method of pumping the fuel up from a boat and into the filler above.

Meanwhile, Sean was spending more and more time in Amsterdam because he was missing his wife. We decided to move the project along so we needed him on Sealand and to achieve this we needed his wife there. Jo was happy to go but said she couldn't leave the dog, as they didn't have anyone to look after her. Even if they could find someone, the poor old thing would pine for her. Wasabi, I should explain, had lived with them in the States and when their work took them to the Caribbean island of

Anguilla, she went there with them. Wasabi was a bit of a Heinz 57 mixture of Labrador and something else her mother had taken a shine to. She had been taken along with them, as she was an important member of the family. As an animal lover myself, I could appreciate their thinking but this created a multitude of problems. Primarily that we couldn't take the dog through the UK without it having six month's quarantine, which it probably wouldn't have survived due to its age.

So we decided to get Sean there working happily, we needed Jo there and to get Jo there, we needed Wasabi there.

A few days later my skipper Paul, my son Liam (then aged eleven) and myself left Leigh-on-Sea heading across the North Sea for the Belgian coast. Paul had worked for me, on and off, for years. He had recently had crises in his life when he and his friends went on a cultural visit to Thailand. He fell hook, line and sinker for a Thai girl. The problem being he was married at the time. He left his wife of many years and got straight back on a plane to Thailand.

As he explained to me afterwards: *"They have a saying in Thailand that a man's body only has enough blood in it to supply either his brain or his penis"* and it was obvious which direction his was flowing. At one point, he was more or less commuting between Thailand and the UK for work. He had done a few trips out to Sealand. It was the funniest thing to watch him sitting opposite you on the inflated sponson of the RIB as it was lifted out of the water high up in the air. A devil may care, macho bloke that was terrified of heights; he would cling to the bar-tight lifting strops, eyes clenched shut and mumbling obscenities. His knuckles white under the strain of clinging on to the strops so tight, as others in the boat and on the fort took the piss out of him and fell about laughing.

"Come on Paul we can't let the side down in front of the Yanks." I quipped.

Always having something to say for himself or cracking a joke, he was good company as we steamed across the North Sea in a moderate south-westerly breeze. We arrived off the Belgium coast in the dark at about ten o'clock at night. We'd arranged to meet Jo at Nieuport; she and the mutt had travelled there the day before from Amsterdam and checked into a hotel.

We tried calling the harbour master on the radio and then tried the phone number we had from the nautical almanac. All to no avail, so we just sailed past the little lighthouse and carried on between the breakwaters until we reached the river that served as a harbour.
About a quarter of a mile up the river there were some dilapidated jetties, which we came alongside carefully in the dark and tied up to.

I phoned Jo and got some sort of confused directions to her hotel. Paul stayed on the boat and Liam, who wasn't feeling so good after ten or so hours rolling across the North Sea, elected to join me on Terra Firma. It soon became clear that the reason these jetties were not inundated with boats was because they must have been condemned. Nearly every plank we stepped on broke or was already broken. Walking along the main beams, we managed to get ashore without falling in. The place was quiet and dark, with just the odd car noises in the distance. Liam and I trudged up the road with a vague idea of the direction when, much to my surprise, there in front of us was the hotel we were looking for. Jo was downstairs in the reception with the large docile dog sitting at her feet by the warm fire.

"Come on then, let's go!" I said, grabbing her bag whilst ushering her and the object of our mission out of the door.

All four of us marched swiftly back down to the dock where we got Paul to manoeuvre the boat to a safer and more dog-friendly part of the jetty. Jo and the dog loaded aboard and tucked up safely in the cabin; we set sail again for Sealand.

I have done some bizarre things in my life in the interest of promoting business, but this was certainly one of the strangest. There was Jo looking tired sitting on a bunk with the rather large hound, who obviously thought he was a lap dog, draped across her. Some eight hours later, approaching the Sunk light vessel and still in international waters, we radioed a coded message to Sealand and the RIB was launched to meet us.

Appearing impressively out of the early morning light at 35 knots with a crew of three dressed in black dry suits and black crash helmets; the RIB roared up alongside us, with Alan at the wheel. First we helped Jo across into the smaller boat and told her to encourage the now nervous dog to jump across. He clearly didn't have salt in his veins and this sea dog thing was starting to look a bit dubious to him. As he tried to retreat further back into the wheelhouse, Paul scooped him up in both arms and deposited him into the rubber clad arms of Tim and the other lads in the RIB. Mission accomplished; the RIB roared off with a very dejected and confused looking animal staring longingly at its owner.

In a freshening breeze, we altered course for the Thames and opened up the throttles.
Uncomplaining little soldier that he was, Liam had been having a bit of a hard time with seasickness on the voyage. He had chundered quite a few times on the way there and on the way back whilst I held onto his collar as he leant over the side. He was not a well boy.
I got Paul to drop us off at Southend Pier so I could take him home. He was starving, but the first food he ate he threw up again. When you have been on a small boat for 36 hours and you step ashore, you encounter a strange rolling feeling for a while. I still get it sometimes to this day.

Out on Sealand the maintenance crew were busy clearing the towers for the hundreds of server racks we were told we would need space for. They even removed the ammunition racks from the bottom-but-one floor.
A high gantry was erected on the south end of the fortress to hold the bank of dishes we would need.

Potential customers were getting fractious because we were not ready to go. One customer had already sent a server for the Tibetan government in exile, that we had promised to host for nothing. It was eventually sent back to its owner in Holland.

The original idea for Havenco included other secure server farms around the world with Sealand as the hub. To this end, Jo Hastings decided to visit an Indian tribe with tribal lands that had a certain amount of independence on the west coast of Canada. I wasn't told she was going until she had gone, which I found strange and I don't think anything came from the meeting.

Sean asked me to accompany him on a fundraising trip to the US. We flew from Heathrow landing at Boston, Massachusetts. It was August and the weather was a bit warmer this time. America is a huge country with huge diversity of weather conditions. I found New England and New Hampshire to be lovely places in the summer months and very reminiscent of the UK.

Avi picked us up from the airport and we were taken to have dinner with some potential investors who pledged some funds. Sean stayed with a friend and I stayed once more with the very genial Avi and Gail.
The next morning we met some more potential investors for breakfast in the Holiday Inn. Again they pledged some funds. Most of the individual investors threw in amounts of $100k or more. This was all just before the Internet bubble burst, so the industry was awash with money and people looking for an interesting and novel project that was going to be the next big one producing more Internet billionaires.

We had booked flights to San Francisco and boarded the plane that morning at Boston's Logan airport. The plane rose from the ground into beautiful clear blue skies. The view was fantastic as we flew over countless lakes and the Hudson River on whose bank sits the great city of New York. After a three and a half hour flight the desolate landscape below changed from mountains to desert and eventually to orderly and uniform farmer's fields before Denver, Colorado to change flights. The plane touched down with a bump and a squeal of wheels in the midday sunshine.

Walking through the terminal to our connecting flight, I was intrigued to see that the airport toilets had a sign over the door announcing that they were designated tornado shelters. We hung around for half an hour before boarding our flight to San Francisco. Two hours later we were at our destination, climbing into the back of a yellow taxi and heading for Sean's old apartment in Oakland, where his friend had stored his car. Having met up with his friend's flatmate, we got the car keys we went for a drive around San Francisco, with its vast array of over 50 steep hills inside the city limits and picturesque trams. The whole thing was straight off the set of the 1968 Steve McQueen film 'Bullitt.' Still recognised as one of the best car chase film sequences ever, where the cars screeched around corners and up and down the steep hills dodging the trams. It is a truly magical city.

We went into Sean's favourite bar, which was more like someone's front room than a pub, where people were sitting around using their laptops. Sean marched up to the bar, chatted to the barmaid, got himself a drink and sat down.
This kind of threw me as you would expect in other countries to be offered a drink, especially in someone else's hometown and their home pub. I realised later that there was no slight intended and this was the way of many young Americans. I am sure if it were the way in Europe, I for one, would be far wealthier!

By now I had visited the States quite a few times but I was still amazed at the depth of poverty there. We only see on the films sanitized versions of America. Where everyone has shiny white teeth, permanent suntans, drive around in big cars, never seems to work, all living in big houses with all the boats, bikes and toys that go with the life style.
The reality is there is a lot of unemployment, with people standing on street corners holding up cardboard signs asking for work or declaring

they were Vietnam War veterans and asking for help. Shopping trolleys are standard transportation for their worldly possessions.

My hotel was very near Berkeley University and there were a lot of rough looking vagrants wandering the streets.

A few weeks previously I had stopped in the street in Philadelphia to try to work out what was going on across the other side of the wide road. There were about fifty scruffy looking people queuing up for something. Thinking I must be missing something good but the rush hour traffic too busy to cross the road easily, I asked a passing girl what it was all about. She looked at me amazed and said *"you are English, right? It's a soup kitchen. The people that live on the streets are being fed."*
Having said all of that, there is vast wealth in America and the bay area of San Francisco had a huge chunk of that.

The next day we had more meetings with some young investors and some chipped in and some didn't.

We were invited to a party in Palo Alto, Silicon Valley. The guy, I was told, was a very wealthy Internet millionaire and it would be good if we went. It was a lovely house in one of the most exclusive and expensive parts of the USA. Walking through the door into the living room, the whole wall was taken up by a huge flat screen television and some children were squealing with delight as they played video games on it. At the back of the house leading onto the garden, there was a bar with a barman dressed up in white dinner jacket serving drinks. I could have sworn it was O.J. Simpson. There was food being served by three or four Geisha girls in traditional Japanese garb, walking amongst the guests with trays. Everybody was dressed in his or her finest, but in the garden looking somewhat out of place was a pale, skinny, spotty boy in a scruffy pair of Bermuda shorts covered in mud. He was bent over on his knees digging around in the flowerbed with a trowel. I naturally assumed he was some kid home from college trying to earn a shilling helping out in the garden. I wondered why his parents let him carry on like that when they had guests here and had spent out so much on this party. That wasn't the case. It was his house and his party. He had sold out his company and made multi-millions. I doubt he was much older than twenty. As it turned out, he was a nice and obviously very bright lad. His family and friends were a pleasure to spend the evening with.

About ten thirty, Sean said we had been invited to a rave in the Bay area and really should go as Sameer, one of our initial investors, was hosting it. He had mentioned it before, but I wasn't keen.
"A rave? Why would I want to go to a bloody rave?" These were things you read about in the paper when the police raid them for illegal drugs or worse. We argued and I said I would get a taxi back to the hotel but Sean was insistent.
"It will be fun" he kept saying, with a twinkle in his eye.

So we said our goodbyes to these very nice people, loaded into Sean's sports car and drove off into the night. We were, it seemed, having a bit of trouble finding this rave. The roads were getting darker and darker as we moved away from the city and Sean was making lots of phone calls to Sameer to get directions. Suddenly out of the blackness a man stepped into the road franticly waving a light stick and gesturing that we should pull over to the left onto an old disused pier jutting out into the bay. It was Sameer himself, his eyes glinting in the dark with his long flowing black hair in the mild fresh breeze.

We pulled in amongst a large pile of rocks that hid other cars behind them. The music was booming out of a speaker and a generator was humming away to one side. Across the dark bay I could see the shape of rows and rows of huge motionless cranes like something out of a science-fiction film and in the distance the Golden Gate Bridge. America is a land of many awesome bridges.

Sameer came over grinning to greet us. He was the DJ and was thoroughly enjoying himself.

I was being introduced to all sorts of people once again while looking for somewhere to get a beer. It seems that most of my fellow ravers were happy with water. Although there were a few pills of some description and other substances being offered around, but hell isn't that what raves are meant to be about?

A friend of Sameer, a man in his thirties, was introduced to me; he had a rucksack full of beer and kindly offered me one. I helped him empty the rucksack as we chatted away into the night; we must have been talking a good hour and a half. He offered me somewhere to stay explaining he was a budding artist and had to do a daytime job in the medical industry until his artistic career took off.

"Ah," he said looking over my shoulder *"I would like you to meet my partner."*

"Oh," says naive old me *"Your business partner?"*

"No, my partner" he declared proudly.

"It's been awfully nice meeting you both" I said, *"but I am going to go before I get my eyes clawed out!"*

The bloke gave me his card and I marched over to Sean, who was looking highly amused and thrust it in his hand.

"Sean you know when I said I would try everything once, well I didn't actually mean everything!"

But then what was I to expect accepting 'sweets' off a bloke in the gay capital of the world?

Somewhat bemused by the loud music and the whole situation. I walked down to the water's edge where I found a Chinaman, with long thinning hair blowing straight out behind him. He was staring out across the bay with his eyes out on stalks, sucking on a colourful child's dummy, or pacifier as the yanks call them. It was attached to his shirt by a plastic chain and clip, in case he lost it I suppose. I couldn't believe this one. I walked around him twice looking into his eyes from just inches away, like a grumpy regimental sergeant major. I tweaked the dummy, to no effect. He wasn't on the same planet.

I hurried back to Sean and his friends, describing my latest experience in the land of the brave, hoping to get an explanation. Apparently it was all normal stuff and whatever the guy was high on, the dummy was to stop him swallowing his tongue.

So that was my very first rave! Not to be repeated again properly until my sons stag do in Ibiza at the age of 61 (but then that's another story).

We must have spent a week in the San Francisco Bay area attending meetings in offices and over many very pleasant breakfasts and dinners.

I was invited to Los Angeles by a Hollywood film studio that wanted to make a film about Sealand and my family. They sent tickets, so Sean and I took the forty-minute flight to LA.

We were met at the airport by a very slim and charming blond lady of an indeterminate age; it was clear that she was fighting off the ravages of time with the help of LA's finest surgeons. She had smooth white alabaster skin that didn't seem to move a lot as she spoke. Clearly facial expressions were a thing of the past; a sacrifice that had to be made.

She took us in a limousine to a swish restaurant near the airport, where her business partner joined us for lunch. After a very pleasant meal, over which they made me an offer for the film rights to consider, they gave us a lift to town. On their advice we got dropped at the Holiday Inn Santa Monica, a stones throw from the famous pier and beach. It looked a great spot. Sean said he was going to try and arrange some investor meetings before we headed back to San Francisco.

We decided in the interest of not wasting investor's money, to share a room. The stereotypical pretty blond behind the desk was struggling with

Sean's description of our requirements.

"Look we want individual beds," I said in an exasperated voice *"its quite simple one room two beds."*

The dark haired manageress sitting with her back to us and obviously listening to the conversation came over to the counter. Speaking knowingly in a hushed, confidential tone. She whispered to the girl *"I think what they really want is a double bed. Book them into a room with a double."*

I looked at Sean with his pale skin and long thick black hair down his back. I caught a glimpse of myself in the mirror behind the counter, twenty odd years older, sun tanned with cropped hair. *Hmmm!*

"Look," I said struggling for a politically correct comment in what was fast becoming a very gay world, *"I'm English, in fact, I'm a Sealander, oh, just give us single bloody beds will you? We are on a business trip, not a fucking gay fest!"* I bellowed in as macho a voice as I could muster. Crestfallen she nodded to the receptionist and silently retired to her desk.

I dumped my bag in the room and went for a walk on the fabulous beach then down the pier, picking up a pair of shorts for the next day.

Up at seven in the morning, I would get a cup of coffee from across the road and sit on a bench overlooking the beach, in the company of the down and outs and nutters. Some spouting religion at me as I tried to make my phone calls to the UK. On the pavement there were beautiful girls in skimpy shorts, some even in thongs, flashing past (in more sense than one) on their roller blades in the early morning sun.

Santa Monica was a terrific place to be but I was missing my children and family. I suppose it was because I had changed flights so many times on the way there and had to do the same on the way back they seemed a million miles away.

Shit, it was like boarding school all over again but in the sunshine. I realised I was homesick!

I had been travelling and staying in odd hotels over six weeks. It was time to go home. I left Sean in San Francisco on the way back and caught a flight to Philadelphia. Collecting yet more cash to pay wages and expenses for the Havenco project. I jumped in a yellow cab and headed for the airport. The driver, a very nice but clearly potty guy, showed me a device that he wanted to take a patent out on. He had strapped the heel end of a flip-flop to his thigh with a piece of Velcro and was steering the car with it as he rolled a cigarette with his hands. Most of this was done whilst staring over his shoulder into the back of the car at me, as we sped along the highway at considerable speed. He mumbled on about how he was looking for an investor to get this world-changing device into production. Along with some revolutionary washing powder he had invented. Clearly driving the cab was just a means to an end until he attained the recognition he rightly deserved. Happy to have escaped from his rambling not to mention terrible driving, I wished him good luck and made my way through the airport terminal to my flight with only minutes to spare. From there I had a direct flight to London Heathrow landing at 5.30 am. Getting back to Southend in time to see my children Charlotte and Liam at my ex-wife's house before they went off to school. My eldest boy James was away at boarding school.

I have done some things wrong in my life and I have done some things right. I certainly wouldn't qualify for angel wings but the best thing I have ever done was have those kids. They are an absolute delight to me!

Havenco Goes Live

Sean had stayed in the US and I was asked by the investors to take over as Havenco's CEO to try to kick the lagging project into life. This was not easy, as I didn't have the technical know how to put it together. However, working with Ryan, I ordered in all sorts of electrical supplies, cables, cable ducting, racks for the servers, switch boxes, etc. I was given free reign of one of the investor's credit card. The local electrical wholesalers were having a field day. Selling us a huge amount of kit that was being shipped out daily and being installed by our team of workers on site that was swelling daily with the workload. Sean and I had been to London a few weeks before and bought a 'UPS' (Uninterrupted Power Supply. Basically, a large bank of batteries that would run the computer servers for ten minutes or so if a generator failed until another one was fired up and put online). This too was now being fitted.

There was to be much tinkering with the microwave radio link that connected the servers on Sealand to the E1 data cables on the east coast of England, from there to Telehouse in London and the World Wide Web. When we eventually got it up and running, Ryan, who had been sitting on the sea wall staring into his laptop looking for the signal packets, became uncharacteristically animated and happy.
Suddenly he was skipping off down the beach towards the RIB. I had been running him backwards and forwards to Sealand over several days as he set it up, but his ebullient mood was a side of him I had never seen.
He was singing, *"I'm rich, I'm rich!"*
"Are you ok Ryan?" I questioned him. By now I was sure he had cracked from his long hours of staring into a computer screen. Alan's request for a straight jacket, just in case we needed one, didn't seem such a daft idea at this point. Good old belt and braces Alan had a nickname himself, *'Five humps'*. If you sent him out to get a camel, he would surely return with one with five humps. A simple two-humped camel would just not do.

Ryan meanwhile had broken into song. He really was very happy as he explained to me that we were up and running and fortunes would now flow into our coffers at a great rate of knots.

I had never seen him smile before, let alone be jumping about with joy.

Amorph 2003

Havenco was sort of up and running when we got an invitation to attend an artistic event centred on a summit of Micronations in Helsinki. This was our first step into the world of artists. We had a great time being shown the city and the museums as well as meeting diplomats from various countries and UN dignitaries from around the world.

A few months later I was invited to the Finnish embassy in London to view a film of our time there. The main event was on Harakka Island, which had been a military chemical weapons research unit in the late 1920s and still had the lecture rooms with theatre like wooden seating. I went with Geoffrey Withers, a onetime advisor to Margaret Thatcher on telecoms law and now one of our advisors, his much younger girlfriend and my son James, who was sixteen.

Whilst there we met the Swedish artist Lars Vilks, who's cartoon of Mohamed has since led to several shootings and attempts on his life by disgruntled Muslims.

Our accommodation was in a huge old house in a beautifully kept park near a lake. The house I would think had been built during the Russian occupation, with massive cast iron fireplaces right up to the ceiling.

On Harakka Island, we were given our rooms to turn into a Sealand Consulate and receive the public. I have always considered myself a bit of a philistine and devoid of any artistic inclination at all, apart from the odd bit of sketching, so the whole artistic scene was totally new to me. Being a very practical man and having been put in quite a few survival situations, art seems superfluous to reality. Something I sometimes struggle to get my head around. I mean, I have been to artistic events around the world since through Sealand and have always had a good time and met some great people. They always give me a badge with my name on it and then the word 'Artist' emblazoned proudly. It gets me into all the events and the restaurants and even a couple of raves. Now and again I am asked to give a talk or meet people but I sometimes wonder why I am there. I love to travel, and it's a great excuse, but I just don't seem to see the art in things the way others so passionately do. Like the pile of bricks on a pallet, I saw at the 'Biennial' at Porto Alegre in Brazil. To me it just looks like a pile of bricks on a pallet (Maybe they were doing some building work and I got that wrong). Another example being the mucky films of a couple having sex being displayed endlessly at the huge 'Sonar' festival event held every year in Barcelona. It just looked like another mucky film to me.

Maybe I will get more sensitive as I get older, but time is running out on that one, and it hasn't happened so far.

Sealand On Fire

Friday the 23rd of June 2006, sitting in the sunshine in Spain having lunch with my parents, the phone rang. The urgent voice on the other end of the line enquired, *"Is that Michael? This is Thames Coastguard. We are receiving reports of flames and smoke pouring from Sealand. Do you know what the situation is? We are getting reports that the whole fortress is on fire, and we can see huge palls of smoke from the Coastguard station at Walton on the Naze!"*

Shocked by the news and the phone call I told them I would call them back. I quickly ended the call and dialled Michael Barrington, the man in charge while I am away. He told me that he was ashore in the UK getting supplies and that his colleague Chris was on Sealand alone. Generator engines are governed to run at a constant speed. For some reason one of them had decided to run away with itself, revving out of control and bursting into flames; igniting the fuel in the day tank before setting fire to the generator shed we had built for Havenco above the North tower. Chris had fought the fire as well as he could, but it was too much for him to deal with and the fire was already raging out of control. The only part-saving grace was that the wind was from the South West and was blowing the smoke and flames away from the main building, and across the sea.

A RAF Air Sea Rescue helicopter had eventually lifted off our chap Chris, fire-fighting tugs had been despatched from Felixstowe and the Harwich lifeboat was on site. It was a little-known fact that for years we had been co-operating with RAF Watisham in allowing the Air Sea Rescue helicopters to practice their skills lifting casualties on and off our helideck. They would telephone and ask permission, sending a confirmation fax to me. These practice runs were intended to simulate lifting injured personnel off of oilrigs and ships. Little did we know that one day it would come in useful for our own people!

All the emergency services did a valiant job. The fire-fighting tug lived up to its name, pumping hundreds of thousands of gallons of seawater up from its powerful water cannons, through the doors and windows quenching the flames.

In between talking to the Coastguard and various other people involved, I managed to arrange an urgent flight back to the UK that evening.

The situation was dire. We had one man in hospital with smoke inhalation and Sealand was unmanned for the first time in forty years and looking at the news footage it was in a serious state.

I sat down with my sons James and Liam and we started planning what to do next.
Clearly the first thing we had to do was get back onto the fortress as soon as possible and assess the damage. This was a whole lot more difficult than it sounds. For the last forty odd years we had been making it difficult, if not impossible, for people to just climb up; it was after all an almost impregnable fortress.

We decided that the only way, bar using a helicopter, was a hook ladder from below on a boat. I phoned up our engineer Peter Johnson and asked him to make a couple of hooks up we could tie onto the end of a ladder. Mike Barrington volunteered that he had just such a set of ladders in his garden and we were welcome to use them.

The next day saw me and my sons roaring out to Sealand in our RIB meeting a small fishing boat on its way there with Mike Barrington, Alan Beale and the boats crew on deck.

I climbed aboard with James as Liam piloted the RIB on a parallel course.

The weather was fine with just a gentle swell rocking the boat as I inspected the ladders. James had already insisted that it was him that was going to climb them. It had never occurred to me to ask either of the boys to do it. I just assumed it would be me climbing back up there, but it seems it had also never occurred to James that he would not be doing it. So there he was standing in front of me *'Chip off the old block'* it was like history repeating itself all over again. So it was my job to see that it was done as safely as possible. We put James in a compact, self-inflating life jacket and he was ready to go.

The ladder was in two sections, so we slotted them together and then tied them so that there was no chance of them coming apart.
The hooks that Peter had made were quite heavy steel and they were S-shaped with a flat top to lie across the flat top of the girder. The hooked end on the top that would keep the hooks in place and stop them sliding off the steelwork was only about two inches deep. I wasn't very happy with them but it was all we had and we were by then committed to our mission.
No one else wanted to tie the hooks on, explaining it was my son so I should do it.

Hooking the bottom half of the S under the one from top rung, I lashed them on as well as I could to the side, so that they wouldn't turn as we manoeuvred it about.

By now the Sealand fortress was quite near and the magnitude of the damage it had sustained becoming ever more apparent. The building was smoke-blackened and the double glazed windows overlooking the sea were gone; collateral damage from the high-pressure water cannon blasted from the fire-fighting tug. What was left of the burnt out shell of the generator shed that had been built for Havenco was just a mass of twisted metal on the skyline. James sat quietly on the boats gunwale, with a serious look on his face gathering his thoughts and psyching himself up for the very daring and dangerous job he was about to undertake.

I looked across at Liam in the RIB steaming along next to us. He was staring forward resolutely with a look of determination on his face. I knew if James didn't have the strength to complete his mission; his brother would be right behind him. I have to say at that moment, looking at my boys, Liam seventeen and James nineteen; my heart could have burst with pride.

I have been very gifted with my children and how all three of them have turned out. They never cease to amaze me and give me a huge amount of pleasure. I feel sorry for less lucky parents.

We lifted what was now, despite being made of aluminium, quite a long and heavy ladder with the iron hooks at the top and placed it against the boats forward wheelhouse to get some support. One man stood on the wheelhouse roof to help lift and steady it. Gary, the skipper, brought the boat into position perfectly and we lifted the ungainly thing straight up between us and tried to hook it on a girder hanging underneath. It was too short. There had been a bit of a cock up with the calculations and it wasn't quite long enough!

This was no good. We had perfect weather conditions high tide and it didn't quite reach. We all climbed on the wheelhouse roof, dragging the ladder with us. Gary once again did a great job in putting the boat in the right place, we all heaved the ladder as high as we could and again it still didn't quite reach. This time it was only inches short, but we couldn't quite get it over the top of the girder. There was a scraping of metal on metal as the hooks slid across the girder but try as we did; we couldn't quite get it to hook on. The boat caught by the now slow moving tide came away from the fortress and we nearly lost the bloody ladder over the side. Everyone was getting exhausted and by now I thought this is really not going to happen. We needed to go ashore and have a re think.
"Just one more go," I said resolutely *"and then we will have to go back to the drawing board."*
Gary put the boat in position; we all took several deep breaths and on the

command we heaved the ladder straight up in the air to chest level with all our combined strength. You wouldn't believe how heavy the thing was. *Clunk!* The hooks went over the top of the girder and had the weight of the ladder.

"Thank Christ for that!" I said gratefully.
James stepped forwards looking up at the ladder with concentration. We lifted him up above our heads onto our shoulders so he could reach a couple of rungs up. He got a grip and hauled himself up further until he managed to get his right foot onto the bottom rung.
"Back up!" I shouted to Gary, *"get clear in case he comes off."*
The boat roared into astern, backing away quickly and James was on his own. Liam brought the RIB in smartly alongside and, as per our pre-arranged plan, I jumped into it and got into the helmsman seat so we could get closer to James and pluck him from the sea if need be; with its speed and manoeuvrability should he fall off.

The higher James climbed, the more the free hanging ladder swung in under the girder it was hooked over. As James got nearer the top, he was horrified to see that the hooks that Peter had made were barely over the girder. When he got to the top the ladder and his legs went further in under the girder, the hooks popped out from behind the girder teetering on the top of it. The whole thing was now balancing and starting to swing like a pendulum on gimbals, ready to fall into the sea with him on it. He told me later his heart was in his mouth and his legs turned to jelly. It took every bit of mental strength and courage for him to reach up to the next girder above his head and get free of the impending disaster he could see unfolding before his eyes.

He was now standing on the girder that held the swinging hook ladder and grabbed hold of a piece of trawl net that was hanging over the side. This had been fixed there originally to stop the RIB being damaged by the rough and abrasive steelwork when we lifted it aboard. I opened my mouth to shout to him not to trust the lashings, as I didn't know how well it was tied on, but he was already climbing up it to the deck above. I thought it best just to shut up and crossed my fingers that he would be clear of it smartly.

His fingers twisted into the green mesh, he was soon at the top and climbing over the side. He gave a shout of triumph and I breathed a massive sigh of relief. A cheer went up from the fishing boat and us in the RIB! Against all odds, he had done it. I looked around at Liam, who was beaming with delight. I had given him the camera to take some pictures of his brother's daring climb.

"I bet you got some good pictures," I said in a relieved tone. He looked down at the large camera in his hand. Then back at me.

"Er... I think I got a couple!" he said. He had been so concerned about his brother that he only took his eyes off him for a fraction of a second to take a couple of pictures of James's finest hour.

James started the diesel hydraulic winch and lowered the Boson's chair down to us below. I jumped into the seat and he winched me up to the deck above. As he pulled on the rope to swing the derrick arm in, the devastation was apparent straight away. It looked like a scene from a disaster movie.

The smell of the fire damage was overwhelming and everywhere. There were empty fire extinguishers laying around, even one up on the helipad, where Chris had struggled to hold back the flames. When we stopped the winch engine, it was eerily quiet and surreal. We carefully entered the building. The stench of burning pervading through everything; we didn't know what damage had been done to the steelwork and gingerly stepped on the heat buckled deck plates. The floor was a mess of black slurry; a mixture of black carbon and water from the fire hoses.

Above the north tower where the fire had started in the generator shed, there were just the heat twisted remains of what had been the framework of the building. In the middle of it, two large burnt-out generators and two smaller ones all totally destroyed. It appeared that the throttle linkage on one of the 'Gardner 6LX' engines had come apart, allowing it to runaway with itself and bursting into flames. The original tarmac deck had all burnt away down to the steel plates below. The nearest room in the main building was the radio room and the transmitted heat had burnt it out, right back to the steel walls that were originally lined with wood. It was gutted. As we moved further along the corridor back towards the south tower, the damage became less and less although all the windows were broken and everything was smoke-blackened. The whole place was a blackened burnt smelling shambles.

We lifted the other men up from the fishing boat and then winched up the RIB with Liam in it. It was heart breaking looking at all the damage the fire had caused.

"You can't live in these conditions." I said to Mike Barrington glumly.
He looked at me with a look of sheer determination and chirped *"We won't let a silly little thing like a fire stop us! Of course I can live here and get things back to how they were before. Now let me dig out my emergency mattress."*

It took well over a year but with the help of friends and associates, the damage was painstakingly cleaned up and repaired.

Reflections and New Horizons

I have been asked to explain in more detail why Havenco failed. I think it was a mixture of the Internet bubble bursting as it was described at the time, and the breakdown of the Soviet Union, which brought in a huge amount of competition to us at discounted prices. Havenco was never going to offer a budget service because of its unique but isolated location. There were also problems getting customers to pay. I was spending more and more time chasing around Europe, Gibraltar and other jurisdictions trying to pull in debts for them. One customer owed about $120k that was never recovered. There was a dilemma when clients got behind with payments; We could shut off their service until they pay, effectively putting them out of business, or keep them trading with a promise of payment. The longer it went on the bigger the problem and greater the debts. Havenco ended up owing millions of dollars to my family. But hey, it was a fascinating project where I met some very interesting people and I have no regrets.

A more modest Havenco has recently been re-started and is in its infancy.

In 2007 I was approached by a Spanish estate agent asking if he could put Sealand up for sale on the world market. It started with a few amusing emails backwards and forwards amounting to very little interest from our side. The next thing I remember was standing in a shop near my Essex home idly browsing the newspaper stand. The front page of 'The Times', the headline shouting out at me: *'Sealand For Sale'*. To say I was shocked would be an understatement! He had put an eye-watering price tag of $1billion on it. I had lost my cell phone the day before and was waiting for a replacement.

I was furious to say the least, and hastily headed straight home to seek an explanation.

To my surprise, large group of journalists stood outside my house, who bombarded me with questions before I'd even opened my car door. I pushed my way through them, slamming the front door shut behind me. My new cell phone had arrived. I opened the box, put the sim card and battery inside and set it down. Buzzing into life on the kitchen table, it began bleeping, vibrating furiously and making all manor of noises, indicating countless messages and voice mails.

Over all the years and interesting incidents that have happened in my life, I have never come across such media frenzy as this created. I could see there was no stopping it and decided to go with the flow. I was giving interviews all day long for several days, at one point I had CNN, a Lebanese and a Japanese film crew waiting in my kitchen, while talking to another Japanese film crew in my lounge.

Then the emails began flowing in from interested parties. One of the most bizarre and interesting ones was arranged for the lobby of the 'Tower Hotel' in London with a group of three Russians. We saw them pull up outside in a chauffeur driven Rolls Royce, where the porter opened the door and ushered them in. All three were wearing immaculate suits and sitting in a row on a sofa. There was the principle, a thick set thuggish looking chap with grazed knuckles on both hands, giving the impression he had been recently battering someone severely. Sat next to him was his interpreter, a slightly built fellow, and another Neanderthal looking type, presumably a minder, who said nothing.

The principle scarcely looked me in the eye during the bizarre half hour meeting, but toyed with a small, very expensive looking mobile phone as he stared down at the floor mumbling in Russian to the interpreter out of the corner of his mouth. I plainly asked the interpreter what his interest was. The answer: *"Boys must have their toys"*.

There were meetings with Chinese, Argentineans and various other interests and nationalities.

None of the people I spoke to including 'The Pirate Bay' from Sweden, who are involved with the misappropriation of proprietary rights, seemed fitting for Sealand and its duty to the international community.

On another occasion we were asked to give sanctuary to Julian Assange by one of his associates, and to host a Wiki leaks server on Sealand. Through much deliberation, I was initially supportive of his revelations and freedom of information, but it soon became clear that such sweeping disclosures could endanger world security, and more importantly to me, British and allied troops serving abroad.

Our international football team the 'Seals' have played in various locations around Europe, including Monaco, the Isle of Man, Alderney and grounds in the UK. We have played the likes of the Chagos Islanders (perhaps not the most sociable bunch of lads, with their war drums and warlike chanting, and not forgetting their penchant for drinking their own cans of beer in the pub after the game, as well as brazenly tipping serving plates full of sandwiches we had provided into their sports bags as soon as they arrived, before heading antagonistically for the door). Our charity celebrity team made up of well-known actors, notable sportsmen and Olympians have played the 'Fulham All Stars' several times at Craven Cottage, raising tens of thousands of pounds for charity.
Our charity cricket team has played at Harrow public school, again raising considerable amounts of cash for 'Help for Heroes'.

Would I change my life if given another crack at it? I don't know; the early years were very hard both physically and financially. I am sure this was a major contributor to the breakdown in my marriage, which I didn't deal with very well. My ex wife is now my best friend and I'm proud to say my children have turned out amazingly. My two sons are my business partners, and I have been lucky enough to travel extensively with my boys, including a six week 6,500-mile road trip around the USA. How many fathers get the chance to do that?

I have met diplomats, politicians, actors, sportsmen, leaders of industry and artists including one with a 'Fatwa' on his head and a vast array of other interesting people. I have been interviewed by literally hundreds of Radio, TV and publications from around the world and even made a 'Sizzle reel' for a docusoap filmed in the UK and Los Angeles with my family. I am in a good place right now and stand ready for the next challenge.

The King Is Dead, Long Live The King

Well, he might not have been a king, as he declared Sealand a Principality, but it was a sad day when my father passed away in October 2012. He had been suffering from debilitating Alzheimer's disease for some years; the doctor had told him that somewhere along the line he had suffered a mini stroke and heart attack earlier in his life. Whether this contributed to his condition, I don't know. With the arrival of Havenco, my parents were able to fulfil a lifelong dream to spend their later years in the sunshine and they moved to Spain.

I know this was a good time for them and they enjoyed the life to the full. Unfortunately, both of their health started to deteriorate. All of a sudden my mother became almost bed bound with arthritis and my father was trying to stick his dentures in with shaving gel. Amusing at first, he would eventually see the funny side, but it soon became a serious problem. Alzheimer's is a horrendous illness; sufferers become frustrated and sometimes even violent with their own inability to cope with normal everyday things that we all take for granted.

My girlfriend at the time helped me look after them both and we arranged the arduous task of getting them home. At one point I thought I was going to have to buy an old ambulance and drive them back. I just didn't see them being able to cope with an international flight. I had struggled to keep them in the sunshine, where they wanted to be, for as long as I could; visiting them more and more frequently to make sure they were ok. Perhaps I had left it a little too late? Eventually I bought two wheelchairs and with the help of friends and British Airways, I managed to get them home. On the day it all went surprisingly easily.

We got them back to their seafront home in Essex and found a team of carers to look after them 24/7. But after a couple of years even the carers could not cope and they had to go into a care home. It was heart breaking.

My father died peacefully on the 9th of October 2012. I was surprised how hard his passing hit me, as I had already resigned myself that we had lost him two years before, when he couldn't even recognise his family or me. *We had been through some great adventures together!*
The death certificate gave the cause of death as Alzheimer's, but he had contracted the MRSA bug about three months before and I am sure that's what eventually finished him off. He was a fighter to the end.

There was a big turnout at the funeral. The coffin, draped with a Sealand flag, was carried by Mike Barrington (a faithful Sealander of many years), Sean Sorensen (a Hollywood film executive and family friend of many years), me, my two sons James and Liam and (to my absolute delight and I am sure my father would have been so proud of her) my beautiful daughter Charlotte; all legs and high heels.
Liam read a very moving eulogy and James read one of his grandfather's poems about a fallen soldier in a foreign land. It was all very touching. Charlotte, absolutely stunning with her model looks, walked me from the Chapel.

My father said to me many years ago *"I am very proud of you son. One day when I am gone, you will be my shadow walking the earth."*
I guess that time has arrived.

Sealand continues with the backing of my sons and I am sure one day my Grandson young 'Freddy Michael Roy Bates' will step into the breach, a fourth generation Sealander. With the passing of Dad and his adventurous life, the prospect of a Hollywood film seems once more to be back on the cards.

Appendix: Birth of Sealand

By George Tupper

From: Crewmember of Admiralty Salvage Vessel DAPPER under the command of Captain Thorpe, 1942.

We were stationed at Southend Pier, known, as HMS Leigh, which was an assembly point for convoys and mine sweepers. We had orders to pick up anchors, chain and marker buoys from Millwall Docks. This we did on a fine sunny morning. We also picked up two high-ranking naval officers and then preceded down-river past Southend and through the boom, which was across the Thames estuary. We then entered the SWIN channel. Two mine sweepers preceded us. Jerry must have had a busy night because mines seemed to be exploding like champagne corks – at least nine or ten of them. I remember that it was a beautiful hot sunny day with a haze bringing visibility down to one mile. We eventually stopped, took soundings and laid the two anchors, chain and marker buoys about twenty-five fathoms apart. From having been in the merchant navy before the war and engaged in the coastal trade, I estimated that we were somewhere off Harwich.

We then steamed back to Greenwich. Early next day, we went across the river to Tilbury Docks with the two naval officers still aboard, where we were met by three large tugs towing this huge concrete structure out of the docks. It can only be described as a gigantic rectangular concrete barge with two tall cylindrical towers arising from the centre with a platform across the top on which stood a large anti-aircraft gun. As soon as the 'unit' as I shall call it met the ebb tideway, everything seemed to go wrong.

Being flat-bottomed, it very slowly sheered from side to side; the tugs were unable to hold it steady or steer it. In other words in became unmanageable. In the bight below Greenwich about a dozen lightships were anchored for the duration of the war. The tugs did their best but were unable to stop the 'unit' from crashing into the first line of lightships, driving 3 or 4 of them from their moorings. After a lot of megaphone shouting between the naval officers and tugs masters, most of it unprintable, it was decided, when practical, to turn the unit head to tide and endeavour to hold it steady until the flood tide, when they thought it would be more controllable.

At the first of the flood, we were under way again, only to carry away part of the boom at Southend. Progress was slow, so the Dapper got a towline on the leading tug and with four towing, progress was better. We eventually saw the marker buoys. The tug masters were very clever in holding the unit in position for the marines on the unit to pick up the mooring chains. I think they were in excess of 30 marines on board the unit. As it was planned to sink the unit at low water, we had to wait until the next day. We, therefore, dropped anchor nearby for the night.

To control the sinking of the unit, there were a series of bulkheads built across the hull, the first about 2ft high, and each successive bulkhead higher than the previous one. The idea being to fill the first compartment which would then flow into the second and so on, rather than the water flowing freely over such a large area. Low water came in the afternoon, and the order was given by the naval officers to open the seacocks in the first compartment. Very slowly and in slow motion, the bows dipped and continued to do so until the water reached the gunwales. The unit then started to list to starboard and continued to do so! Panic stations! This was not planned. The angle increased dramatically – the marines on board could not now stand upright, grabbing any handhold they could find. Others slid to the other end of the decking – a few tried to scramble into the lifeboat which was on the lower side. A large searchlight broke free from its mounting and crashed into the sea. It seemed that at any moment, the huge structure was going to capsize, an awesome sight. Then at the very last moment, the deepest corner of the unit touched bottom. The listing stopped and very, very slowly, the unit settled upright, to the relief of all around. After making sure that there were no casualties, we recovered the marker buoys, wished everyone on the unit the best of luck, gave several blasts on the ship's whistle and proceeded back to Southend. I still have a picture in my mind of the twin towers rising from the sea platform across the top and a gun turret in the centre.